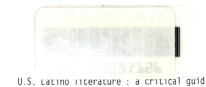

U.S.
LATINO
LITERATURE

U.S.
LATINO
LITERATURE

A Critical Guide
for Students and Teachers

Edited by Harold Augenbraum
and Margarite Fernández Olmos

Under the auspices of the
Mercantile Library of New York

GREENWOOD PRESS
Westport, Connecticut • London

Library of Congress Cataloging-in-Publication Data

U.S. Latino literature : a critical guide for students and teachers / edited by Harold Augenbraum and Margarite Fernández Olmos under the auspices of the Mercantile Library of New York.
    p. cm.
Includes bibliographical references and index.
ISBN 0–313–31137–4 (alk. paper)
    1. American literature—Hispanic American authors—History and criticism.
    2. Hispanic Americans in literature. I. Augenbraum, Harold. II. Fernández Olmos, Margarite. III. Mercantile Library Association of the City of New York.
PS153.H56U7 2000
810.9'868—dc21   99–462065

British Library Cataloguing in Publication Data is available.

Library of Congress Catalog Card Number: 99–462065
ISBN: 0–313–31137–4

First published in 2000

Greenwood Press, 88 Post Road West, Westport, CT 06881
An imprint of Greenwood Publishing Group, Inc.
www.greenwood.com

Printed in the United States of America

The paper used in this book complies with the Permanent Paper Standard issued by the National Information Standards Organization (Z39.48–1984).

10 9 8 7 6 5 4 3 2 1

Copyright Acknowledgments

The author and publisher gratefully acknowledge permission for use of the following
material:

Excerpts from Margarite Fernández Olmos, *Rudolpho Anaya: A Critical Companion*. Westport,
Conn.: Greenwood Press, 1999. Greenwood Press is an imprint of Greenwood Publishing
Group, Inc.

Genaro M. Padilla, "The Self as Cultural Metaphor." *Journal of General Education* 35, no. 4,
pp. 242–258. Copyright 1984. By The Pennsylvania State University. Reproduced by permission of The Pennsylvania State University Press.

Poetry by Tomás Rivera is reprinted with permission from the publisher of *The Searchers,
Collected Poetry* (Houston: Arte Público Press—University of Houston, 1990).

Poetry by Pat Mora is reprinted with permission from the publisher of *Borders* (Houston:
Arte Público Press—University of Houston, 1986).

Poetry by Pat Mora is reprinted with permission from the publisher of *Chants* (Houston:
Arte Público Press—University of Houston, 1984).

Poetry by Pat Mora is reprinted with permission from the publisher of *Communion* (Houston: Arte Público Press—University of Houston, 1991).

For Lucy and Phil Suarez

Contents

Introduction

One of the most compelling stories of North America's origins—a dramatic tale of ambition, adventure, hardship and transformation—and one of the first to document the intercultural accommodations required for survival in North America is largely unknown to present-day students and teachers of American literature. Alvar Núñez Cabeza de Vaca's *Relación* (*The Account*), which details the disastrous results of the ill-fated Spanish expedition to the North American mainland in 1527 that forced the survivors to spend eight years wandering westward from Galveston Island in the first transcontinental crossing of North America by Europeans, continues to intrigue historians, anthropologists, archeologists, ethnobotanists, and others for its detailed observations of the peoples and places of what is now the southwestern United States. From a literary perspective, the work is foundational. As the forerunner of U.S. Latino literature, *The Account* represents the beginning of a long and rich cultural tradition born in America, a tradition bred of hope, dreams, and, in some cases, desperation, of persons willing to wager all to attain their goals in a land of promise.

Had the adventures published by Cabeza de Vaca in 1542 taken place in the northeastern United States among Anglo literary cultures, they would undoubtedly have assumed a significant role in the U.S. literary imagination. To date, however, *The Account*, as well as the works of many U.S. Hispanic/Latino peoples produced prior to the 1960s (and even most produced after the 1960s), remains merely a curious footnote in some U.S. literary education texts, despite the growing evidence that the Latinos resident in the United States—native-born, immigrants, and exiles living here for extended periods of time—have forged a significant literary culture throughout the past 450 years.

This work is our contribution to the growing body of scholarship that seeks to correct that omission. Our 1997 anthology, *The Latino Reader: An American Literary Tradition from 1542 to the Present*, was the first historical collection to trace this important body of American letters from the Spanish colonial era in North America beginning in the early 1500s through the period after 1848 when, as a result of warfare between the United States and Mexico, the Treaty of Guadalupe Hidalgo forced Mexico to cede to the United States almost half its territory, to the Spanish Cuban American War of 1898 which left Cuba and Puerto Rico under U.S. domination, and to the twentieth century with its sporadic and ongoing waves of immigration from the Caribbean (Cuba, Puerto Rico and the Dominican Republic in particular), Mexico, and more recently Central and South America. The destinies of Latino peoples, and their relationship vis-à-vis the United States, have always been intricately linked to imperial territorial expansion and the vagaries of geopolitics. Despite the thematic, aesthetic, and political diversity of Latino literary culture, a common historical subtext permeates this multivocal and even multilingual literature.

Describing this varied population with one term, "Latino," is disputable and warrants some clarification. Although loosely united by a common heritage as native Spanish speakers from the Americas or their descendants, the numerous Latino groups in the United States are ethnically, racially, and socioeconomically heterogeneous; each Latino subgroup represents a distinct culture and geographical area of the Americas. Using the terms "Latino" and the more official "Hispanic," which the U.S. Census Bureau began to use in 1970, to describe the cultures of peoples from Mexico and the countries of Central and South America and the Caribbean is problematic in several respects. The term "Hispanic" is rejected by many authors as too reductive in its association with Spain and Spanish culture, thereby ignoring the indigenous and African heritage of many Latin American and Caribbean peoples. The term "Latino," which is perceived as a more useful, if still unsatisfactory, label, is based more neutrally on an identity shared through the use of language. "Chicano" and "Nuyorican," which are more recent, are occasionally interchangeable with "Mexican American" and "mainland Puerto Rican," although the former in particular reflects a political expression of ethnic pride and the latter is now geographically limiting. As in *The Latino Reader*, we have given preference to "Latino" until a more precise term emerges.

It is important to recognize that the peoples described above constitute an ever-increasing segment of U.S. society. By all accounts the United

States is currently undergoing one of the most profound demographic shifts in its ethnic and racial makeup since the late nineteenth century, which is creating a multicultural society of unparalleled diversity. The Latino/Hispanic population is playing a major role in these changes. According to 1995 Census Bureau figures, Hispanics comprise 10.2 percent of the total U.S. population and, at present rates of growth, they are expected to make up one quarter of the population by the year 2050.

Today the Hispanic presence has emerged, seemingly suddenly, as a pervasive fact of American life. History is filled with unintended consequences, and one of the ironies (a "latent destiny"?) of the history of a nation that expanded its influence and "manifest destiny" into Latin America and the Caribbean is that, in significant numbers, their diverse peoples have come to the United States and themselves become "Americans."[1]

Being "American" and becoming "Americanized" is one of the thematic conflicts that define the Latino literature of the 1960s and 1970s, the era of the emergence of Latino writing in the United States. It is the period in which Latinos began to forge a distinct tradition in poetry, drama, and fiction, the fruits of efforts sown painstakingly generations before by writers, scholars, and researchers. The writing that emerged from the Chicano and Nuyorican barrios or neighborhoods affirmed values in direct contrast to mainstream Anglo culture; autobiographical narrative usually reflected the tensions and conflicts inherent in the drive toward assimilation and the pull to remain loyal to one's ethnic group. The works produced during this period were often characterized by militant calls for social change; the task of writing was perceived as promoting political struggle and serving as a stimulus for action against social injustices. Some of the most prominent names in U.S. Latino writing emerged in this era, several of which continue to resonate today: Piri Thomas, Tomás Rivera, and Rudolfo Anaya, for example, are among the writers who helped to forge a distinct literary path for Latino peoples.

In the final decades of the twentieth century, Latino literature reflects the increasing diversity of the Latino population itself. The defiant social and occasionally rhetorical stance that characterized much of the literature of the 1960s has given way to a greater aesthetic flexibility. The writing has become more inclusive, with women and gay and lesbian authors creating a space for themselves, contesting the limitations of the dominant society and of their own cultural groups. Such authors as Richard Rodriguez, Sandra Cisneros, Cristina Garcia and Julia Alvarez illustrate the aesthetic flowering that has broadened the expanse of a Latino writing no longer circumscribed aesthetically, linguistically, or ideologically. As a result, U.S. Latino writing has enjoyed substantial critical and commercial success in the United States and abroad in recent years, and it is beginning to receive the critical recognition it deserves.

Will our cultural and educational institutions be prepared to meet the challenges of our multicultural society? The studies included in this book, arranged chronologically by date of the subject-text's publication, are designed to assist educators and their students in that task by providing biographical and critical information about representative Latino authors and their works. The general format of the essays herein, with some variation, includes a brief biography of the authors, an analysis of the themes and forms of the work(s) selected, suggestions for teaching, and a section on criticism and related works for further study or classroom use. We were influenced by the ground-breaking work of John R. Maitino and David R. Peck, *Teaching American Ethnic Literatures* (1996).[2] Our book adds an appendix with a sample course on U.S. Latino literature, web sites, and other resources for classroom and research use. The need for such a work is clear: much of this material is not available elsewhere. For some readers, the Latino world described herein will be familiar. Others, however, will become modern-day explorers, discovering an unknown terrain, a parallel U.S. tradition, within their own society.

The works included in this book, on which the critical essays were based, were suggested by a group of 15 high school teachers who participated in a year-long series of seminars on U.S. Latino literature that took place at the Center for World Literature of The Mercantile Library of New York during the academic year 1995–96, which was funded by a Humanities Focus Grant from the National Endowment for the Humanities. Of the 22 texts these teachers were asked to read, discuss, and analyze, the following were selected by those teachers as those most relevant to the lives, reading levels, and school curricula of their students, although many others could have been included. We would like to thank Anthony Castelli, Carole Dalton, Gwyneth DeGraf, Olga Economos, Lydia Nagle, Pat Peacock, Barbara Peiser, Estrella Pujadas, Alan Ravage, Zacarias Rivera, Jr., Jordan Ronson, Marceline Rogers, Steve Shreefter, Barbara Stroud, and Roberto Vega, the teachers who participated in our seminars and whose invaluable assistance made this book possible. We would also like to thank Charles Sterne for his help in preparing the manuscript and Angela Spellman for her development of the list of web sites.

One should also note that there has often been some confusion about classifying these works as "Latino." They are indeed different from the Latin American texts that are also used in the classroom. Stemming from an intercultural literary tradition with influences from European, Latin American, and, often, U.S. "ethnic" fiction, U.S. Latino literature has elements of each but belongs in its own category.

Last, but not least, we would like to thank Lucy and Phil Suarez for their generous support in making the compilation and publication of this book possible.

NOTES

1. Rubén G. Rumbaut, "The Americans: Latin American and Caribbean Peoples in the United States" in *Americas: New Interpretive Essays*, ed. Alfred Stepan (New York: Oxford University Press, 1992), 275.

2. John R. Maitino and David R. Peck, *Teaching American Ethnic Literatures* (Albuquerque: University of New Mexico Press, 1996).

1

Literary Strategies in Alvar Núñez Cabeza de Vaca's *The Account*

Harold Augenbraum

ALVAR NÚÑEZ CABEZA DE VACA was born between 1488 and 1492 in the south of Spain, most likely in Jerez de la Frontera, which later became known as the center of the sherry wine industry. His maternal grandfather, Pedro de Vera, was the well-known conqueror of the Canary Islands. The fourth son of a prominent family, Cabeza de Vaca was a successful soldier in the service of King Carlos V on various military expeditions in the Mediterranean. His name (in English, cow's head) originated with a thirteenth-century ancestor, a shepherd, who marked a secret pass through the mountains for King Sancho of Navarre with a cow's skull, which enabled Sancho to defeat the Moors in a decisive battle.

Cabeza de Vaca traveled to the New World twice. In 1527 he sailed with Pánfilo de Narváez through Cuba to La Florida. His work *The Account* (*La relación*, 1542 and 1555) recounts the disastrous events of that trip and the subsequent seven years that he spent attempting to contact Spanish settlements north of Mexico City. Cabeza de Vaca's second trip, which began in 1541 when he was named governor of the Río de la Plata region in South America, resulted in the mutiny of several of his lieutenants, and Cabeza de Vaca was interned and sent back to Spain, where he was tried for his "crimes," which most likely were nothing more than his attempt to establish just government for both Spaniards and Amerindians. This experience resulted in the publication of the second part of his memoirs, *Comentarios Reales* (*Royal Commentaries*, 1555) and a pension from the crown. He is believed to have died in Seville, Spain, sometime between 1556 and 1564.

ANALYSIS OF THEMES AND FORMS

In 1527 Emperor Carlos V awarded the governorship of Florida, which extended from the southern coast of the present state, north to contemporary North Carolina, and west to the Pacific, to Pánfilo de Narváez, a veteran of American campaigns whose claim to fame had been that he had failed in a mission to Mexico to arrest the conquistador and Marqués del Valle Hernán Cortés for insubordination. The expedition sailed from San Lucar de Barrameda, at the mouth of the Guadalquivir River in southern Spain, on the seventeenth of June that year. After stopovers on Hispaniola and Cuba, where a hurricane devastated part of their small fleet, five ships, about 450 men, 10 women, and several dozen horses made their way north and landed in the vicinity of present-day Tampa Bay. Cabeza de Vaca, as he called himself in his own introduction to the memoir, was appointed *tesorero* (treasurer, who would be responsible for supplies) and *alguazil mayor* (provost marshal).

Almost immediately, the effort went awry. With the idea that the explorers would find riches similar to those found in Mexico, according to Cabeza de Vaca's account, Narváez proceeded to make one faulty decision after another, all of which Cabeza de Vaca questions but accedes to in order to preserve his honor. One of these decisions resulted in the landing party's becoming separated from the ships, which stranded several hundred men in a hostile environment with winter approaching.

Undaunted, when told by the natives that a town to the north held great wealth in gold and silver, Narváez pressed into the interior, toward the village of Appalachee, where the Spaniards met with armed resistance. They were hungry, tired, and unprepared for the weather. When they finally returned to the coast, where they were unable to reconnect with their ships, they decided to build boats to sail to Panuco, the Spanish settlement to the west, which their unreliable pilots had reckoned to be between 30 and 50 miles away, even though there were no experienced shipbuilders in their group. The crafts experienced a series of mishaps and were destroyed one by one, leaving several dozen men marooned without supplies on a small island in the Gulf of Mexico off the coast of the Florida panhandle. Within months, only four of the original 600 were still alive: Cabeza de Vaca, Alonso del Castillo, Andrés Dorantes, and Estebanico, a dark-skinned African, who would one day be made famous by his adventures in New Mexico.

For the following seven years, Cabeza de Vaca and his mates, separate and together, wandered slowly toward the west, where they believed the Spanish settlements to be. Most of that time, under extraordinary conditions, they were forced to serve native Amerindian masters, beaten, and threatened with death. As they escaped from one tribe or another, on their westward tack, their differentness became an asset. In an odd turn of events, Cabeza de Vaca became known as a healer. The natives believed that his breath could heal the sick and even bring the dead back to life. He developed a following of hundreds of natives and was fêted wherever he went. Finally, in 1536, he and his three fellow travelers stumbled upon several Spaniards who had come from Mexico City to gather slaves. Cabeza de Vaca returned to Mexico City and later to Spain where, in 1541, he was awarded the governorship of the Río de la Plata (Peru and its surroundings).

At first, Cabeza de Vaca's Río de la Plata tenure produced an improvement in the manner in which the colony was run. Cabeza de Vaca's time among the natives of the north had convinced him that the indigenous peoples of the Americas deserved better treatment than they had received from the Spanish, which had included enslavement, rape, and unjust appropriation of land (Fray Bartolomé de las Casas came to similar conclusions later in the century and campaigned vigorously on behalf of the Amerindians). The Spaniards in the expedition disagreed and trumped up charges against him. He was sent back to Spain in chains, where he was tried, censured, and impoverished. In 1555, after the publication of the second edition of his heroic memoir, Cabeza de Vaca was somewhat rehabilitated and in 1556 was awarded a small stipend to help him live out his days.

The facts of Cabeza de Vaca's life, as much as they are known beyond his own memoir, are important in the examination of the memoir itself, as well as how and why it was composed. The first edition of the memoir was published in 1542, though it—and the earlier deposition, which was taken in the Americas and corroborated by one of Cabeza de Vaca's companions—was written and previewed before he was awarded the governorship of the Río de la Plata. After returning to Spain in 1546, Cabeza de Vaca underwent two trials in the space of five years. In both cases, his ability to call witnesses in his favor was denied and he was convicted of various crimes. By 1555 he was penniless, disgraced, and exiled from court.

At that point, it appears that he decided to bring out another edition of *La Relación*, which appeared in 1555, with only minor changes in the text. By mid-1556, Cabeza de Vaca had been awarded a state pension. In other words, the composition and publication of his *Account* seems to have resulted in a partial rehabilitation of his reputation and position. The significance of Cabeza de Vaca's life, and work, is that he was able to translate himself, through his writing, from a naked wanderer in the middle of the American wilderness to a genuine Spanish hero, from a failed conquistador to a valuable arbiter in the development of the New World. That he was able to do this after both his failures—in North and South America—is owed to the textual strategies he employed in his writing, as well as the changes that were wrought upon him and that led him to develop a new way of expressing the new man that he had become.

In the introduction to the recent translation of *The Account*, Martin A. Favata and José B. Fernández, in order to develop the thesis that *The Account* is indeed a literary text, emphasize the author's "vivid descriptions, personal tone, and down-to-earth style." This, of course, presupposes that other texts of the period do not reflect these three traits, which, for the most part, is indeed the case. Chronicles—the sixteenth century's method of reporting on its explorations—were generally limited in their subject matter and the manner in which they were related. They were most often unexciting lists of flora and fauna, which were thought to be disinterested observation. In addition to these were diaries of the expedition itself: lists of men, sequenced movement through little-known country, and encounters with the native peoples, from the Spanish point of view. Chronicles were meant to embody truth, from a supposedly impartial point of view. Details of individual thoughts and experiences were generally omitted.

In Cabeza de Vaca's case, however, scholars have long noted that *The Account* expands the limited composition of these texts, seeing in it the same literary, novelesque qualities noted by Favata and Fernández. In *The Account*, for example, the main character undergoes a paradigmatic, transforming journey, politically and spiritually, the relation of which is heightened by the inclusion of dramatic events that affect his own circumstances and outlook. Recent scholars have also noted the parallels with contemporary immigration stories, such as José Antonio Villarreal's *Pocho*, Edward Rivera's *Family Installments*, and Oscar Hijuelos' *Our House in the Last World*, in which unfamiliar topography confuses the immigrant until, through his or her own transformation and cultural sacrifice, adaptation of one sort or another is made.

The Account, however, is not purely memoir or spiritual awakening. In order to develop his "case," to readjust himself and reinvent himself as a successful explorer despite the obvious failures, Cabeza de Vaca redesigns the genre itself. He *mixes* the chronicle and the spiritual memoir, thereby creating counterpoints that he will use to convince the reader, and those who have the power to rehabilitate him in the social and political world, that he is offering observed truth. He employs multiple voices, memoir and chronicle being the most effective, since one or the other alone would not be sufficient, and thus he develops a hybrid, intergeneric text. This use of textual strategy will make *The Account* the first truly literary document of the Americas, written by a European, who has been changed by his American experiences, and following European literary models. Cabeza de Vaca will be seen as the first Latino author, who refashions himself as a Euro-American, an intercultural man creating an intergeneric literary form.

La Relación can be divided into five segments: preparation for the voyage, misadventures in Florida, attempts to survive on the Isle of Misfortune, slow movement toward the Spanish settlements of the west and events during that time, and reunion with the Spanish of New Spain. These differ in both content and style. However, Cabeza de Vaca's argument, an *apologia pro vita sua*, actually begins in the Proema, or Prologue, a dedication to the monarch, which in this case also serves as an introduction, an opening salvo.

Since most sixteenth-century readers of both the 1542 and 1555 editions of *The Account* would already have known of Narváez's death, incompetence, and failure in the Americas, Cabeza de Vaca's outline would not be new, though he also follows the convention of bringing "news that has never before been heard." In order to clarify his own role and to promote his own interests, Cabeza de Vaca would have to reduce Narváez in the reader's eyes through specific events complete with details, while enhancing himself.

To begin the defense of his role in the debacle of the Narváez expedition, Cabeza de Vaca sets up a dichotomy between himself and Narváez, both implicitly and explicitly exalting his own talents while diminishing those of Narváez, invoking, metonymically, the name of the king and giving the reader a clue to his intentions, "Since my counsel and my diligence were of little avail in accomplishing the task for which we went in the service of Your Majesty" (28). Through this, Cabeza de Vaca conveys to the reader a forethought that, had Narváez listened to his advice, the entire tragedy could have been avoided. He follows much of the accepted rhetoric of the Proema—self-reduction or humbling, exaltation of the monarch—but he will let no opportunity pass that can help his cause.

He continues these attacks throughout the first segment, the first few "chapters" of the book (the work has no real titled chapters; in most translations, breaks in the text have been used to denote chapters for textual clarity), as he implies his own loyalty to the crown and his heroism and denigrates those of Narváez. When a storm develops while they are anchored in the port of Santiago de Cuba, Cabeza de Vaca refuses to leave the two ships under his control, although he has given permission to many of his men to do so. Personal sacrifice thus enters into his own decision-making practices. Only at the repeated urging of the ships' pilots who, according to Cabeza de Vaca, hoped that his presence on the island would "hasten the transfer of provisions" so they could presumably leave the vicinity and ride out the storm in safe harbor or at sea, does he go ashore. The ships are destroyed, and only those who had gone ashore—including Cabeza de Vaca—survive.

Narváez is also portrayed as a terrible evaluator of men. He contracts a ship's pilot to lead the expedition to the mainland of La Florida. The pilot's advice leads them to disaster:

At this time the governor (Narváez) arrived with a brigantine he had purchased in Trinidad, bringing along a pilot named Miruelo. He had taken him because he said that he knew, and had been at, the River of Palms and that he was a very good pilot of the entire north coast. (33)

By also noting that the pilot claimed to have knowledge of the coast to which they were going, and which will form the next segment of the story, Cabeza de Vaca links the two segments, again damning Narváez's abilities.

In the following segment, misadventures in Florida, the reader then learns that Narváez is a poor military strategist and leader of men; the reader can remember that he selected a pilot who turned out to know very little of the coast itself, claiming that the Spanish settlements of the west are nearby. Then, despite the advice of Cabeza de Vaca and others to the contrary, Narváez decides to split his expeditionary force: the ships to sail north along the coast and the foot soldiers and cavalry to go inland. The foray results in another disaster, this one irreparable. The men who go inland are never able to rejoin the ships.

Rather than continue the story of the expedition itself, however, just after he relates the story of how the Spanish marched into the town of Apalachee, Cabeza de Vaca begins to describe, in detail, the surrounding flora and fauna:

From the place where we landed to this village and land of Apalachee, the country is mostly flat, the soil sandy and firm. Throughout it there are many large trees and open woodlands in which there are walnut trees and laurels. . . . The animals we saw in those lands were three kinds of deer, rabbits and hares, bears and lions and other wild animals, among which we saw one which carries its young in a pouch on its belly. (42)

Through this passage, after which he returns to the adventure at hand, Cabeza de Vaca reestablishes himself as an observer who notes the unembellished truth of his surroundings.

The Spaniards soon build rafts to sail to Panuco, the Spanish settlements north of Mexico City, which they mistakenly believe is not far from their current position. Throughout this event, Narváez's loyalty to his men will be questioned. At one point, the rafts are in danger of being swamped. Narváez, who has taken the healthiest and strongest men on his own raft, is driving toward the shore, leaving the others behind:

When I saw this, I asked the Governor to throw me a line so I could follow him, but he answered that it would be enough of a struggle for them to reach shore that night themselves. . . . He told me that each of us should do what seemed best to save his life, since that is what he intended to do. (53)

In the third segment, when they have been shipwrecked on an island, which they name the Isle of Misfortune, Cabeza de Vaca returns to the chronicle format:

The people we found there are tall and well built. They have no weapons other than bows and arrows. The men have one nipple pierced from one side to the other, and some have both pierced. . . . Each one has a recognized wife. (59)

A description of the Amerindians and their customs ensues before Cabeza de Vaca returns to the discussions of their own attempts to survive. At one point, he discontinues his own story for an extended period of time (85–90) to present a detailed account of the Amerindians he has encountered and with whom he has sojourned since he left the Isle of Misfortune. He ends this extended passage, on the sexual and military practices of the natives, with the following:

I wanted to relate this, not only because all men wish to know the customs and habits of other people, but also to warn anyone who may encounter these people about their customs and cunning—very useful information in such cases. (90)

The aforementioned linkages between distinct segments and a return to the chronicle format demonstrate how Cabeza de Vaca seeks to validate his personal strategic objectives by providing "corroborating evidence." There may have been other objectives, as well. According to the scholar Beatriz Pastor Bodmer, Cabeza de Vaca and other chroniclers of failed expeditions refused to let their tragic misfortunes be forgotten; in essence, they wrote themselves into permanent history. This, to an extent, might also have been Cabeza de Vaca's intention.

Cabeza de Vaca, however, born into a family of conquerors, named for a well-known sea captain, and apprenticed to war by the age of 17, would have also needed to reclaim his social, economic, and political place through his writing. This represented his only recourse, writing, as it were, to save the life he had known, the one he had envisioned, and the one he was forced to reenvision. As the scholar Juan Bruce-Novoa pointed out in *Bendíceme, América: Latino Writers of the United States*, Cabeza de Vaca, through his writing, needed to "re-invent" himself as a "cultural product." He will convince the reader of the truth of this "account," by taking on the guises of chronicler and memoirist, using more than one voice as a strategy to complete his point. In *The Account*, Cabeza de Vaca proposes this new self through a multiple mode of expression of that self's experiences.

TEACHING THE WORK

1. Cabeza de Vaca writes to develop the story of his own life as his triumph in a deteriorating situation not of his own making. How can one rewrite one's life in order to convince the reader of one's success?

2. In writing a résumé about one's success, turning failure into success, Cabeza de Vaca uses two genres—memoir and chronicle. How can one develop a similar method today, using a variety of genres that are meant to dispense truth (e.g., journalism and video evidence)?

3. The immigrant, who is often thought of as "the other," needs to develop a way to use his or her talents and differentness to appeal to the dominating society. How does the immigrant do this today?

4. When Cabeza de Vaca rejoined the Spanish in Mexico, he was so changed physically that he was almost unrecognizable as a Spaniard. When he returned to Spain, and then was sent to Río de la Plata, his decisions were based on a new understanding of the Amerindian, which brought him trouble, including charges of disloyalty to the Spanish explorers. He was no longer a Spaniard, but he had not become an Amerindian either. This "intercultural being" needed to prove himself in order to be accepted in the general order of Europe. How does he do this with his writing?

5. Students can catalogue the way in which Cabeza de Vaca links the segments of his experience and find passages he wrote that might be intended to influence how he was perceived in the Spanish court.

CRITICISM AND FURTHER READING

Bishop, Morris. *The Odyssey of Cabeza de Vaca.* New York: Century, 1933.
———. *Cabeza de Vaca's Great Journey.* Washington, D.C.: Pan American Union, 1942.
Bruce-Novoa, Juan. "Naufragios en los mares de la significación: De La Relación de Cabeza de Vaca a la literatura chicana." *Plural* (febrero 1990): 12–21.
———. "U.S. Latino Literature: An Overview." In Harold Augenbraum, Terry Quinn, and Ilan Stavans, eds: *Bendíceme, América: Latino Writers of the United States.* New York: Mercantile Library of New York, 1993.
Cabeza de Vaca, Alvar Núñez. *La Relacion.* Houston: Arte Público Press, 1993.
Clayton, Jay. *The Pleasures of Babel.* New York: Oxford University Press, 1993.
Favata, Martin A., and José B. Fernández. "Introduction" to *The Account* by Alvar Núñez Cabeza de Vaca, ed. and trans. by Martin A. Favata and José B. Fernández. Houston: Arte Público Press, 1993. (All page numbers in the text refer to this edition.)
Hallenbeck, Cleve. *Alvar Núñez Cabeza de Vaca: The Journey and Route of the First European to Cross the Continent of North America 1534–1536.* Glendale, Calif. Arthur H. Clark, 1940.

Pastor, Beatriz Bodmer. *Discurso narrativo de la conquista de América*. La Habana, Cuba: Casa de las Américas, 1983.

Pupo-Walker, Enrique. "Introduction" to *Castaways*. Berkeley: University of California Press, 1993.

Rodman, Maia. *Odyssey of Courage: The Story of Alvar Núñez Cabeza de Vaca*. New York: Atheneum, 1965.

NOTE

Students may also be interested in viewing the 1992 film *Cabeza de Vaca*, directed by Nicolas Echevarria and starring Juan Diego, in Spanish with English subtitles, which is available on video.

2

Trials and Tribulations: The Life and Works of María Amparo Ruiz de Burton

Beatrice Pita

MARÍA AMPARO RUIZ DE BURTON was born in Baja (Lower) California on July 3, 1832. She was the granddaughter of Don José Manuel Ruiz Carillo, the governor of Baja California, and related, through her grandmother, to the most prominent Spanish-speaking families of Alta California (now the state of California). Her father's surname, Arango, is known, but his full name and lineage—as well as why she chose to place her mother's name first on her marriage certificate—remain a mystery. At the age of 16, when the United States and Mexico signed the Treaty of Guadalupe Hidalgo, which ended the Mexican-American War and forced Mexico to cede half its territory to the United States, Ruiz de Burton and her mother moved from Baja to San Francisco, along with several hundred other refugees. There she met Captain Henry S. Burton, who was 28 years old and a widower. Though she was Catholic and he Protestant, they were married, in both civil and religious ceremonies. At the outbreak of the Civil War, Burton was posted to the East. During his southern campaign, he contracted malaria, from which he later died, in Rhode Island in 1869, leaving Ruiz de Burton with two children.

Considered one of the most beautiful women in the West, Ruiz de Burton was believed to be the model for the young woman in the ballad "The Maid of Monterey," which for years was sung by Mexican veterans of the war. In historian Hubert Howe Bancroft's *California Pastoral* (The History Company, 1888) and in various newspaper articles published in the 1930s, the marriage of Ruiz and Burton was described in great detail and characterized as one of the great romances of the time.

Ruiz de Burton's first known work was a five-act comedy based on the adventures of Don Quixote, but it was her novel, *Who Would Have Thought It?* (J. P. Lippincott, 1872), that showed her extraordinary talent. Written in highly assured English prose, it is now believed to be the first novel written by a Mexican American and certainly the first to be written in English. *Who Would Have Thought It?* was published without the author's name on the title page (a not uncommon occurrence of the time), but it was registered at the Library of Congress under the names of H. S. Burton and Mrs. Henry S. Burton. A diligent reporter discovered Ruiz de Burton's authorship and made it known to the public. Her second novel, *The Squatter and the Don* (1885), was published with the name C. Loyal (*ciudadano leal*, or loyal citizen) listed as author on the title page. Ruiz de Burton died in 1895.

ANALYSIS OF THEMES AND FORMS

The relative dearth of information on nineteenth-century Latino/Chicano literary history in the Southwest is slowly being remedied by the recovery of long-neglected texts such as those written by María Amparo Ruiz de Burton (RDB) and other nineteenth- and early twentieth-century writers. These texts will undoubtedly have a central place in the growing canon of Latino/Chicano literature. RDB presents us with the case of an extraordinarily talented woman, a writer with a powerful voice who addressed crucial issues of ethnicity, power, gender, class, and race. Writing for publication in English from the vantage point of an acculturated Californio, RDB dialogues with a number of contemporary nineteenth-century discourses—political, juridical, economic, commercial, and literary—to create a narrative space for the counterhistory of the subaltern and to voice the bitter resentment of the Californios faced with despoliation and the onslaught of Anglo-American domination in the aftermath of annexation to the United States. Seen in this light, RDB is clearly a precursor of Chicana/o literature as her novels investigate issues at the core of Chicana/o history and literature. As a woman writer, her work is of special significance, for it brings to the discussion of nineteenth-century U.S. literary historiography the perspective of someone who was both inside and outside the dominant U.S. culture. In fact, *The Squatter and the Don*, RDB's second novel, published in San Francisco in 1885, almost 40 years after the United States invaded and occupied the Mexican Southwest, appears at this point to be the first published narrative—written in English—giving the perspective of the conquered Mexican population that, despite being granted full rights of citizenship by the 1848 treaty, was, by 1860, a subordinated and marginalized national minority.

Readers need to keep in mind that RDB's background afforded her a certain critical distance and alternative points of reference from which to view and to critique the transformations taking place in the United States; her extended stay in the East provided her an opportunity for firsthand observations and assessment of the U.S. republic, its westward movement, its Civil War, and the aftermath. While living in San Diego in the early 1850s, RDB had written, produced, and later published a five-act comedy based on *Don Quixote*. Several years later, in 1872, her first novel, *Who Would Have Thought It?*, was published by J. B. Lippincott in Philadelphia. The title page gives no author, but the book is listed under Mrs. Henry S. Burton by the Library of Congress. Clearly the ever-enterprising RDB hoped that she, like other women writers of the period, would be successful with her writing and overcome her precarious financial situation.

Considering the content of the novel, however, one can well understand why she would elect *not* to publish her name on it. Her first novel is a bitingly satirical text, a caustic parody of the United States during the period of the Civil War. Amongst other critiques, the novel scrutinizes the pettiness and racism of a Northern abolitionist family and foregrounds the issues of democracy, liberalism, women's suffrage, imperialism, political opportunism, and religious hypocrisy—all analyzed from a dual insider/outsider perspective. The Mexican spectator here is a child whose mother, from an aristocratic Mexican family and pregnant at the time, is—in true romance fashion—kidnapped by the Indians. The child, rescued by a Yankee geologist exploring near the banks of the Gila River, is brought to the East to live with his family on the eve of the Civil War. In this text, as in her second novel, *The Squatter and the Don*, we find history and romance bound up together in the narrative, with the romance serving allegorically to configure national, political, economic, and cultural contradictions.

Focusing more directly on California issues, RDB's second novel, *The Squatter and the Don*, was published 13 years later in 1885 under the pseudonym "C. Loyal": "C." for *Ciudadano* or "Citizen," and "Loyal" for *Leal*, a Loyal Citizen. This term was commonly used to close government correspondence in Mexico during the nineteenth century. The English pseudonym, the indeterminacy of the author's gender, and the designation of the author as a "loyal citizen" provide an ironic twist, considering that the work is severely critical of the political structures of U.S. society. If, in the Treaty of Guadalupe Hidalgo, the United States agreed to respect the rights of Mexicans subsumed into the United States, it did not recognize the validity of the Spanish-Mexican land grants outright. On the contrary, it called all land titles into question with the Land Act of 1851. The novel traces how the burden of proof fell not on the government, nor even on the squatters who "located" on the land, but on the Californio landowners. The law, in effect, forced Mexicans off their lands by encouraging squatters. In the end, many of the Californios' titles were declared valid after numerous court appeals, but by then most of the Californios had lost their property to the banks, to loan sharks, to lawyers and speculators, or to the state itself for failure to pay the taxes levied on their property. Thus it is an open question whether the 1851 Land Commission furthered the recognition of property rights or was in fact the principal mechanism leading to Californio land loss. The Alamar family narrative given in *The Squatter and the Don* fictionally reconstructs the fortunes of many Californio families and the legal problems they faced in retaining their lands; it is a composite of many different cases of land loss to squatters and litigation.

The Squatter and the Don is a historical romance that details not only the repercussions of the Land Act of 1851 after the U.S. invasion of California but the rapid rise of the railroad monopoly in the state. The novel's action, which roughly covers the period from 1872 to 1885, traces the trials and tribulations of the two star-crossed lovers from the Alamar and Darrell families. The narrative builds on the tension between the romantic and the historical as it reconstructs conflicts between Californios of Mexican descent and the invading Anglo squatters by focusing on two families: the family of Don Maríano Alamar, owner of a 47,000-acre ranch in the San Diego area, and the family of William Darrell, one of the numerous squatters on the Alamar ranch. Amidst the dispossession and disempowerment of the Californios, the youngest daughter of the don, Mercedes, and the eldest son of the squatter, Clarence, fall in love, and while the romantic plot is resolved happily by novel's end, the historical issues posed, especially in relation to disempowerment of the Californios and the rise of corporate monopolies and their power over government policy, are not as easily reconciled.

The Squatter and the Don—like all romances—textualizes a quest that necessarily involves conflict and resolution, given here as the trials and tribulations standing in the way of the felicitous union of a romantic couple. Because the novel is also marked by its historicity, however, the quest is not merely for the love of a maiden, but also for land and justice. The narrative thus follows two tracks, one historical and one romantic, with the latter serving to frame the reconstruction of a critical period in the history of the Southwest. In this regard, RDB's novel is eclectic much like other nineteenth-century historical romances, but while focusing on the demise of a heroic society (the aristocratic/feudal Californios), it differs in that it is not written from the perspective of the conquerors, with the usual portrayal of a "backward" people constrained by an outmoded feudal order and unable to cope in the modern post-feudal state. On the contrary, this novel, written from the perspective of the conquered, questions whether the new order indeed brought progress to the region, and if so, at what cost, in view of the crassness and immorality of much of the invading population, whether squatters or monopolists, its corrupt political leaders and their legislation, and its reprehensible treatment of the conquered who are willing to accommodate to the new structures. From the invasion of Californio lands, the novel goes on to address other forms of "invasion" in which the space being invaded is as much economic and political as geographical. By the novel's end, the victims are seen to be not only the Californios and their immediate antagonists, the squatters, but also the city of San Diego and, in the long run, the entire state population, subject to the tyranny of the railroad monopoly—the "white slaves of California"—who suffer the consequences of the collusion of state government, Congress, and the monopolies, as figured in the Big Four: Stanford, Huntington, Crocker, and Hopkins. The story of the railroad monopoly and its willingness and capacity to crush all competition figure preeminently in *The Squatter and the Don*. The text narrates the demise of the promise of prosperity for San Diego that comes with the failure of the townspeople to have their city be the western terminus of "the shortest transcontinental railway," ruled out when the Big Four, in collusion with Congress, ensure the failure of the Texas Pacific railroad.

The Squatter and the Don is not, of course, the only novel written about nineteenth-century California dealing with the righteous dispossessed or with the voracious monster, the Railroad Trust, described by Frank Norris in *The Octopus* as "an iron-hearted monster of steel and steam, implacable, insatiable, huge—its entrails gorged with the life blood that it sucked from an entire commonwealth" (322). Although RDB's novel does not focus on the dispossession of farmers in the San Joaquín Valley, as does Norris' 1901 novel, it does—years before Norris' account—provide a critical portrayal of the railroad monopoly that thwarted the construction of the Texas and Pacific Railroad to San Diego, ending with a mention of the Mussel Slough massacre of 1880, which is the subtext of *The Octopus*. But unlike the Norris novel, in which the "Spanish-Mexicans" are described as "decayed, picturesque, vicious and romantic," RDB's novel presents a capable, cultured, even heroic people who were unjustly deterritorialized, economically strangled, linguistically oppressed, and politically marginalized after 1848. It is precisely to rail against the cultural defamation of Mexicans and Californios—as much perhaps as the material dispossession—that RDB writes.

The RDB novel decries the precluded agency of individual entrepreneurs and the immoral "principles of business" of the Big Four and expresses outrage at the lack of governmental action to control "the hydra-headed monster." The powerlessness of the American public and their betrayal by political bodies, ostensibly working in their interest, but instead controlled and bought off by powerful corporations, are two crit-

ical subtexts found throughout the novel. The novel's heroic moral struggles are played out generally within the public sphere, although not
exclusively, for social, cultural, and economic battles are fought out
within the home as well. The real battles however are primarily fought
in Congress, in the court rooms, in state legislatures, and in interactions
between squatters and Californios; these come into the reader's view
through detailed accounts and numerous intercalated texts, be they congressional bills, treaties, laws, the infamous *Colton suit* letters, or reports
of what transpired in the attorney general's office. In the narrative, the
repercussions of this legal, legislative, and congressional action on the
Californios, on the settlers, on the squatters, and on the public in general
are viewed directly and extensively, but are always given within the
narrative paradigm of the romance and enclosed within an ethical framework which is always explicit in what is at times heavy-handed didactic
calling for a "moral" nation and a "gentler and kinder" form of capitalist
development. Thus while inveighing against corruption, the novel, in
keeping with a reformist stance that has no basic quarrel with capitalism
in and of itself—nor with patriarchy, for that matter—argues for the full
enforcement of existing laws guaranteeing the righting of wrongs and a
more principled capitalism and politics.

At bottom, the problem in *The Squatter and the Don* is seen to be political rather than economic. What stands out most notably in the novel,
in terms of narrative as well as ideological strategy, is that several conflicts come to a head with the handicapping of male agency. Women's
intervention arises in fact as a corollary to this "emasculation," be it
derived from economic, political, or physical causes. This disabling,
whether the crippling of Victoriano, the fall of Gabriel, the illness and
death of Don Maríano, the suicide of Mechlin, the shooting and crippling
of George, or the moral blindness and consequent crippling of the trans-
gressor Darrell, constrains men from action and feminizes them. The
crippling and freezing of the Californios, a motif woven throughout the
novel, serves as a metaphor for the political disempowerment and subsequent proletarianization of the Californios. Readers will find that another crucial aspect of RDB's novels is her countering of the prevailing
racist representation of Californios and Mexicans generally as a "mongrel
race" unfit for membership in the republic. In both novels these negative
stereotypes are subverted and partially inverted: the Mexicans or Californios are constructed as a heroic, cultured people who were economically, linguistically, and politically marginalized after 1848.

The California novel, as does *Who Would Have Thought It?*, takes note
of the ongoing social struggle for women's suffrage; intelligent and en-
lightened men, like the hero Clarence, are said to recognize an inequity
and inequality in rights, and to be aware that women have little or no
say in matters, and are being forced to operate at a distinct disadvantage.

Men too, however, are shown to be subject to external, socially imposed constraints. The "incapacitation" of men, and thus their figurative emasculation in the novel, serves not only as a symbolic act to reproduce the handicapping of an entire collectivity—the Californios—but, inversely, to expose as well the social handicaps and gender constraints under which women—perceived as "incapable" of exerting agency except in discrete "feminine spaces"—constantly find themselves. Excluded from participating in the power struggle at the public level, women are reduced, however resentfully, to exerting their power in interpersonal relations. If only to underscore "the tyranny" of partriarchy, the novel here falls back on the notion that in the domestic sphere and in the emotive domain women find a playing field on which they have the upper hand.

A writer who witnessed the disappearance of the old order and the disruption of everyday life with the disintegration of past structures, shifts in power relations, and the rapid capitalist development of the territory, RDB would seek to reconstruct a bracketed history and to question dominant Anglo-American ideological discourses. Unwilling to adopt a position of resignation or to ensconce herself in nostalgia for the past, RDB, through her novels—despite their contradictions—takes a forthright and vocal stand, whether it be in denouncing the despoliation of the Californios or satirizing the presumed superiority of the Anglo-Americans. At a moment when the few histories narrated by Californios themselves remained in manuscript form and were even then already collecting dust in archives, the very act of writing and publishing this historical romance was a call to action and at the same time a form of empowerment for the collectivity. So too today the recovery of these texts has an important role to play in tracing back the literary and ideological history of the Southwest and its inhabitants, highlighting issues that are still very much with us today.

TEACHING THE WORK

Rushes for both gold and land characterized the mid-nineteenth century history of California. Within the history of what was the Mexican Northern territories and is now the U.S. Southwest, these often lawless times came just on the heels of the end of the Mexican-American War. The Anglo population, for example, increased by tenfold within a few years after the discovery of gold. Many of those who stayed tried to take land from the large estates held by Mexican and, later, Mexican-American landowners.

1. Students can be asked to compare the image of the California Gold Rush, told mainly by Anglo-American historians, and the little-written history from the point of view of the Mexican population that was already in California.

2. Appropriation of land has been an ongoing theme of American western expansion, first against Native Americans, then against Mexicans in Texas and California. Teachers should introduce the idea of Manifest Destiny and its repercussions for the populations whose land has been conquered.

3. Mexican Americans have rarely had access to equal legal representations, in the legislature or in the courts. In *The Squatter and the Don*, how can it be shown that even with adequate funds and legal representation, execution of decrees and legal decisions can sometimes lack power?

4. Within the context of land use and corporate power, in *The Squatter and the Don*, women provide a reasonable voice from the private sphere, which influences the public one. What roles are women allowed to play in *The Squatter and the Don*, and are they different in Anglo and Mexican households?

5. The works of RDB have recently been rediscovered by North American feminists and others. A comparison between her novels and those of such contemporary authors as Harriet Beecher Stowe and Helen Hunt Jackson (whose 1884 novel *Ramona* in defense of Native Americans so entranced the Cuban poet and patriot José Martí that he translated it into Spanish) may be an illuminating exercise to contrast their female positions (two being from outside the cultures they defend and one, RDB, presenting an insider's perspective) with regard to such issues as cultural assimilation and accommodation, racism, minority and ethnic identities in the United States, and government policies in regard to race, ethnicity, and gender.

SUGGESTIONS FOR FURTHER READING

Works by María Amparo Ruiz de Burton

Don Quixote de la Mancha: A Comedy in Five Acts, Taken from Cervantes' Novel of That Name. San Francisco: J. H. Carmany, 1876.

[C. Loyal]. *The Squatter and the Don: A Novel Descriptive of Contemporary Occurrences in California.* San Francisco: Samuel Carson, 1885. Reprint Houston: Arte Público Press, 1992, with introduction and notes by Rosaura Sáchez and Beatrice Pita.

Who Would Have Thought It? Philadelphia: J. B. Lippincott, 1872. Reprint Houston: Arte Público Press, 1995, with introduction and notes by Rosaura Sánchez and Beatrice Pita.

Other Sources

Bancroft, Hubert Howe. *California Pastoral, 1796–1848.* San Francisco: The History Company, 1888.

García, Mario T. "The Californios of San Diego and the Politics of Accommodation." *Aztlán* (Spring 1975): 69–85.

Gutiérrez, David G. *Walls and Mirrors: Mexican Americans, Mexican Immigrants and the Politics of Ethnicity.* Berkeley: University of California Press, 1995.

Monroy, Douglas. *Thrown Among Strangers: The Making of Mexican Culture in Frontier California.* Berkeley: University of California Press, 1990.

Norris, Frank. *The Octopus: A Story of California.* New York: Doubleday, Page & Company, 1901.

Pitt, Leonard. *The Decline of the Californios: A Social History of the Spanish-Speaking Californians, 1846–1890.* Berkeley: University of California Press, 1970.

Saldívar, José David, and Hector Calderon, eds. *Criticism in the Borderlands: Studies in Chicano Literature, Culture and Ideology.* Durham, N.C.: Duke University Press, 1991.

Sánchez, Rosaura. *Telling Identities.* Minneapolis: University of Minnesota Press, 1995.

Sánchez, Rosaura, and Beatrice Pita. Introduction to *The Squatter and the Don.* Houston: Arte Público Press, 1992.

———. Introduction to *Who Would Have Thought It?* Houston: Arte Público Press, 1995.

Weber, David J. *Foreigners in Their Native Land: The Historical Roots of the Mexican Americans.* Albuquerque: University of New Mexico Press, 1992.

3

Piri Thomas' *Down These Mean Streets*: Writing as a Nuyorican/Puerto Rican Strategy for Survival

Asela Rodríguez de Laguna

PIRI THOMAS, originally named John Peter Thomas, was born in 1928 in New York City, the son of a Cuban father and a Puerto Rican mother. Thomas was the first mainland-born Puerto Rican narrator to achieve national, mainstream recognition in the United States for his autobiographical work, *Down These Mean Streets*, in 1967. The autobiography is a forceful portrait of Thomas' difficult life in the streets of Spanish Harlem from the Depression era to the early 1960s. His experiences as a child in the barrio and as a teenager in an Italian section of East Harlem and later in Babylon, Long Island, forced him to confront issues of racial and ethnic identity. *Down These Mean Streets* traces his early initiation into gangs, violence, drugs, and sex, as well as time spent in a maximum security prison after his conviction for armed robbery. In fact, Thomas began writing in prison.

The popularity of *Down These Mean Streets* converted him into a spokesperson for the Puerto Rican community in the late 1960s, with frequent appearances on television and radio. The autobiography emerged at a time in which there was a growing market for works that could help U.S. readers comprehend the social unrest taking place around them; it remains as powerful and controversial today as it was when first published. Thomas' self-documentation continues in two autobiographical sequels, *Savior, Savior Hold My Hand*, published in 1972, and *Seven Long Times* (1975).

ANALYSIS OF THEMES AND FORMS

Rereading Piri Thomas' masterpiece bildungsroman *Down These Mean Streets* (1967) elicits different and conflicting critical reactions. At a time when the postcolonial is giving way to neocolonial experience and criticism, and within an academic climate richly diverse in competing interpretations of the role of the text among canonists and multiculturalists, *Down These Mean Streets* necessarily takes the reader nostalgically and historically back to the beginning of an emergent Puerto Rican minority literary production in the mainland. A new reading of the text also critically questions the essence, nature, and perdurability of several of the signals encoded in this autobiographical text, particularly if examined by adherents or theorists of feminist, gender, and queer studies, or any other transcolonial approach.

More than 30 years after its publication, *Down These Mean Streets* remains an important canonical, albeit controversial, text within the fabric of Puerto Rican literature written in English. Its publication signaled the beginning of what later became the Nuyorican "ethnic" literary experience, and it established itself as a pioneer text. It brought immediate fame to its author, contributing to the displacement of a voiceless and marginal writer, representative also of a voiceless community, from no place to at least the periphery of mainstream American letters, and it was acclaimed as a classic in the growing-up-in-the-barrio genre. It also opened up the path to future Latino writing.

Down These Mean Streets is the tale of a mulatto Puerto Rican youth in search of his racial definition and cultural identity who wanders uncomfortably in the contested social, cultural, and racial spaces of the home, the school, and the "mean" streets. The encounter and ensuing conflicts between the mixed-race Puerto Rican family and the racist American society of New York during the 1940s and 1950s are narrated against the backdrop of the author's personal experiences. This is the first autobiographical novel written by a Puerto Rican prisoner turned writer, enraged by the fury of "hate," "rejection," and "invisibility." Piri, like the author Piri Thomas, ends up in jail. However, "jail" becomes a metaphor not only of punishable incarceration, but, most important, of creative freedom and redemption. It is the experience of incarceration that opens up the opportunity to write and encounter religious conversion. It is, thus, a tale of hope and salvation. On another level, this text is also about writing as a process of catharsis and, therefore, of creatively coming to terms with rage, anger, hate, and invisibility.

Like many other autobiographical narratives, *Down These Mean Streets* is a didactic novel, marked by a positive and optimistic outlook regarding a young man's struggle for individuality, personal responsibility, justice, human dignity, acceptance, and, above all, recognition. This search becomes a very passionate and honest invitation to penetrate the unknown world of Piri—his Puerto Rican–American experience in El Barrio, Hispanic Harlem, a neighborhood community characterized by "garbage-lepered streets" (xi),[1] violence, drugs, crime, prejudice, and poverty. In combining the didacticism of the genre with the pioneering depiction of an antiheroic figure within a ghetto space, Piri Thomas initiated an ethnic literary trend that enjoyed the support of a major publishing company partly because the text maximized the basic elements of a commercially successful work. However, behind the drugs, crime, sex, verbal and physical violence, streetwise mentality, and expected stereotypes, there is a very direct and compelling voice that captivates by transcending those contingencies and by forcing the contemporary reader to question the issues of race, sexual behavior, and gender relations.

The invitation of the protagonist in the prologue to enter his world is therefore a window to Piri's space—both exterior and interior: "Hey, World—here I am. Hallo, World—this is Piri Thomas. That's me" (xi). The tension between spaces—that of a soul in search of affirming its own binary identity and a hostile environment—further exposes the thorny topic of racial differences. It is through writing that the protagonist learns to temper his conflicting existential and sociopolitical demands and accept what he is. In exploring the space that fluctuates between locations—Puerto Rico and El Barrio, home and the streets, his inner but troubled self and the ugly outside world—the author manages to produce a rich and provocatively dynamic text. *Mean Streets* illuminates, from the perspective of the marginalized, the pains of racism, the struggle to survive pain, self-hate, violence, aggression, invisibility, and social oppression, while questioning both the individual and the society.

The anguish resulting from racial differentiation and the struggle to understand it is first experienced and enunciated at home—a microcosm of the "racialized differentiation among Puerto Ricans within their own communities" as Marta E. Sánchez has expressed it (120). It is precisely in the home—the family space par excellence at the core of Hispanic culture and values—where Piri ironically initially encounters loneliness, rejection, and invisibility. He is the darkest of all his siblings, and because of his color he is the target of his black father's cold treatment and resentment. Thus, color becomes the category that sets Piri apart from the others—his immediate family—among whom he feels "like a stranger" (23). The most blatant victimizer is the father who prefers the others who are white and blames Piri for almost everything that happens at home. It is important to point out that it is the "black" father who discriminates against the dark son, not the "white" mother who indeed accepts him for what he is. Piri's nuclear family is emblematic of a typically Puerto Rican mixed family: Puerto Rican society privileges those with fairer complexions for their closeness to being white. Piri's brothers and sister seem to identify with the white world within their community. His father and siblings make alliances with the white world, symbolized by the father taking a white woman as a mistress and by the family moving to suburbia. By doing so they desert their black origins and align themselves instead to their Indian ancestry.

Piri runs away from home at the age of 12 but carries Harlem within him. The first time he runs away no one in the house notices his absence—a doubling of the marginality and invisibility of the streets at home. A sense of rejection and uncertainty about himself are the basis of a journey which leads him to different racial identifications and designations that intensifies when he begins to keep company with American blacks. "I felt shame creep into me. It wasn't right to be ashamed of what one was. It was like hating Momma for the color she was and Poppa for the color he wasn't" (129). However, his friend Brew, a black from the Deep South, claims Piri is just one of them: "Ah only sees another Negro in fron' of me" (130). When Piri finally adopts blackness as his color identity, his dumbfounded mother, who is far removed from the context of American racism corrects him by pointing out the difference of hybridization: " 'You are not black,' Momma said, 'you're brown, a nice color, a pretty color' " (45). Piri's attempts to find himself in his family are aborted. When he chooses to identify himself as black his brothers reject him. Puerto Ricans, as defined by his brothers, are non-blacks: "You're crazy, stone loco. We're Puerto Ricans, and that's different from being *moyetos*" (154). His brother José reiterates the differences that separate them in the context of the American society:

"I ain't black, damn you! Look at my hair. It's almost blond. My eyes are blue, my nose is straight. My mother . . . lips are not like a baboon's ass. My skin is white. White, goddamit! White! Maybe Poppa's a little dark, but that's the Indian blood in him. He's got white blood in him and—"

"So what the f . . . am I? Something Poppa an' Momma picked out of the garbage dump?" (155)

The father exposes the strategy he has adopted to survive North American racism:

" '—I got pride in you, *hijo*' he said slowly. . . . Poppa's eyes were on his hands, . . . 'I ain't got one colored friend,' he added, 'at least not one American Negro friend. Only dark ones I got are Puerto Ricans or Cubans. I'm not a stupid man. I saw the look of white people on me when I was a young man, when I walked into a place where a dark skin wasn't supposed to be. I noticed how a cold rejection turned into an indifferent acceptance when they heard my exaggerated accent. I can remember the time when I made my accent heavier, to make me more of a

Puerto Rican the most Puerto Rican there ever was. I wanted a value on me, son' " (164).

Thus, the father desires to be recognized as a person, as a being with *value*, that is with respect, dignity: someone visible. This is why he tries to maintain himself within familiar territory—the other Spanish-speaking communities. Foreign language and a heavy accent are the marks of difference, a difference much more accepted than the color difference which seems to be much crueler in alienating a person from the social, public, and political space. For father, son, and the other siblings the very place of identification, caught in the tension of demand and desire, is a space that creates a splitting into opposite directions: one, opting for a supposedly blind Puerto Rican color mentality that inclines more toward the white, and another that chooses blackness as a dwelling space. In either instance, however, one's born reality is not affirmed. Rather the subject constructs an identity based on exterior expectations. This is made explicit in Piri's encounter with a prostitute in an "only for white brothel" in the South where he has been admitted as a Puerto Rican. Upon leaving, however, he yells at the prostitute that she has been with a "nigger," "a black man." This ought not to be confused with an "act of adolescent bravado" as Eugene Mohr has stated (1982, 50), or much worse as a very mean sign of getting even through sex, but rather as an affirmation of his identification (he now sees himself as a black man).

In this text, Thomas forcefully exposes a theme that up to the 1950s and 1960s was barely touched within Puerto Rican literature written in Spanish with the exception of Francisco Arriví's dramatic trilogy *Máscara puertorriqueña* (Puerto Rican Masks, composed of *Bolero y plena* [1956], *Vejigantes* [1958], and *Sirena* [1959]) and Pedro Juan Soto's novel *Usmaíl* (1959). In these texts forms of discrimination based on the shade of one's skin color serve to expose racism as a social and political phenomenon, a fact not openly admitted given the familiar belief that there is no racial prejudice in Puerto Rico. *Down These Mean Streets* undermines the widely accepted myth of one single, happy, color-blind Puerto Rican cultural family.

Through the rough journey of drugs, violence, fights, robbery, crime, prostitution, and all the evils associated with the subculture of poverty—beginning in Harlem and then on to Long Island, to the South, back to New York, and ultimately to jail—there is also a quest for self-searching and for achieving manhood. It is a journey that evolves from feeling himself a part of the "shadows" of the city (the Harlem of lights, noise, cars, music, curses) to a liberation of self. It is in Harlem that he begins to listen to the "sounds inside me" (xii) which culminate with his finding the Bible as a source of content, accepting faith in Christ, and finally defining himself as a man with self-respect and dignity (354). Religion and education have been liberating forces toward the self-realization of the character in the same way that writing has been the strategy for survival for the author.

Down These Mean Streets is considered a classic (see Ilan Stavans, "Race & Mercy: A Conversation with Piri Thomas"). Although it is a text many have heard about or have referred to in papers on the subject of Nuyorican literature, very few critical studies have been made of the text. James B. Lane exalts it as a "provocative autobiography" that "dramatically captured and transmitted the reality of growing up in the Puerto Rican 'Barrio' district of New York during the 1940s and 1950s" (814). Most critics have praised the text for Thomas' graphical etching of East Harlem, capturing the colors, sounds, passions, and moods of the teeming tenements, portraying the barrio as both liberator and enslaver (Lane 814). If the text offered the first glimpse of the Puerto Rican barrio, its protagonist conveyed the "inner conflict facing a youth who hoped to achieve self-esteem and respect" (Lane 814). Piri's life exemplified a stereotype, the life of a member working within and trying not to succumb to a world of violence, drugs, cynicism, and jail. When the work appeared it was hailed as a black cultural-nationalist text or alternatively as a mainstream narrative of rehabilitation.

One of the most provocative studies that has been done on the work is Marta E. Sánchez's "La Malinche at the Intersection." She uses the trope of "La Chingada" and exposes the "negotiations of racial and gendered discourses" in the memoir from a Chicana feminist approach. The trope, based on the figure of La Malinche, the Mexican Indian translator and consort of the Spanish conquistador Hernán Cortés, considered by the Mexican people as an "Eve" or traitor, has been reevaluated in recent decades by feminists. From being an icon of destructive social and sexual agency, La Malinche/"La Chingada" is now considered an agent of affirmation, as a cultural bridge and translator. Applied to a Puerto Rican text, the trope serves to point out how Thomas "appropriated the signs of the dominant black-white model of race to represent himself and his life ways to the larger metropolitan culture" by "generating intercultural linkages among Anglo-Americans, African Americans, and Puerto Ricans years before the concepts of hybrid, heterogeneity, and difference gained academic and social repute" (119).

TEACHING THE WORK

1. There are many approaches to teaching *Down These Mean Streets* because it is a text that can be used to explore not only many themes

but also several analyses (psychological, Freudian, feminist, linguistic) that go beyond a sociological one in which the protagonist and his environment are studied only as a typical representation of the Puerto Rican community in the Bronx. To provide a more rounded cultural personality of El Barrio, students could be asked to read one or two sketches of Jesús Colón in *A Puerto Rican in New York and other Sketches* and of Nicholasa Mohr's *El Bronx Remembered* or *In Nueva York* to compare Piri Thomas' literary depiction of the barrio. These readings could be a beginning for the discussion of Puerto Ricans in the diaspora from a historical and sociocultural perspective: reasons for coming to New York in different periods (early in the century and later in the 1940s and 1950s); the socioeconomic backgrounds of the immigrants; and the family and social relations established between the Puerto Rican community and others.

2. Discuss: Are the characters all stereotypes? What mechanisms does the author employ to represent the characters and the barrio? Which images are privileged? Against the background of El Barrio how does the image of native Puerto Rico appear? How is the island described? Consider images, colors, the attitude, and tone in references to the island.

3. In preparing students to discuss "machismo," "donjuanismo," and "sexism," what is the role of the woman (mother/daughters/sisters/ girlfriends/American acquaintances) in this text? Discuss gender, race, and class and expose commonalities and differences.

4. How do the Puerto Rican characters view miscegenation and their relation vis à vis blacks and whites. Pay attention to the uses of language, the metaphoric and poetic, versus street and foul language, and the use of Spanglish.

NOTE

1. All page numbers noted in parenthesis in the text refer to Piri Thomas, *Down These Mean Streets* (New York: Knopf, 1967).

CRITICISM

Lane, James B. "Beating the Barrio: Piri Thomas and *Down These Mean Streets*." *English Journal* 61 (1972): 814–23.

Mohr, Eugene. "Lives from El Barrio." *Revista Chicano-Riqueña* 8, no. 4 (1980): 60–79.

Sánchez, Marta E. "La Malinche at the Intersection: Race and Gender in *Down These Mean Streets*." *PMLA* 113, no. 1 (January 1998): 117–128.

Stavans, Ilan. "Race & Mercy: A Conversation with Piri Thomas." http://www.cheverote.com/stavansinterview.html.

SUGGESTED READINGS

Acosta-Belén, Edna. "Beyond Island Boundaries: Ethnicity, Gender, and Cultural Revitalization in Nuyorican Literature." *Callaloo* 15 (1992): 979–98.

———. "The Literature of the Puerto Rican Minority in the United States." *Bilingual Review/La Revista Bilingue* 5, no. 1–2 (1978): 107–16.

Alegría, Fernando, and Jorge Ruffinelli, eds. *Paradise Lost or Gained: The Literature of Hispanic Exile*. Houston: Arte Público Press, 1990.

Cardona, Luis A. *History of the Puerto Ricans in the U.S.* Alpharetta, Ga: Carreta Press, n.d.

Cintrón, Humberto N. *Frankie Cristo*. New York: Taino, 1972.

Colón, Jesús. *A Puerto Rican in New York and Other Sketches*. New York: Monthly Review Press, 1961.

Darder, Antonia, and Rodolfo D. Torres. *The Latino Studies Reader: Culture, Economy & Society*. Malden, Mass.: Blackwell, 1998.

Flores, Juan. *Divided Borders: Essays on Puerto Rican Identity*. Houston: Arte Público Press, 1993.

Hernández, Carmen Dolores. *Puerto Rican Voices in English: Interviews with Writers*. Westport, Conn.: Praeger, 1997.

Kanellos, Nicolas. *The Hispanic Almanac: From Columbus to Corporate America*. Detroit: Visible Ink Press, 1994.

Mohr, Eugene. *The Nuyorican Experience: Literature of the Puerto Rican Minority*. Westport, Conn.: Greenwood Press, 1982.

Mohr, Nicholasa. *El Bronx Remembered*. New York: Harper & Row, 1975

———. *Felita*. New York: Dial Press, 1979.

———. *Going Home*. New York: Dial Press, 1986.

———. *In My Own Words: Growing Up Inside the Sanctuary of My Imagination*. New York: J. Messner, 1994.

———. *In Nueva York*. New York: Dial Press, 1977.

———. *Nilda*. New York: Harper, 1972.

———. *Rituals of Survival: A Woman's Portfolio*. Houston: Arte Público Press, 1985.

Ortiz Cofer, Judith. *An Island Like You: Stories of the Barrio*. New York: Puffin, 1995.

Rodríguez, Clara E. *Puerto Ricans Born in U.S.A.* Boulder, Colo.: Westview Press, 1991.

Rodríguez de Laguna, Asela, ed. *Images and Identities: The Puerto Rican in Two World Contexts*. New Brunswick, N.J.: Transaction Books, 1987.

Soto, Pedro Juan. *Spiks*. Trans. Victoria Ruíz. New York: Monthly Review Press, 1973.

Stavans, Ilan. *The Hispanic Condition: Reflections on Culture and Identity in America*. New York: HarperCollins, 1995.

Torres, Edwin. *After Hours*. New York: Dial Press, 1979.

———. *Carlito's Way*. New York: Saturday Review Press/E P. Dutton, 1975.

Urciuoli, Bonnie. *Exposing Prejudice: Puerto Rican Experiences of Language, Race and Class*. Boulder, Colo. Westview Press, 1996.

Vega, Ed. *Casualty Report*. Houston: Arte Público Press, 1991.
———. *The Comeback*. Houston: Arte Público Press, 1985.
Wagenheim, Kal, and Olga Jiménez de Wagenheim, eds. *The Puerto Ricans: A Documentary History*. Princeton, N.J.: Markus Wiener Publishers, 1994.

4

Un Mundo Entero: Tomás Rivera and His World

Evangelina Vigil-Piñón

TOMÁS RIVERA is the celebrated, highly acclaimed, and beloved Chicano author, best known for his masterpiece, . . . *y no se lo tragó la tierra/ . . . And the Earth Did Not Devour Him*, about the social and economic struggles of a community of Texas migrant farmworkers. Considered a landmark of Chicano letters, the novel has been critically acclaimed for its innovative form, thematic complexity, and linguistic vitality. In addition to this classic, Rivera's work includes extraordinary short stories, eloquent poetry, and profoundly visionary literary essays. Tomás Rivera was deeply mourned when he died of a heart attack in 1984 at the age of 48, still in the prime of his life. His literary legacy lives on as a source of knowledge, history, and inspiration for present and future generations.

Rivera received a B.S. in English and Education in 1958 from Southwest Texas State University, an M.Ed. in 1964, and a doctorate in Romance Literatures from the University of Oklahoma in 1969. He was Chancellor of the University of California at Riverside, the first Mexican American to attain such a prestigious rank in higher education. Rivera was at the height of his career at the time of his death, as a man of letters and an exceptionally efficacious academic administrator deeply committed to the cause of promoting higher education for his own people and for all.

ANALYSIS OF THEMES AND FORMS

Deeply evocative, at once disturbing and inspiring, ... *y no se lo tragó la tierra/* ... *And the Earth Did Not Devour Him*[1] is a story of human suffering, of strength and survival. Set in the late 1940s to mid-1950s, Rivera's novel presents a poignant portrait of a disenfranchised community of Texas Mexican-American seasonal laborers working in the Midwest migrant stream. The story draws from the author's personal experiences growing up in his native town of Crystal City, Texas, in a rural settlement known as Winter Garden, an impoverished community of Mexican and Mexican-American laborers who lived at the mercy of farm owners and agribusiness contractors. Seeking work, entire families traveled the seasonal migrant stream—to Iowa, Wisconsin, Minnesota, Utah, and other areas of the Midwest—to earn a living at back-breaking stoop labor. The harsh social experiences that this community faced and their enduring hope and determination to seek a better life is the focus of *tierra.*

In addition to *tierra,* Rivera produced remarkable short fiction, collected and published posthumously in *The Harvest: Short Stories by Tomás Rivera,*[2] the reading of which can provide an important insight into Rivera's themes and style. Among the most famous stories in the collection are "El Pete Fonseca," about a sly pachuco (a Chicano "slick") who cons "la Chata" and fools the town; "Las salamandras" (The salamanders), an allegorical tale about a metaphysical struggle to the death with nature; and "Zoo Island," about a disenfranchised, landless, migrant community that fathoms the collective power of a "counted" populace. An interesting note by the collection's editor Julian Olivares is that "El Pete Fonseca" and "Eva y Daniel" are known to have been in the original drafts of *tierra.*

A complete collection of Rivera's poetry is contained in *The Searchers,*[3] published posthumously, also edited by Julian Olivares. The poetry is marked by a spareness of words effecting abstraction and complementing the persona's quiet, reflective voice. Major themes present in *tierra* resonate in this evocative poetry, including a struggle for survival, justice, and human dignity, while the power of hope underlies the theme of social struggle. Another theme deals with the search for truth and understanding through reflective thought in the realm of solace, where poetry originates. In "Poetics," which opens the collection, Rivera describes the power of poetry: "Poetry gives me pure feelings—time, beauty, man, and original death."

Poetic expression is an aesthetic element of central significance in *tierra.* In one of the novel's vignettes, Bartolo the poet alludes to both the inward source of poetic inspiration and its exteriorization when he tells the people to read the verses aloud because poetry is "the seed of love

in the darkness." Poetic expression surges in the novel, often in the lyrical voice of the child protagonist who is yet innocent and full of wonder.
The boy's poetic utterances both contrast with and transcend the harsh
social environment. In "Cuando lleguemos" (When we arrive), while others curse their predicament, stranded on a highway roadside, the boy's
thoughts transcend reality in the space of a poetic moment: "Lo silencio
de la madrugada hace que todo esté como de seda" (68) (The silence of
the morning twilight makes everything look like it's made of satin) (144).
While the people await daybreak, fatigued and dejected, the boy finds
diversion, gazing at the multitude of stars: "Está tan silencio que hasta
me parece que los grillos les están hablando a ellas" (69) (It's so silent,
it seems like it's the stars the crickets are calling to) (145). Poetry is moon
dust and magic in "La noche estaba plateada" (A silvery night). Having
realized the truth about the devil, the boy heads back home under the
silvery glow of the moon, enchanted: "El viento que sonaba las hojas de
los árboles parecía acompañarle los pasos. No habia diablo" (29) (The
sound of the wind rustling the leaves of the trees seemed to accompany
his every step. There was no devil) (106). Whereas lyricism and poetic
expression abound in the text of the novel, the vignettes interspersed
throughout the work are sheer poetry—cryptic, illusory, and timeless.

   "The Searchers" is Rivera's epic masterpiece and the title poem of his
collection. Rivera scholar Julian Olivares calls it the summa of Rivera's
poetic achievement. As conveyed by the title, the people live a life of
search—for sustenance, justice, self-realization. Readers will find in this
poem direct and implicit references and allusions to a story told in *tierra*,
"Cuando lleguemos" (When we arrive). In this chapter, Rivera portrays
the severe hardships experienced by migrant workers, loaded in
crowded trucks like beasts of burden, transported across the land of
plenty, seemingly always arriving but getting nowhere in a cycle of poverty. We "hear" the people's inward expressions of frustration, desperation, and dejection—the human spirit on the brink of defeat. Yet, a
profound sense of hope persists, collectively articulated in the solemn
and celebratory. The poetic voice invokes the people's noble courage to
tread forward in their search, the "passion of prophecy" in their eyes. In
tierra, the refrain "when we arrive" reflects expectation. In the epic poem
the refrain intones "we were not alone," reinforcing the power of unity
in the search. The refrain also affirms that cultural memory keeps the
past alive and unites the living with those who have died in the struggle.
Significantly, both the novel and the epic poem project the community's
consciousness of its historic struggle spanning centuries, a past of mythological dimension. At another level, the search is also for a mode of
expression. In "The Searchers," the people's invincible spirit is documented in the form of a traditional heroic epic; in *tierra*, the boy recon-

structs the symbolic "lost year," gaining a new vision. In *tierra*, the main development is psychological. The boy recalls the "lost year" and, through this process, retrieves time and gains a new understanding.

The theme of the inseparability of life and literature is reflected in the novel, as the young boy retreats to the cool darkness under the house. There he recalls the people and events of his "lost year" deciphering meaning through an imaginative process. The epiphany is his moment of truth and discovery:

Encontrar y reencontrar y juntar. Relacionar esto con esto, eso con aquello, todo con todo. Eso era. Eso era todo. Y le dio más gusto (75) (To discover and rediscover and put things together. This to this, that to that, all with all. That was it. That was everything. He was thrilled) (152).

Rivera stresses the power of language and its vocalization as an act of self-affirmation: "We must ritualize our existence through words" ("Fiesta of the Living," *The Complete Works* 340). In the novel, the child is a listener of words. He remembers the voices and expressions of the people. Through his internalization of the voices of others, his own voice is vitalized. Through language, his story is told. For Rivera the community maintains folk traditions through a "remembering, retelling and reliving" of its past. Cultural vitality is conveyed through language. The Tejano Spanish spoken by the characters in the novel, for example, features many folk expressions ("no'mbre," "vieja," "no, pos si") and words adapted from the English language ("jamborgues"/hamburgers, "bulegas"/bootleggers, "morolti"/model T). Through the language of dialogue, Rivera conveys the people's sensibilities and the nuances of their perceptions regarding such symbolic and thematic elements as family values, social customs, and religion. *Tipos de personas*—types of persons— function as archetypes: the pachuco, the nameless and faceless *mojado* (wetback), the cunning traveling salesman, and the weird couple.

The first chapter of *tierra* is introduced by an objective omniscient narrator who introduces the young boy. It becomes increasingly apparent that the boy is the work's protagonist. The narration penetrates the child's psyche in this opening chapter and reveals a recurring sequence that the boy has been experiencing. His thoughts flow, entering and exiting contiguous depths of perception: full consciousness, a subconscious dreamlike state, the state of awakening from sleep within a dream, the state of sleep within a dream within another dream, an infinite depth of the subconscious. This mental sequence leads the boy to a state of uncertainty. The dream state as reality then emerges as another psychological scape in which the boy hears the voice of his unconscious, a surrealistic, ghostly experience. He experiences confusion, a loss of memory, then a surge of fear, as he realizes that the voice calling him is his own. Several depths of conscious perception are then introduced as the narrator observes that the boy is thinking, then thinking about thinking, then about never thinking (a negation or subtraction of thought). This mental exertion causes him to blank out and fall asleep. "But before falling asleep," the narrator intones, "he saw and heard many things" (83). Remarkably, in less than a half-page of text, Rivera sets a tone of mystery and suspense, establishing the unconscious, subconscious, and conscious dimensions of thought as "setting" for this psychological novel.

Tierra is divided into twelve parts, corresponding to the twelve months of "the lost year" to which the narrator refers in the first section. In his introduction to *Tomás Rivera: The Complete Works*, editor Julian Olivares takes account of the twelve stories, noting their temporal and symbolic significance: "The temporal dimension of some of the episodes indicates a past more remote than one year; hence, the months and year are to be taken as stages of existence and, in some cases as an individual's or even a group's entire past" (17). Interspersed between the twelve chapters are thirteen vignettes which have been described as cinemagraphic "miniatures" that encapsulate the novel's thematics and aesthetics. Marked by brevity, some of the vignettes are in the voice of an objective narrator; others seemingly are in the voice of the child protagonist. Some contain short clips of dramatic conversation in the voices of unknown personages, reading much like Chicano *teatro* "actos" (short set pieces used extensively in late-nineteenth- and early-twentieth-century Mexican-American theater), as noted by Nicolas Kanellos.[4] These dynamic pieces range from impressionistic sketches to cryptic representations of the people's everyday existence. Collectively, the vignettes present a poetic quietude and an elusive, seemingly remote reality marked by deep irony, satire, dark humor, and human pathos.

In *tierra*, the story is told from multiple perspectives in a chorus of voices. A third-person omniscient narrator opens the novel. The voice of the child protagonist emerges, advancing the story from first-person and third-person perspectives. The child's voice is also presented as internal monologue, dialogue, and stream of consciousness. Kanellos observes that, as the story progresses, the objective omniscient narrator gradually adopts the voice of the main character. Other voices of the community are heard in the form of dialogue, dramatic monologue, interior dialogue, and stream of consciousness.

One of the most profound aspects of *tierra* is the presence and dynamics of silence. In an article entitled, "The Discourse of Silence in the Narrative of Tomás Rivera,"[5] critic Lauro Flores reveals the awesome power and complex function of silence in the novel. The brevity of the text and the laconic tone of the narration are indeed constructs of silence. It is significant how little is said, the manner in which it is expressed, as well as how much is left unspoken in the telling of the story. The expression of thought versus its suppression comes into question. As a sector of the "invisible" Mexican-American minority, the community of migrant workers has no voice in American society, yet their silenced actions—thinking (consciously and subconsciously), remembering, fearing, hurting, daring, understanding—propel the story with a vitality that defies their repressed social status.

Another fascinating aspect of Rivera's novel is its existentialist vision. This thematic bent is most dramatically portrayed in the title chapter, "... y no se lo tragó la tierra" (... And the Earth Did Not Devour Him) in which the boy curses his fate and God and challenges the faith of his mother. This is his most profound volitional act, and it represents a break with traditional Catholic belief. The boy is freed from the repressive forces of the Church and is placed, at once, "alone in the universe." Yet he is left free to find "grace" and spiritual strength within himself and his own people.

The most conspicuous of the novel's formal aesthetics are the author's manipulation and fragmentation of time and space, his reliance on evocation allusion, the use of multiple voices and character perspectives, and the permeation of various levels of consciousness. Such literary strategies challenge the reader to read interactively and to read and reread in order to decipher meaning. Rivera's *tierra* tears open earth, space, and time in a search to find truth.

TEACHING THE WORK

1. The most salient feature of ... *y no se lo tragó la tierra* is its structure, which fragments the story and makes the text consciously literary and self-referential. Comparing this work and its structure to other consciously literary texts (e.g., Sandra Cisneros' *The House on Mango Street*) shows the Latino writer's search for new ways to present the Latino experience. Other texts that mix English and Spanish and various genres also attempt to present Latino experience in an intergeneric way. Students should compare these works to more traditional narratives and discuss the value of each mode of presentation.

2. Another feature of *tierra* is the attempt made to present the boy's conscious and unconscious thoughts. Combing through the text, students can see which voice is being used and note any patterns.

3. *Tierra* presents a succession of themes: confusion, loss, superstition, the degradation of poverty, and racism among them, in the specific environment of agricultural migrant workers. Students may refer to other sources to investigate the migrant worker's world, including biographies of César Chávez, the video of Edward R. Murrow's series "Harvest of

Shame," and the history of "El Teatro Campesino" ("Theater of the Peasant"), founded by Luis Valdez.

4. Another outside area of study developed in *tierra* is the Chicano involvement in U.S. wars, also dealt with in Rudolfo Anaya's *Bless Me, Ultima* and Rolando Hinojosa's Klail City Death Trip series of novels. The Korean War was the first U.S. war in which Chicanos played a major part in the American armed forces. In the movie *Giant*, for example, the Chicano (played by Sal Mineo) enlists in the service and is killed in action. Discuss.

5. The Roman Catholic sacrament of first communion is a recurring theme for Latino authors (see Edward Rivera's *Family Installments* for a hilarious episode). Students may be asked to share their own experiences in preparing for their communion, including family involvement, or to put together an oral history anthology of first communion experiences (or confirmation or bar mitzvah experiences) of people they know.

NOTES

1. Tomás Rivera, . . . *y no se lo tragó la tierra / And the Earth Did Not Part*, trans. Tomás Rivera, Herminio Rios, and Octavio I. Romano-V. (Berkeley: Quinto Sol Publications, 1971); Tomás Rivera, . . . *y no se lo tragó la tierra / And the Earth Did Not Devour Him*, trans. Evangelina Vigil-Piñón, 3rd ed. (Houston: Arte Público Press, 1992). Subsequent references are to the latter edition, cited in this article as *tierra*. Published bilingually, the English translations come from the same edition.

2. Tomás Rivera, *The Harvest: Short Stories by Tomás Rivera*, ed. Julian Olivares (Houston: Arte Público Press, 1989).

3. Tomás Rivera, *The Searchers, Collected Poetry*, ed. Julian Olivares (Houston: Arte Público Press, 1990).

4. Nicolas Kanellos, "Language and Dialogue in . . . *y no se lo tragó la tierra*," in *International Studies in Honor of Tomás Rivera*, ed. Julian Olivares (Houston: Arte Público Press, 1986).

5. Lauro Flores, "The Discourse of Silence in the Narrative of Tomás Rivera," in *International Studies in Honor of Tomás Rivera*, ed. Julian Olivares (Houston: Arte Público Press, 1986).

SUGGESTIONS FOR FURTHER READING

Works by Tomás Rivera

La Cosecha, Cuentos de Tomás Rivera / The Harvest, Short Stories by Tomás Rivera, ed. Julian Olivares. Houston: Arte Público Press, 1988.

The Searchers, Collected Poetry, ed. Julian Olivares. Houston: Arte Público Press, 1990.

Tomás Rivera, The Complete Works, ed. Julian Olivares. Houston: Arte Público Press, 1992.

. . . *y no se lo tragó la tierra / And the Earth Did Not Devour Him*, trans. Evangelina Vigil-Piñón. Houston: Arte Público Press, 1987.

Related Works

Calderón, Héctor. "The Novel and the Community of Readers: Rereading Tomás Rivera's *Y no se la tragó la tierra*." In *Criticism in the Borderlands: Studies in Chicano Literature, Culture, and Ideology*, ed. Héctor Calderón and José David Saldívar. Durham, N.C.: Duke University Press, 1991.

International Studies in Honor of Tomás Rivera, ed. Julian Olivares. Houston: Arte Público Press, 1986.

Kanellos, Nicolas, and Claudio Esteva-Fabregat. *Handbook of Hispanic Cultures in the United States: Literature and Art*, ed. Francisco Lomelí. Houston: Arte Público Press, 1993.

Lattin, Vernon E., Rolando Hinojosa, and Gary D. Keller, eds. *Tomás Rivera, The Man and His Work*. Tempe, Ariz.: Bilingual Review Press, 1988.

Leal, Luis. "Mexican American Literature: A Historical Perspective." In *Modern Chicano Writers: A Collection of Critical Essays*, ed. Joseph Sommers and Tomás Ybarra-Frausto, 18–40. Englewood Cliffs, N.J.: Prentice Hall, 1979.

Olivares, Julian, ed. "Introduction." *Tomás Rivera: The Complete Works*, 13–46. Houston: Arte Público Press, 1992.

Pino, Frank. "The Outsider and 'El Otro' in Tomás Rivera's . . . *y no se lo tragó la tierra*," *Books Abroad* 49 (1975): 453–58.

Sommers, Joseph. "Interpreting Tomás Rivera." In *Modern Chicano Writers: A Collection of Critical Essays*, ed. Joseph Sommers and Tomás Ybarra-Frausto, 94–107. Englewood Cliffs, N.J.: Prentice-Hall, 1979.

5

Historical and Magical, Ancient and Contemporary: The World of Rudolfo A. Anaya's *Bless Me, Ultima*

Margarite Fernández Olmos

RUDOLFO A. ANAYA was born on October 30, 1937, in a small village in the eastern llanos or plains of New Mexico, a barren, desolate area of mournful winds and tough vegetation that materializes in many of his writings. His roots in the region run deep. Anaya's ancestors were among the original settlers of the area and thus the cultural richness of one of the oldest communities of the Americas informs Anaya's literary worldview.

As a student at the University of New Mexico Anaya wrote several novels, some quite extensive, which he later destroyed. In 1963 he graduated with a B.A. degree in English and American Literature, and in 1968 he completed an M.A. in English and earned another M.A. degree (1972) in guidance and counseling which he supported by his work as a high school teacher. Anaya's quest for a unique literary voice led him to spend seven years, from 1963 to 1970, to complete his first novel. That work, *Bless Me, Ultima* (1972), one of the very few Chicano best-sellers, established Anaya's reputation as an author and as one of the founders of the contemporary Chicano literary movement.

By the time Anaya had published his second novel, *Heart of Aztlan*, in 1976, he was no longer a high school teacher. In 1974 the English Department at the University of New Mexico invited him to become a member of the faculty to teach creative writing. *Tortuga* (1979) is the third novel of what the author has called his New Mexico trilogy. *Heart of Aztlan* and Anaya's later novellas from the 1980s, *The Legend of La Llorona* (1984) and *Lord of the Dawn: The Legend of Quetzalcoatl* (1987), are closely inspired by Aztec mythology and symbolism, but

Anaya's writings embrace a variety of genres and styles, including a travel journal, *A Chicano in China* (1986), as well as plays, short stories, poetry, edited anthologies, and essays.

In 1992 Rudolfo Anaya published *Alburquerque*, the recipient of a PEN-West Fiction Award, a suspenseful story of a young boxer's quest for his family's origins. The following three novels, *Zia Summer* (1995), *Rio Grande Fall* (1996), and *Shaman Winter* (1999), represent Anaya's incursion into the genre of detective fiction and a dramatic change in subject matter and style. Less mystical and lyrical than his earlier novels, but more easily read, Anaya's recent novels explore sociopolitical, ethical, and environmental problems that result from the power struggles inherent in rapid economic growth and development. *Jalamanta*, his novel published in 1996, is the tale of a spiritual leader banished from the "Seventh City" who returns with wise teachings and challenging beliefs. While not directly related to his suspense/detective novels, initiated by *Alburquerque*, *Jalamanta* nonetheless reflects the quest for truth that pervades all of Anaya's writings.

ANALYSIS OF THEMES AND FORMS

The celebrated Mexican-American novelist, poet, playwright, and essayist Rudolfo A. Anaya has described his literary work as a quest to compose the Chicano literary worldview. As a student of the classics and of contemporary literature in the English/Anglo American traditions, Anaya was well acquainted with the myths and symbols of King Arthur's Court, a metaphor the author uses in his essay "An American Chicano in King Arthur's Court" for the communal memory of Anglo Americans whose history and culture have been almost exclusively associated with American identity. But the voice he was searching for, the worldview he wished to discover in literature, was not to be found in those works nor in any others of the time. His creative voice as an author of his Hispanic/ Indian/New Mexican identity Anaya would have to discover on his own. That quest resulted in his 1972 novel, *Bless Me, Ultima*, still considered among the most memorable works of Chicano fiction.

Anaya has portrayed his "meeting" with the fictional character of his first novel, "Ultima," as a type of spiritual or magical encounter. He had begun to work on the story of a young boy, Antonio, and his relationship with his family. The story, however, never seemed to coalesce. The author found it difficult to uncover the symbols and patterns of his own culture. The pathway to that process, he claims, was opened up to him by Ultima's "appearance." "That strong, old curandera [folk healer] . . . came to me one night and pointed the way. That is, she came to me from my subconscious, a guide and mentor who was to lead me into the world of my native American experience. Write what you know . . . learn who you really are" ("An American Chicano" 115). From that moment, the ideas for the novel flowed as Anaya rediscovered the collective symbols of his Hispanic, indigenous heritage. In the author's first novel he turned to his life experiences for inspiration. The story of the awakening of a young boy's consciousness growing up in a small New Mexico town shortly after World War II closely parallels the author's own experience. At the same time, however, *Bless Me, Ultima* is a highly original work with a unique story and a universal appeal that has established Anaya's international reputation.

Bless Me, Ultima is considered by many the quintessential Chicano bildungsroman or coming-of-age novel. In *Bless Me, Ultima*, as in other works of this genre, the reader observes the process of the maturation of the main character through a series of rites of passage that affect the hero profoundly. In Anaya's novel the passage of time is limited to the main character's experiences from ages six to eight, much briefer than in the traditional bildungsroman. Young Antonio learns much in those two years, however, thanks to his apprenticeship with the old folk healer who guides his growing consciousness. Writers like Rudolfo Anaya from ethnically and racially marginalized groups in the United States take full advantage of the genre's potential. Often the coming-of-age novel as expressed in their works reflects the identity and adjustment problems of the protagonist to the dominant cultural society. The novel reveals the influence of objective cultural values on the moral maturation of the central character. In asserting an identity not always condoned or accepted by the power structure of his or her society, the ethnic or minority writer attempts to create new standards and perspectives from his or her position on the periphery of mainstream society.

Bless Me, Ultima blazed a path within the Chicano literary tradition in the category referred to as "novels of identity" in which the main characters must redefine themselves within the larger society from the vantage point of their own distinct ethnicity. In identity novels the character is always aware of his or her cultural heritage (often questioning it as well) and attempts to forge some type of reconciliation with the larger society while maintaining a distinct identity. In *Bless Me, Ultima* the figure of Ultima in this context is crucial. As young Antonio's guide and mentor, her teachings not only bring him into contact with a mystical, primordial world but also with a culture—his own Hispanic/Indian culture—that he must learn to appreciate if he is ever to understand truly himself and his place within society.

How can a story told from the vantage point of a seven-year-old boy express profound insights and complex ideas? *Bless Me, Ultima* accomplishes the task by being an extended flashback, that is, by assuring the reader from the very beginning that the events described, although seemingly occurring in the present, in fact occurred at an earlier time; the narrator is therefore, by implication, an adult. Anaya is able to maneuver this tension of the older implied narrator and the younger voice of the child-protagonist Antonio by carefully recreating the reactions of a small boy. Antonio's comments reflect the expected limitations of a child of that age. For Antonio, World War II is a "far-off war of the Japanese and the Germans," for example, and other historical events are explained in an equally simple age-appropriate manner. The reader is informed that Ultima came to stay with Antonio's family the summer that he was almost seven years old. Her arrival marks the beginning: "the beginning that came with Ultima" (1), and indeed Antonio's story begins and ends with her. Subsequent references in the same chapter to a time "long after Ultima was gone and I had grown to be a man" (13) affirm the fact that, although the story is presented in the voice of a young boy, it is actually the tale of a remembered youth. Time and chronology assume additional significance; time is described as "magical," it "stands still" and is linked with the character of Ultima. She represents origins and beginnings; her very name implies extremes and the extent of time and distance that Antonio will travel on his passage from innocence into awareness.

Bless Me, Ultima is an accessible novel despite its grounding in Chicano folk culture and myth and its occasional use of Spanish. It follows a linear or straightforward story development, a plot line that is clearly defined, and avoids the more experimental prose styles of other writers. Levels of narration are clearly delineated for the reader by the use of italics, a frequent Anaya device. Antonio's dream sequences, for example, are separated from the rest of the narration by italics, indicating a different dimension of consciousness. The first chapter serves important functions in plot development and structure. It gently guides the reader toward essential story elements, such as setting, characters, and historical background, and introduces the major conflicts that will form the basis for the dramatic tension throughout the novel. The technique of foreshadowing, which can often provide structural and thematic unity to a work, first appears in the introductory chapter. In *Bless Me, Ultima* foreshadowing ranges from statements that openly indicate future events to symbolic premonitions in dreams that suggest them. After Antonio's home is described in chapter one as a place that offers the young boy a unique vantage point from which to observe family incidents, he refers to the tragedy of the sheriff's murder that has yet to occur, the anguish of his brothers' future rebellion against their father, and the many nights when he will see Ultima returning from her moonlit labors gathering the herbs that are a folk healer's remedies. Ultima, who rarely speaks and whose words are therefore significant, states that "there will be something" between herself and Antonio, suggesting a strong and important relationship yet to come. But the most effective foreshadowing technique is found in Antonio's dream sequences throughout the novel, the first of which occurs in chapter one. They express the dread and anxiety of his inner world but are also frequently premonitions of the future. Antonio's dreams provide both a structural and thematic framework for the novel as they illustrate past events and suggest future conflicts.

Family history and New Mexican history are inextricably linked in *Bless Me, Ultima*. Antonio's father teaches the young boy about his past, which is tied to the Spanish colonial period of the region. His father, Gabriel, is a *vaquero* or cowboy. More than an occupation, it is a calling that has united his father and his paternal ancestors to the New Mexican plains, described as being as vast as the oceans. (Antonio's father's surname, Márez, derives from the Spanish word *mar* meaning the sea.) Social and economic changes in the state severely curtailed the free-spirited, aggressive lifestyle of the vaqueros when Anglo settlers took control of the land. The novel refers to such background information as part of the process of Antonio's education concerning his family's past; these facts also serve, of course, to provide readers with the cultural and historical foundation that will broaden their appreciation of events in the novel.

Antonio's mother is also linked with local culture but from a different perspective, as her own surname implies; she is a Luna, a people of the moon, tied to the land as farmers. The Lunas represent a different tradition within the rural U.S. Hispanic culture of the Southwest—the farming tradition, settled, tranquil, modest, devout, tied to old ways and customs. Antonio's mother, María, had convinced her husband to leave the village of Las Pasturas, and a lifestyle she considered coarse and wild, and move the family to the town of Guadalupe where better opportunities existed for their children. The move separates Gabriel from the other vaqueros and the free llano life he loves. He becomes a bitter man who drinks to soothe his hurt pride and his loneliness. The differences between these two cultures forms the basis for the first major conflict that affects Antonio's family. These tensions, as one discovers throughout the work, are presented as dichotomies: Márez/Luna, vaquero/farmer, free spirited/settled. Antonio must find a balance to these divided forces which tug at him from opposite directions.

The first dream sequence in chapter one illustrates his anxieties. Antonio describes a dream in which he witnesses his own birth assisted by an old midwife. After he is born she wraps the umbilical cord and the placenta as an offering to the Virgin of Guadalupe, the patron saint of the town (and of Mexicans and Mexican Americans in general). In his dream Antonio observes a terrible quarrel between the two branches of his family. The Lunas hope that the baby will become one of them, or possibly even a priest (his mother's fervent hope); the Márez uncles smash the symbolic offerings of fruits and vegetables brought by the mother's clan and replace them with their own emblematic gifts of a saddle, a bridle, and a guitar. They hope Antonio will follow their free-spirited ways. Both families frantically attempt to take hold of the placenta hoping to control the baby's destiny by disposing of it in their own allegorical fashion. The Lunas would bury it in the fields, tying the boy to the earth; the Márez family wish to burn it and scatter the ashes freely to the winds of the llano. The families have nearly come to blows when the old midwife steps in to claim her rights, as the person who brought the young life into the world, to dispose of the afterbirth herself. "*Only I know his destiny*" (6).

That old midwife is, of course, Ultima, the *curandera* who eventually comes to live in their home. One issue upon which both parents agree is their obligation to provide and care for the elders, respecting customs and traditions. Therefore, when Antonio's father discovers that Ultima will be living alone in the llano when the people abandon the village of Las Pasturas, he and Antonio's mother decide to invite her into their household in gratitude for her years of service to themselves and the community. Ultima is a respected figure, referred to as *la Grande*, the old, wise one. Outside of the family, however, Ultima is feared by some. Her healing powers are suspect and she is considered a *bruja* or witch. The suggestion of witchcraft brings a shudder of fear to Antonio and is a warning to the reader as well; the idea that witches can heal but can also place and lift curses with evil powers is another example of Anaya's foreshadowing of things to come.

Ultima is associated with ancient traditions and wisdom; in *Bless Me, Ultima* she is also equated with the forces of nature. Her meeting with Antonio is accompanied by a whirlwind, an oft-repeated motif representing magical power or warning of danger. And, as in traditional witch stories, Ultima is identified with a specific animal—in this case, an owl. The animal is reputed to be a disguise assumed by witches, but Ultima's owl does not frighten Antonio. On the contrary, her owl protects, defends, and soothes him, an observation legitimized by another of Antonio's dreams in which the owl flies the Virgin of Guadalupe on its wings to heaven.

Throughout *Bless Me, Ultima*, Antonio's dreams serve several functions: they sometimes anticipate events to come but more importantly they are an index to the main character's emotional and psychological development. Anaya has skillfully blended the "external" plot events with Antonio's frequent introspective musings and his world of dreams, a combination of personal experience, fantasy, and mythical legend. Antonio's dreams pervade his waking hours; each of them influence to some degree his conduct and attitude. In chapter nine, aware that his brothers frequent Rosie's house, the town brothel, Antonio's musings on his older brothers' behavior mirror his own apprehensions with regard to women and sexuality, innocence, and the concept of sin. The young boy represses his disturbing feelings which translates them into a dream about his brothers' restlessness as they experience the restraints of a small town and their parents' aspirations. Their behavior is rationalized in the novel, in great part, by their lineage; the notion of blood and heredity is a motif throughout *Bless Me, Ultima*. Just as Antonio's father's aggressiveness and his wife's gentle, subdued behavior are understood as hereditary qualities—in the "blood"—his brothers' attitudes and behavior are attributed to their father's character: "The Márez blood draws them away from home and parents" (72). Antonio's mother attempts to link his destiny with that of his Luna ancestor, a priest who supposedly established the town of Guadalupe generations earlier. In his dream, Antonio's brothers declare him to be a Luna who will become a farmer-priest like their maternal ancestor for their mother's sake. The dream sequences serve as a good example of the crossweaving of the external and internal conflicts that drive the plot.

Inquisitive and courageous, sensitive and thoughtful, Antonio's character evolves on several levels. On the objective, external plane his character passes through a variety of experiences, some typical of most young boys, some highly unusual. Many of his experiences can be compared to those of other rural Hispanic children in the U.S. Southwest of a certain era: he is raised in a Spanish-speaking home where traditions are maintained and respected; he confronts an Anglo-oriented school system where he is linguistically and culturally socialized into mainstream society; and he is indoctrinated into the Catholic religion even as he is surrounded by competing influences.

Other experiences are less typical and even extraordinary: in a short period of time, Antonio confronts violence and murder, tragic death, witchcraft, and supernatural phenomena. He will actively participate in ritual healing and even experience a symbolic death and rebirth as a part of his spiritual and psychological maturation. What Antonio cannot face or understand on a conscious level is deciphered in his dreams. His doubts and uncertainties are echoed on the subconscious level and occasionally resolved there as well. His reactions to these events as expressed in his dreams are the most revealing insights into the growth and evolution of the character; they provide a thematic framework of his gradual transformation.

As noted earlier, Antonio's first dream is of his own birth; both his biological mother and his spiritual mother (Ultima) are present. The dreams that follow reflect concerns about family and fear of losses (of people and illusions) that prepare him for his passage into adulthood and individuality. The critic Vernon E. Lattin divides the nine remaining dreams that follow the birth sequence into groups that reveal the path to Antonio's destiny. Dreams three (1978, 45), five (70), and seven (140) reflect the fear of loss: Antonio foresees that he will not become the priest his mother had hoped for, his innocence will be lost as he faces the temptations of sexuality, and the vision of Ultima in her coffin foreshadows the loss through death of his spiritual mother. Dreams two (25), four (61), and nine (235) reflect anxieties concerning Antonio's brothers and the larger world beyond, foreshadowing the experience of loss that he must assimilate in order to attain adulthood. In dreams two and four Antonio's brothers confront their own destinies beyond the family. With Antonio's help they can face the dangers of the treacherous river, but Antonio comes to realize that he cannot always assist these giants of his dreams, and by dream nine he resigns himself to the fact that they are lost to him and his parents. Like the souls of the Comanche spirits calmed by Ultima's ritual cremation, the souls of his brothers are put to rest in Antonio's anguished psyche.

Dreams six (119), eight (172), and ten (243) are considered by Lattin and other critics to be the most significant: "the dreams most homologous with the experience of the sacred, and as they present the dark night of the soul, they prepare the soul for its rebirth" (Lattin, "Horror of Darkness" 55). Dream six is the calm of reconciliation after the storm, an important step in solving Antonio's dilemma of good versus evil. The eighth dream becomes progressively more violent as despair and destruction are vividly communicated to the young boy—his home is set afire, his family is destroyed, Ultima is beheaded by an angry mob, and all life around him disintegrates. From this cosmic nothingness regenerative powers emerge. Although Antonio's final dream is filled with terror of death, the reader senses that he is now more prepared to accept and understand the realities of life. Having witnessed by now so much of Ultima's healing power, the messages of her teaching and his own dreams have revealed themselves to him. Toward the novel's end he reflects: "And that is what Ultima tried to teach me, that the tragic consequences of life can be overcome by the magical strength that resides in the human heart" (249).

A less-developed character than Antonio, Ultima is crucial nonetheless. She is once a stabilizer and a catalyst for growth and change, and the story revolves around the transference of her knowledge and worldview to Antonio. In Ultima, Anaya has created a fascinating character who embodies the combination of indigenous traditions, ancient beliefs, and shamanic healing. Ultima is seer and natural scientist, teacher and herbal doctor. And despite her never having married or having had children of her own, she is a symbolic mother figure who represents the mysteries of life, death, and transformation.

Ultima is a conciliatory force in the novel who guides Antonio between the extremes of his parents and the myriad other tensions he must attempt to resolve. Respected as "a woman who has not sinned," she is also feared. Her skills were acquired from a renowned healer, "the flying man of Las Pasturas," and hence many consider her a witch. Ultima's characterization goes beyond the usual expectations regarding the gendered roles for men and women because she is a *curandera*; she is afforded a place in the public world not usually given to women in traditional patriarchal cultures. Her power comes in part from her knowledge of herbal remedies, spiritual healing, and magical rituals. And her spiritual approach is syncretic: it derives both from modern medicine and time-honored Native American curative practices, Christianity, and pagan traditions. The complexity of this character derives from these differing sources that are blended in her. Ultima represents a Mexican Amerindian tradition that has often been preserved precisely by women *curanderas*. Though uncommon in U.S. letters, *curanderas* have been a part of the Hispanic tradition for centuries and are familiar characters for many Hispanic readers.

Given the density of symbolism, myth, and cultural references in *Bless Me, Ultima*, it is not surprising that the novel has inspired a variety of critical responses. On the most fundamental level, of course, the novel's major theme is the coming-of-age and self-realization of a young Hispanic boy in New Mexico. Other obvious topics are the quest for personal and cultural identity, the significance of Chicano tradition and myth in spirituality and healing, and the role of mentors and guides in psychological and spiritual growth and development.

A standard approach to *Bless Me, Ultima* emphasizes the protagonist's need to reconcile the opposites in his life. The novel offers numerous conflicts the young boy must confront and presents them as seemingly irreconcilable opposites. The most evident is the clash between his father's pastoral lifestyle and his mother's farming tradition. The differences between the two, repeated throughout the novel, are underscored by their very surnames—Márez and Luna. Other striking examples are the conflicts between male and female, good and evil (personified in the beneficent mother-figure Ultima versus the evil father Tenorio), love and hate, town and country, and the Christian God versus the golden carp. Some critics have also noted the message of reconciliation, synthesis, and harmony that is also apparent in the novel. Conflicts and imbalances find a solution in harmony, balance, and a message of oneness; synthesis resolves opposites and mediates differences. Generally the balance and mediation are brought about by Ultima or Antonio; in other instances, the wisdom of nature itself restores harmony.

Some readings of the novel portray it as a nostalgic text, romanticizing an era that has little relevance for contemporary Chicano readers who are largely urban and for whom the conflicts among rural Hispanic traditions are issues of the past. Other critics disagree. For Horst Tonn, *Bless Me, Ultima* can be read on another level at which "the novel constitutes a significant response to relevant issues of the community. In broad terms, these issues are identity formation, mediation of conflict, and utilization of the past for the exigencies of the present" (2). U.S. society at the time Anaya was writing his work was experiencing a crisis of values similar to that portrayed in the novel in the mid-1940s. The theme of the pressure of change portrayed in the novel that Tonn identifies is underscored in the scene in which the townspeople react to the detonation of the first atomic bomb near Alamogordo, New Mexico, in 1945: "They compete with God, they disturb the seasons, they seek to know more than God Himself. In the end, that knowledge they seek will destroy us all" (190). The disruptive effects of World War II on veterans and their families, as well as on the internal migration from rural areas to the cities, have their counterpart in the social upheavals of the 1960s when Chicanos participated in movements for social change and began to question their cultural values and identities. *Bless Me, Ultima* proposes responses to the contemporary crisis of values based on the need for healing and reconciliation. Just as Antonio and Ultima function as mediators, healing a community suffering from strife and disruption, "the novel itself can be said to share in and contribute to a mediation process at work in the Chicano community during the 1960s and early 1970s" (Tonn 5). Juan Bruce-Novoa agrees that *Bless Me, Ultima* is truly a novel reflective of its era. In the midst of conflict and violence some present at the time proposed the alternative responses of "love, harmony, and the brotherhood of all creatures in a totally integrated ecology of resources . . . *Bless Me, Ultima* belongs to the counterculture of brotherhood based on respect for all creation" (Bruce-Novoa, "Learning to Read" 186).

Among the more popular approaches to the analysis of *Bless Me, Ultima* are those based on myth theory and criticism, a viable alternative given the emphasis that the novel places on the developing dream life of its protagonist, Anaya's familiarity with the theories of Carl G. Jung regarding universal archetypes, and the author's expressed affinity for myth: "One way I have in looking at my own work . . . is through a sense that I have about primal images, primal imageries. A sense that I have about the archetypal, about what we once must have known collectively" (Johnson and Apodaca, 422). *Bless Me, Ultima* offers ample opportunities for archetypal interpretations. The archetypal feminine principle—the intuitive, loving, life-affirming protector and nurturer—can be attributed to Ultima, the Good Earth Mother, and on another level, to the Virgin of Guadalupe who appears often in Antonio's dreams and is his mother's spiritual protector. The Terrible Mother—the frightening female figure, emasculating and life-threatening—corresponds to "La Llorona," a legendary mother in the Hispanic tradition who destroyed her own children and threatens those of others.

Antonio's character has been interpreted as that of the classic boy-hero who must successfully complete the universal rite of passage of separation, initiation, and return. He must depart the comforts of his mother's hearth and cross the bridge into the wide world of the town with its perils and challenges. His trials will extend from Lupito's murder to his Uncle Lucas' ritual exorcism for which the hero will sacrifice himself to save another. After three days of agony he will emerge as if reborn, a new, more mature boy who can reconcile himself with his father and mother, as well as the world around him. Ultima provides him with the symbolic tools (her pouch of herbs) and the spiritual weapons (her teachings) that will assist him in his ordeals.

A Jungian approach to *Bless Me, Ultima* could run the risk of leading to a static, unchanging mythical perception, however, one that certainly would not be faithful to Anaya's views on mythology. For the author, mythology is not simply a refashioning or retelling of ancient or universal tales and patterns. Myths should speak to our contemporary lives, give significance to a community. Historically constructed over generations, myths can help us understand contemporary realities and conditions. A more dynamic approach to myth criticism in *Bless Me, Ultima* is described by Enrique R. Lamadrid as "an ongoing process of interpreting and mediating the contradictions in the everyday historical experience of the people" (Lamadrid 103). In the novel this would be manifest in the dichotomies and binary oppositions (good and evil, love and hate, etc.) that are mediated by Ultima and Antonio. Their role is to reconcile these contradictions to arrive at harmony and synthesis and, in keeping with the original role of myth, resolve the internal contradictions of their community.

A myth criticism interpretation of *Bless Me, Ultima* should bear in mind, therefore, that Anaya describes a specific culture, a particular belief system. An analysis of the character Ultima may reflect universal principles, but it must be remembered that Ultima, as a shaman/*curandera*, represents an actual vocation, that of a healer/spiritual leader, a role with a useful and important function in an authentic culture. The role of a shaman and the role of a *curandera* are often indistinguishable. Both can resort to dreams and visions for help and guidance, and both practice medical, magical, and spiritual arts. A specialist in the use of spells and incantations as well as herbal remedies, the shaman is believed to have the power to change her or his human form into that of an animal or spirit. The curative practices of a *curandera* are intertwined with religious beliefs and respect for nature. Disharmony and imbalance cause a disruption of health; healing is a return to oneness and harmony with nature. These alternative healing values have endured for centuries and continue to provide contemporary answers to age-old questions. *Bless Me, Ultima* demonstrates that myth criticism and a culturally specific approach to a work of literature need not be mutually exclusive. Anaya's novel is historically relevant and magical, ancient and contemporary.

TEACHING THE WORK

1. *Bless Me, Ultima* was among the first published Chicano bildungs-roman. An interesting comparison might be made between Anaya's novel and the works of other Chicano authors, such as Tomás Rivera and Richard Rodriguez, particularly with regard to the protagonists' relationships to their ethnicity, language, and family relations. A comparison with other Latino authors such as Piri Thomas might also prove fruitful if the focus then becomes the influence of the world outside the family on the development of the young male protagonist. How significant is being a member of a specific cultural group compared to issues of race, social class, and environment?

2. The topic of identity could be extended to gender. How do the dilemmas faced by the male protagonist of *Bless Me, Ultima* compare to the issues proposed by such female authors as Sandra Cisneros and Esmeralda Santiago in their works with female protagonists? Are the social tensions they confront complicated by gender?

3. The figure of Ultima represents a shamanic/folk healer culture that has long been a tradition in the U.S. Southwest. Her use of natural plants and herbs to heal reflects a curative practice, *curanderismo*, that is ancient but has gained popularity recently among those with an interest in alternative healing practices in the larger mainstream society. Robert T. Trotter's *Curanderismo, Mexican American Folk Healing* (Athens: University of Georgia Press, 1981) is useful for this approach. Students could research this fascinating area of study, listing some of Ultima's remedies and suggesting family cures from their own ethnic or family traditions. How is the use of magic significant in healing?

4. Additional student projects could include (1) consideration of what might be Antonio's chosen profession as an adult (despite his parent's dreams, can we imagine what Antonio eventually decided to do with his life?); (2) researching the time and place discussed in the novel, recalling that this was the sight of the first atomic bomb test (why is that significant? How might it affect the inhabitants of the region and the land so cherished by Antonio's family?); (3) consultation of a dictionary or interviewing a Spanish speaker to understand Anaya's Spanish terms and expressions to see the novel from an "insider's" perspective; and (4) consideration of how events might be portrayed differently if narrated by characters other than Antonio.

CRITICISM AND RELATED WORKS

Works by Rudolfo Anaya

"An American Chicano in King Arthur's Court." In *Old Southwest/New Southwest: Essays on a Region and Its Literature*, ed. Judy Nolte Lensink, 113–18. Tucson: Tucson Public Library, 1987.

Bless Me, Ultima. New York: Warner Books, 1994. (All page references in this chapter correspond to this edition.)

"La Llorona, El Kookoóee, and Sexuality." In *The Anaya Reader*, ed. Rudolfo A. Anaya, 417–28. New York: Warner Books, 1995. Here he discusses La Llorona as a cultural icon.

"Mythical Dimensions/Political Reality." In *The Anaya Reader*, ed. Rudolfo A. Anaya, 345–52. New York: Warner Books, 1995.

"The Writer's Landscape: Epiphany in Landscape." *Latin American Literary Review* 5, no. 10 (Spring-Summer 1977): 98–102.

"The Writer's Sense of Place: A Symposium and Commentaries." *South Dakota Review* 26, no. 1 (Winter 1988), 93–120.

Other Sources

An extensive number of books, articles, book chapters, and interviews have been published on Rudolfo A. Anaya; he is the most studied Chicano writer to date. The following list, therefore, is selective, having been chosen with *Bless Me, Ultima* and themes revolving around the work as its focus. In some cases, they are cited in this chapter.

Bruce-Novoa, Juan. *Chicano Authors: Inquiry by Interview*. Austin: University of Texas Press, 1980, 183–202. An early but still relevant interview with a trailblazing author in the Chicano literary tradition.

———."Learning to Read (and/in) Rudolfo Anaya's Bless Me, Ultima." In *Teaching American Ethnic Literatures*, ed. John R. Maitino and David R. Peck. Albuquerque: University of New Mexico Press, 1996, 179–91. An excellent analysis of *Bless Me, Ultima* with highly useful suggestions for teaching the work.

Candelaria, Cordelia. "Rudolfo A. Anaya." In *Dictionary of Literary Biography: Chicano Writers*, ed. Francisco Lomelí and Carl R. Shirley. Vol. 82. Detroit: Gale Research, 1989, 24–35.

———. "Rudolfo Alfonso Anaya (1937–)." In *Chicano Literature: A Reference Guide*, ed. Julio A. Martínez and Francisco A. Lomelí. Westport, Conn.: Greenwood Press, 1985, 34–51.

Colby, Vineta, ed. *World Authors 1985–1990*. New York: H. W. Wilson, 1995, 10–14.

Crawford, John. "Rudolfo Anaya." In *This Is About Vision: Interviews with Southwestern Writers*, ed. William Balassi, John F. Crawford, and Annie O. Eysturoy. Albuquerque: University of New Mexico Press, 1990, 83–93.

Fernández Olmos, Margarite. *Rudolfo A. Anaya: A Critical Companion*. Westport, Conn.: Greenwood Press, 1999. A critical work dedicated exclusively to Anaya's novels and novellas. Includes biographical information on the author, a study of Anaya's role within the Chicano literary tradition, and analyses of themes, characterization, plot, and a variety of critical approaches applied to Anaya's novels. For students, teachers, and general readers.

González, Ray. "Songlines of the Southwest: An Interview with Rudolfo A. Anaya." *Bloomsbury Review* 12, no. 5 (September-October, 1993): 3, 18.

González-T., César A., ed. *Rudolfo A. Anaya: Focus on Criticism*. La Jolla, Calif.: Lalo Press, 1990.

Gunton, Sharon R., and Jean C. Stine, eds. "Rudolfo A(lfonso) Anaya 1937–" *Contemporary Literary Criticism*. Vol. 23. Detroit: Gale Research, 1983, 22–27.

Johnson, David, and David Apodaca. "Myth and the Writer: A Conversation with Rudolfo Anaya." In *Rudolfo A. Anaya: Focus on Criticism*, ed. César A. González-T. La Jolla, Calif.: Lalo Press, 1990, 414–38.

Jussawalla, Feroza F., and Reed Way Dasenbrock, eds. *Interviews with Writers of the Post-Colonial World*. Jackson: University Press of Mississippi, 1992, 244–55.

Lamadrid, Enrique. "Myth as the Cognitive Process of Popular Culture in Rudolfo Anaya's Bless Me, Ultima: The Dialectics of Knowledge." In *Rudolfo A. Anaya: Focus on Criticism*, ed. César A. González-T. La Jolla, Calif.: Lalo Press, 1990, 100–112.

Lattin, Vernon E. "The 'Horror of Darkness': Meaning and Structure in Anaya's Bless Me, Ultima." *Revista Chicano-Riqueña* 6, no. 2 (Spring 1978): 51–57.

———. "The Quest for Mythic Vision in Contemporary Native American and Chicano Fiction." *American Literature* 50 (1979): 625–40.

Newkirk, Glen A. "Anaya's Archetypal Women in Bless Me, Ultima." *South Dakota Review* 31, no. 1 (Spring 1993): 112–50.

Rogers, Jane. "The Function of La Llorona Myth in Rudolfo Anaya's Bless Me, Ultima." *Latin American Literary Review* 5 (Spring 1977): 64–69.

Tonn, Horst. "Bless Me, Ultima: Fictional Response to Times of Transition." In *Rudolfo A. Anaya: Focus on Criticism*, ed. César A. González-T. La Jolla, Calif.: Lalo Press, 1990, 1–12.

Vassallo, Paul, ed. *The Magic of Words: Rudolfo A. Anaya and His Writings*. Albuquerque: University of New Mexico Press, 1982.

Further Reading

Augenbraum, Harold, and Margarite Fernández Olmos, eds. *The Latino Reader: An American Literary Tradition from 1542 to the Present*. Boston: Houghton Mifflin, 1997.

Lattin, Vernon E., ed. *Contemporary Chicano Fiction: A Critical Survey*. Binghamton, N.Y.: Bilingual Press, 1986.

Saldívar, Ramón. *Chicano Narrative: The Dialectics of Difference*. Madison: University of Wisconsin Press, 1990.
Sommers, Joseph, and Tomás Ybarra-Frausto, eds. *Modern Chicano Writers: A Collection of Critical Essays*. Englewood Cliffs, N.J.: Prentice-Hall, 1979.
Tatum, Charles. *Chicano Literature*. Boston: Twayne Publishers, 1982.

6

The Self as Cultural Metaphor: Oscar "Zeta" Acosta's *The Autobiography of a Brown Buffalo*

Genaro M. Padilla

OSCAR "ZETA" ACOSTA was born in El Paso, Texas, in 1935, according to his application for the California Bar. After serving in the U.S. Air Force, he attended college and graduated from law school. In 1970 he ran for sheriff of Los Angeles County for La Raza Unida party. Acosta disappeared in Mazatlán, Mexico, in 1974. The circumstances of his disappearance have never been explained.

Acosta was a friend of Hunter S. Thompson, and he appears as Dr. Gonzo in Thompson's *Fear and Loathing in Las Vegas* (1971). In the early 1970s, he produced two books, the first of which focuses on his own search for his identity as a Chicano: *The Autobiography of a Brown Buffalo* (1972). The second, *The Revolt of the Cockroach People* (1973), focuses on the politics of Chicanismo in the late 1960s and early 1970s. As part of Acosta's self-proclaimed public persona, he took the nickname "Zeta" (the name of the letter "Z" in Spanish).

In recent years, Acosta's reputation has been revived. In 1996 the critic Ilan Stavans published *Bandido*, an appreciation of Acosta's life and work. In 1996 he edited a collection of Acosta's unpublished stories, which was published by Arte Público Press at the University of Houston.

ANALYSIS OF THEMES AND FORMS

Oscar "Zeta" Acosta is dead, but he has never been buried and there is no death certificate. The author of two books that summed up his life and his short-lived involvement in the Chicano social movement in Los Angeles in the late 1960s, Acosta simply dropped from sight in late 1974, or early in 1975, and has never been heard from again. He is probably dead, but given his style of frenetic movement, he may be playing the ultimate dropout road adventure somewhere in Mexico, Central America, or some nameless barrio; but whatever happened, he is gone.[1] If he is on the road again, however, he is now as elusive and insubstantial as the vanishing hitchhiker.

Like Ralph Ellison's invisible man, he disappeared altogether to speak to us from a lower frequency, and the result was *The Autobiography of a Brown Buffalo* (1972) and *The Revolt of the Cockroach People* (1973), an interconnected literary record of one Chicano's development of a cultural identity and a forceful, if exaggerated, political consciousness. Whatever his faults, which, according to his enemies and friends both, were often grievous, excessive, and even inimical to the social movement, the books stand beyond the actual Chicanos' continuing struggle for dignity and self-definition. No matter how botched the personal life may have been, Acosta's writing was aimed toward freedom. It is the examination of that personal life in *The Autobiography of a Brown Buffalo* that is the subject of this chapter.

In writing his autobiography, Acosta documented the process through which he reintegrated the disparate parts of his cultural sources, realigned himself with his people's historical experience, and came at last to understand some truth about the reality of life for Chicanos in North America. What he learned is that the individual and the community are not separate entities, that even when the individual is trying hardest to sever his relations with his people he is still responding to the dictates and shared life of that community. The historical experience of a cultural group, then, shapes for better or for worse the personal experience of the individual. Unlike the traditional notion that the autobiographical "I" stands isolated, consumed in scrutinizing an autonomous self, the fundamental identification between the "I" and the "we" is a principle of ethnic autobiographical consciousness for writers like Acosta. In fact, it is in moving away from the "I," away from isolation and sickly self-consciousness, that the Chicano shapes a personal identity, an "I" capable not only of living with a troubled historical legacy, but also of acting to redirect that legacy.

In *Design and Truth in Autobiography*, Roy Pascal emphasizes the unavoidable relationship between the individual and society which underlies the autobiographical impulse. While the self is always at the center of the narrative, Pascal says that "the outside world must appear, so that, in give and take with it, the personality finds its peculiar shape." For the Chicano, the shape of the personality may indeed be peculiar, the result of a troubled give and take with society. As Pascal writes, the autobiography "establishes certain stages in an individual life, makes links between them, and defines, implicitly or explicitly, a certain consistency of relationship between the self and the outside world (or consistency of misrelationship)."[2]

Within this parenthetical qualification lies the generating force of Acosta's *Autobiography*. The tension between individual desire, what the self believes it is or may become, and the recognition of the Chicano's *place* in America simultaneously shatters the personality and leads to its locus of identity. For the Chicano, much as, say, for the black, the "consistency of misrelationship" with American society is the very principle of experience that leads to self-knowledge. Since relations with the outer world are tenuous, if not simply antagonistic, one can fairly say that Acosta comes into being as a result of the way in which American society has repeatedly defined and limited him to a type, and likewise as a result of his often misdirected recoil against such limitation. Always a "greaser" regardless of desire or achievement, the Chicano comes into being largely as a response to a perverse interplay with the outer world. For Acosta, as for many Chicanos, the effects of such hostile relations with society include contradictory responses: first, feelings of anger and willful detachment from whites, then feelings of confused self-image, hostility toward the self for not being American enough, and a self-deluding effort to resolve the conflict by acting as American as possible. When he fails to satisfy America's demands, as he must, he withdraws, escapes, and runs from the self he is not allowed to be.

Acosta's life history begins with the description of a large, brown man looking into the mirror with repugnance on the morning of July 1, 1967, the day he decides to make good his escape from his legal work, his friends, and himself. As one of LBJ's legal-aid attorneys in the War on Poverty, Acosta realizes in one moment that his legal knowledge and whatever social ideals he can muster have come to nothing. If on July 1, 1967, he can no longer take the confusion and pain of his work on behalf of the dispossessed, it is because he has been forced to concede a terrible truth: the circuits of the legal system are a complex configuration of loopholes and multiple interpretations meant to keep the class structure intact. Overwhelmed by the daily procession of the poor, as well as by his feelings of inadequacy, Acosta is reduced to an empty, pill-popping, booze-guzzling husk. Laughed at, cut off, and denied professional courtesy, he is stripped of his dignity along with the rest of the dispossessed. Tired of being an "overburdened, mealy-mouthed, chickenshit lawyer who wouldn't know what the hell to do with a real case" if his license depended on it (20), he just wants to drop out, escape, forget.

Before the narrative takes up Acosta's road adventure, the first five chapters describe in graphic detail his last day in the city of confusion. An obsessive confessional impulse informs the narrative with a tone of despair, loneliness, and self-disgust, as well as self-pity, and an irresistible comic madness. Not afraid of skimping on the details of his bleeding ulcer, his troubled bowel movements, his "gurgling vomit," or his schizoid arguments with imaginary characters (his Jewish shrink, Bogey, Cagney, and various women), he conveys all too well the excess into which his life has fallen. Yet Acosta's intention is neither to nauseate nor to shock.

It is as though, before he recounts his stature as the "famous Chicano lawyer" of *The Revolt of the Cockroach People*, he must lay bare his long alienation from his culture. This confessional impulse is both a means of purgation and a way of seeking the forgiveness of those from whom he was so long at odds. The autobiographical act, then, is a ritualistic process that mends the bond between the autobiographer and those whom he has called upon to be his confessors. Focusing upon the sordid details of his life during a time when he was suffering a spiritual crisis is a way of making concrete the isolation that accompanies cultural alienation. He wants to make amends for having earlier run out on his people, but more, he wants the underlying social and racial causes of his fragmentation to be understood as an example and as a warning to others.

When the writing achieves this level of self-recognition, it proceeds beyond crass apologia and is directed toward a liberating end for his people. When the autobiographer, in this case the Chicano autobiographer, begins to see that his alienation was not simply a personal malady, an illness formed in a vacuum, but a disturbance tied directly to his place in the world, he exposes the external influences that shaped his personality. In so doing, he brings the *Autobiography* into alignment with the experiences encountered by other Chicanos in their dealings with the world.

Beginning nonchronologically with an episode from Acosta's maturity, the *Autobiography* forces us into a Daliesque dreamscape of drug hallucinations and drunken revelry in which the main character is a thirty-three-year-old man at the edge of emotional collapse. Acosta's immediate autobiographical strategy is to recreate an emotive scream of anguish at a time when he was one step away from personal destruction. Only after we have retraced Acosta's life through the latter sections of the book do we realize why the first five chapters are so necessarily written as they are. Only then do we see that Acosta's method is a conscious strategy for telegraphing the meaning of early life events. It is a way of bringing the later sections of the autobiography into alignment with the fragmented individual we find in the book's opening pages. For instance, the physical manifestations of Acosta's alienation—the bleeding ulcer, the vomiting, the boozing—all prove to have their source in events that occurred years earlier. Moreover, his ulcer, that chief symbol of modern-day stress and angst in a bourgeois society, becomes a recurring image of his alienation both from white society and from his own people. Alienated from the legal system, from a classist, racist society and its victims, but mostly from himself, he begins a frenzied movement away from San Francisco, the location of his present fragmentation, hoping to find something to hold on to, some magic to restore his belief. What he discovers, however, is what he must discover if he is to be whole again. His various road adventures throughout the West are little more than the loutish, aimless wanderings of a man on the run from the realities that confronted him in the city. The escape route, he discovers, only leads back in circuitous fashion, via the act of remembering his troubled development within the social nightmare of America, to the self he wishes to escape. By recalling those events that constitute his concrete historical experience, he initiates the very process that makes escape impossible and, ultimately, undesirable.

Leaving a trail of dust and beer cans, Acosta leaves San Francisco and lunges into the desert in search of his past. While driving alone toward random points on the map of the West, Acosta recalls the story of his early life in Riverbank, California. All at once, the remembrance of cultural ambivalence and conflict is established in the autobiographer's memory. One is immediately impressed with the degree to which he was aware, as a child, of the boundaries that separated him from other people—even of his own kind. Having been born in El Paso, Texas, he is bewildered when his family moves to California where, he discovers, Mexican people are different: they are *pochos* (Mexican immigrants who have undergone some assimilation), who speak English, act like gringos, and make life difficult for newcomer Mexicans who don't act the same way (77).

As he grows up in California speaking mostly English himself, he will, surely enough, forget his mother tongue and eventually be accused of acting like a gringo as well when he returns to El Paso at age thirty-three. Drawn into the common intracultural conflicts that arise from differences in regional dialects, customs, fashions, and other lifestyles, he learns early that not all is secure within the confines of the group. Nevertheless, he recalls that the conflict with his own people was a minor brush when compared to the larger hostilities that awaited him on the other side of the town. The real fight was with the Okies (poor white trash, called Okies because so many had migrated from the dust bowl of Oklahoma). Although he and his brother are fighting for respect against their *pocho* neighbors, they put up a solid front when they confront the Okies for whom all Mexicans are "greasers, spics and niggers" (78).

Acosta learns early that he and all other brown-skinned people who live across the tracks are simply lumped into one dark mass—Mexicans. Continuously the stubborn student of this lesson in American racial relations, Acosta will be "knocked aside the head" repeatedly in his encounters with the white world. The fights with the Okies, an outcast group themselves, are only emblematic of the fights he will have with the whites who wield real power, for the Okies engage in warfare with the Mexicans as a way of assuaging their own inferior status. As he recalls, "in my corner of the world there were only three kinds of people: Mexicans, Okies, and Americans. Catholics, Holy Rollers, and Protestants. Peach pickers, cannery workers, and clerks" (78). While the Okies and Mexicans engage in daily dogfights, the American, Protestant clerks look on in amusement. They hold out the bitter illusion of the American dream and watch as the Okies and Mexicans tear into each other. The Mexican boy recognizes this divided world, but he fails to understand the fragmenting impact such divisions produce in his own life. He refuses to concede to the Okies, but he submits again and again to the clerks.

It is, for instance, while he is fighting an Okie, Junior Ellis, who calls him a "fucking black nigger," that his attention is drawn to a blue-eyed girl who is watching. For all of his fury to assert himself before the "enemy," there is a division in the Chicano that comes about as a result of wanting to prove his mettle for an Anglo girl whom he secretly desires. As Acosta confesses throughout the *Autobiography*, the blue-eyed, Anglo girls he knew usually assumed the stature of white goddesses for whom the fat, brown Mexican boy was willing to give up anything, including his Mexicanness, to be accepted. It is through such white goddesses that he projected a bright future in America, where, riding on the power that comes with blue eyes, he might rise to the top of the social and economic ladder. They are nothing less than fleshly symbols of the "American Dream" and all that it represents, including a romantic love that erases the divisions of color. America, in the form of its blue-eyed girls, however, is oblivious to the Mexican boy's dreams. Later that day in the classroom, proud of his feat and sure that the girl of his dreams has noticed his bravado against Ellis, he waits for a sign of affection from the girl, only to hear her ask the teacher to have him put on his shirt because he stinks (94). It is more than just sweat and fat; it is his skin, his own dark self, which is rejected (95).

Somehow, Junior Ellis has won the fight after all. For no matter what the Chicano does to prove himself, he will always be the "greaser, spic, nigger." This particular scene points forward to a pattern of self-negation that Acosta continues to feel well into adult life. Such assignation of formative value to childhood experiences is the central function of the autobiographical process. He may exaggerate the events of the past, but he does so with the purpose of emphasizing certain shaping experiences. It was at this point, Acosta sees, that he began to accept the negative images of himself and accept the ugliness he is accorded by white America. Writing about Maya Angelou's *I Know Why the Caged Bird Sings* (1969), as well as about black autobiography in general, Sidonie Ann Smith describes the pattern of self-rejection that the child of color feels when comparing the mirror-self with American ideas of beauty. What Smith says of black girls in this case applies also to Mexican boys:

> In a society attuned to white standards of physical beauty, the black girl cries herself to sleep at night to the tune of her own inadequacy. At least she can gain temporary respite in the impossible dreams of whiteness. Here in the darkened nights of the imagination, that refuge from society and the mirror, blossoms an ideal self. Yet even the imagination is sometimes not so much a refuge as it is a prison in which the dreamer becomes even more inescapably possessed by the nightmare, since the very self she fantasizes conforms perfectly to society's pre-requisites.[3]

This view of the black autobiographical self is disturbingly paralleled by the Chicano autobiographer who remembers his own childhood. Acosta's early adolescent desire to be accepted by the blue-eyed girl is shattered when he sees himself as all that is unacceptable in those blue eyes. The feminine blue eyes symbolize that immense barrier between the dark-eyed Chicano and the fulfillment of his dreams. He can remember tearing into Junior Ellis' eyes, but before those of Jane Addison he is powerless; she reminds him most cruelly of what he cannot possess.

Additionally, as Smith suggests, instead of seeking a positive self-image within the context of one's own race and culture, the dark child often builds an imaginative but self-denying ideal of whiteness. With some variation, this is the labyrinthine pattern into which Acosta falls. He makes himself forget the incident and its humiliating implications; he continues to idealize America's blue-eyed girls. Willfully self-blinded, he pursues a course that increasingly leads him away from his culture and from himself. He still wants to believe that if he proves himself worthy, he will be accepted. In short, he lies to himself, again and again, about what he can be in America.

Only by denying and rejecting some elemental part of the self can the Chicano's relationship with America prove to be propitious and, even then, propitious only in the eyes of the self-deluding protagonists. Afraid of his own reflection, he conjures up an acceptable image for himself, an image he can display before the world he secretly wishes to inhabit. When he is in high school, for instance, he tries harder than ever to out-gringo the gringos. Although when he was younger they were considered the "real enemy," separated from him by clear boundaries, now the Anglos with whom he plays football are his only friends. He may still be fat, but he has added some muscle and has put his size to work in athletics. He may still be dark, but he is bright in class and has musical talent. He is able to barter his cultivated talents for some measure of acceptance by his white classmates. In fact, he is so successful at forging a new image, his cultural self-denial, that he forgets about being a Chicano, a brown buffalo, and falls into a pattern of gringo behavior and forgets his Mexican grade school friends (112). How different from his earlier awareness of the boundaries that divided his world from that of the Okies and the Americans: for his old friends, the boundaries are still real enough, but for this "hard-working" Mexican boy the boundaries have been broken down, or so he believes.

By this time he has also forgotten that the blue-eyed American girls are inaccessible. Not only are they still the ideal standard of the beauty he wishes to possess, but they are also, by comparison, the epitome of what the Mexican girls he knows fail to be. Dating Chicanas is simply out of the question, because, like his old friends Johnny and David and Ben and Alfonso, they stay to themselves and hold back, avoiding participation (112). And, needless to say, "they were homely and square." These Mexican girls are a reflection of the self he wants to forget. In the mind of the self-denying Chicano adolescent, they represent everything Oscar fears will obstruct his progress toward acceptance. They prefer to remain to themselves, they refuse to participate in Anglo activities, and, therefore, they seem to have no aspirations. Worse, they are ugly; the Anglo girls symbolize the feminine ideal.

When he falls for Alice Joy, he thinks that he is within reach of completing the success story of the dark boy who has been allowed to cross the racial lines of romance. Although Alice, unlike Jane Addison, returns his affection, Acosta soon realizes that all of his gains are rendered meaningless when it comes to convincing her parents of his worth. When Alice asks her mother if he can take her to a movie, everything is all right until she discovers the sure giveaway—Oscar's last name. Oscar is disappointed but hardly discouraged. After all, he assumes, he can simply change his name to go along with the rest of the disguise he is wearing. When he asks his mother what she thinks of a name change, she is caught off guard:

She stopped patting the dough for the tortillas and stared me right in the face. "You will go to hell if you change your family name. And your dad will probably hang you again."

"Geez, you can't take a joke at all, ma." (117)

In a sense, Oscar *is* joking. This is evident given the comic tone of the scene, but there is something disturbingly serious about the joke. It would not be that unusual for him to change his name; after all, countless people have hurdled the last barrier to full citizenship simply by changing their strange, foreign-sounding names to something that sounds genuinely American. For Oscar, the joke is that even if he did change his name his dark skin and his cultural background would still betray him. That his mother is making tortillas during the scene symbolizes the manner in which his culture remains vital even when he is trying hardest to forget it.

Of course, even that fails to stop Oscar and Alice, who continue to see each other secretly until one fateful night, after a school dance, when they are confronted by the town police chief, who has followed them at the behest of the girl's outraged father. As he recalls the incident years later, Acosta remembers that what angered him more than the threat of arrest was the condescending way in which he was treated by the police chief:

"... now, I known you for ... since you was just a tyke ... but under the law, if I catch you, I'll take you in. ... Savvy?" He tried to smile.
Perhaps if he hadn't thrown in that "savvy" bit I'd have kept still, but as it stood, I lashed out: "*Chinga tu madre, cabron!*" (119)

The reverberation of that scream—*Chinga tu madre, cabron,*—the Mexicano's gravest outcry against his enemy—sounds to the center of Oscar's self-deluding dream and reveals his long-repressed awareness of the fate that society has accorded him. All at once the Chicano vents his rage against all the external forces that seek to limit his movement in the world. His outburst, however, is a cry not only against the police chief and all that he represents, but against his own self-betrayal. In one moment of time, the standout tackle, the leading man, the solo clarinetist, the dark-skinned boy who aspired to another condition has exposed himself as a dupe. Denied the level of his desires, he realizes in retrospect that his painful shout that night signaled the beginning of his feelings of emptiness, the initial letting of ulcerous acid, the germination of his long alienation (120).

After that night, Acosta is catapulted into a chaotic search for meaning that does not lead to self-reconciliation until he finds himself in El Paso years later. He leaves home after graduation to join the Air Force, where, feeling lonely and betrayed, he turns to religion to fill in the emptiness. Before long he is debating scripture with a Baptist friend, and not only is he converted but he becomes a Bible fanatic who preaches to anyone who will stand still for a moment. When the Air Force sends him to Panama, he takes up the call of the Lord and begins a career as a missionary sent out into the jungle to bring the "heathens" into the fold. For two years, all of his energy is invested in saving the souls of dark-skinned natives. He is so successful that he is called a "Mexican Billy Graham." Still, he "never got invited to the home of any church member." He is good enough for the Lord, but, as usual, not good enough for the white folks. Eventually, his doubts begin to outrun his faith, and he gives up on "Jesus and the Baptist Church" as quickly as he was converted. His religious escape route from the self has led only back to disillusionment and more emptiness.

After his stint in the service, he enrolls in creative writing classes. At the behest of his instructor, who feels he has talent, he hits the road in search of experience and material for a book he wants to write. He spends time in Los Angeles, where he almost becomes a cop; he drifts to San Francisco, where he again studies creative writing; and, on the run again, he ends up in Saint Louis, where he works as a recreational therapist. Finally back in San Francisco in 1960, he finishes the book he has been writing—something called *A Cart for my Casket*—and when it is rejected, he enrolls in night classes at San Francisco Law School. For five years he works days as a copy boy for the *Examiner*, attends classes, and fails to pass the bar the first time but passes it the second time in 1966. He goes to work for Legal Aid in 1967. The life history is rounded out to the present, which Acosta is just leaving as the *Autobiography* begins.

What one cannot fail to notice is that the road adventures of the 1967 self, after he drops his Legal Aid job, are simply a continuation of the restless drifting that Acosta had undertaken for the last fifteen or so years since his confrontation with the chief of police. His stint in the Air Force, his conversion to the Baptist faith, his "Mexican Billy Graham" period, the creative writing classes, the zany adventures with various friends in Los Angeles, San Francisco, and Saint Louis, his decision to become a lawyer, his decision to throw his license in the wastebasket, and his ramblings in the West with hippie friends have all been a series of attempts to hide behind one or another mask.

As Roger Rosenblatt points out in his excellent article, "Black Autobiography," the madness that surrounds the autobiographer often leads to reciprocal gestures of madness on his part. On the night the police chief utters the ridiculing, limiting, imposing word "Savvy?" the Chicano also enters a madhouse from which he cannot easily extricate himself, and in which he will do anything to survive. What Rosenblatt contends for the black also holds true for the Chicano autobiographer:

The sense of circus or madhouse that controls much black autobiography inevitably controls the decisions of the main characters themselves. Recognizing an elusive and unpredictable situation, they adapt it for survival, becoming masters of both physical and psychological disguise, in part to avoid their hunters. Malcolm X moves from one mask to another in his autobiography. He is variously known as Malcolm, Malcolm Little, Homeboy, Detroit Red, a prison number, even Satan, until he reaches the identification of Brother, which to him is not a mask but himself. Conversely the Invisible Man finds his identity in Rinehart, the con man and quick-change artist whose being is nonbeing, who is all things to all people. Sonny of *Manchild in the Promised Land* wears the mask of house nigger when it serves him, as does Bigger. In both black autobiography and black fiction the final discarding of masks is a character's primary goal because such an act is a demonstration of selfhood and freedom.[4]

Much like his black predecessors, Acosta moves from one disguise to another. He is the Baptist preacher saving souls in Panama, the aspiring writer hitting the road in search of material, the frustrated attorney representing the poor, the dropout hippie cavorting with numerous strangers on the road in the late 1960s. Even more emblematic of his failure to fix upon a single identity is the success with which he wears different brown masks. At various times he passes for a Samoan; in a bar in Ketchum, Idaho, he is Henry Hawk, a blackfoot Indian Chief; and, paradoxically, in Mexico he passes for a Mexican, until he opens his mouth and betrays himself as a gringo. In fact, at one point in *Autobiography*, this interchangeability of dark-skinned identities forces him to pose the self-confronting question of just who or what he really is, having been mistaken all his life for "American Indian, Spanish, Filipino, Hawaiian, Samoan and Arabian. No one ever asked me if I'm a spic or a greaser. Am I Samoan?" (68).

Acosta, of course, plays the ironic game here, since it is and always has been clear that those who call him a spic or a greaser are hardly interested in asking him if he is a spic or a greaser. Always placed within one or another category of darkness, the man of color begins to wonder whether there really is any difference. He is everyone, but he is no one. Perceived as a variable but always dark-skinned *foreigner*, the individual finds his perception of the self to be confounded, distorted by the racially insane situation in which he finds himself. The masks he must wear not only hide him from hostile eyes, but, tragically, shatter the inner man, leaving him with little or no personality of his own. His existence, that of running, remaining elusive, ends up being precisely the fate his oppressors have planned for him. For Acosta, as for Ellison's invisible man, the plan is to "keep him running." Only when he finally discards the protective protean mask can he reconcile himself to the identity into which history and cultural circumstances have shaped him. Like Malcolm X, who in reaching the identification of Brother discovers not another mask but himself, so Acosta discovers himself when he achieves identification as a Chicano.

It is, predictably enough, in the city of his birth, El Paso, Texas, that he finally begins to come to terms with himself and his ancestry. When he arrives, the city scene rekindles memories of his early childhood, before the family moved to *pocho* California. There is the normal chagrin with things that have changed over the years, but the old neighborhood evokes vivid memories of the child's rushing life in a Chicano barrio. Across the river in Juarez, the crowded streets filled with brown-skinned people stir feelings of nearly forgotten pride in his own dark self. For the first time in his adult life, he regards Mexican women as life-giving and beautiful. The obsession with the white goddesses of his youth is finally obliterated (188). In one sweep, he is reunited with his "sisters," "cousins," "aunts," and, significantly, the "seven Chicanas" from high school whom he once shunned as "homely and square." As he looks at these Mexican women, enchanted and "blinded by love," he imagines that they, symbolizing his rediscovered Mexicanness, possess the curative for his pain (189).

The mood of this and other early passages in the chapter is one of lyrical nostalgia. However, having romanticized the Mexican source, there is a startling but inevitable discovery Oscar must make while he is in Juarez. If in the eyes of his *fellow* Americans he always has been and always would be a "greaser," in Mexico, once he is divested of his darkness, he is only another gringo. After a week in Juarez, and at just about the time when he has started to feel at home, he gets into trouble and ends up in jail for acting like an arrogant gringo before a hotel clerk. When he comes up before the magistrate, he tries to invoke his status as an attorney and an American citizen to ease himself off the charges. His illusions about his Mexicanness are further deflated by the magistrate's refusal to speak to him in English, even though she speaks "perfect English." Acosta is forced to admit his "gringo arrogance and *americano* impatience" (193). As a final biting remark, the magistrate lets him go by asking why he doesn't go home and learn his father's language (194). Disillusioned with the dream of Mexicanness, he makes his way back to El Paso, the American sector, but he is stopped and challenged by the American border guard who, as usual, refuses to believe that he is a citizen and tells him that he doesn't look like an American.

Truly without any identification and confused and exhausted, he takes a cheap room and, as he did at the beginning of his search, stands naked before a mirror, stripped, without any more disguises. He begins to sob and falls into a long sleep (195). It is during this 33 hours of sleep that the 33-year-old searcher, in a silent, deathlike state, undergoes a symbolic rebirth which reconciles the fragmented parts of the self and generates a renewed vision of his place in the world. He awakens to renewed strength, with his emptiness, alienation, and multiple identities burned away.

Rejecting the definitions that have been imposed upon him, he realizes that he must renegotiate the terms of his search for identity. If he has failed to find the answer to his questions, it is because he has allowed himself to be bandied about between extremes. "One sonofabitch tells me I'm not a Mexican and the other one says I'm not an American," he complains. But it is in realizing that he is neither Mexican nor American that he finds his identity, an identity that Juan Bruce-Novoa has aptly termed "the space (not the hyphen) between the two.[5] It is within the space between Mexican American that an identification of the self as Chicano is realized. Acosta finally locates his experience in that space realizing, "I am a Chicano by ancestry and a Brown Buffalo by choice" (199).

While marking the location of a distinct cultural identity, the space between Mexican American is wide enough to allow Acosta his own personal identity. That the two, however, are inextricably tied together is apparent. As the Brown Buffalo, Acosta may roam the terrain of his own life, but his freedom to do so, he now realizes, is largely determined by the circumstance of the herd itself. Almost instinctively, he knows that, like the buffalo "who were slaughtered, butchered and cut up," the Chicanos face spiritual and cultural extinction, if not outright physical extinction, unless they band together. Acosta may refuse to compromise those parts of the self that give distinction to the personal life; he may remain outrageous, angry, even destructive; but once he comes to understand his cultural-historic identity, that energy is given purpose, and if he is bent on destroying anything it is a corrupt social system instead of the self.

Having defined the terms of his own freedom, in the final pages of *Autobiography*, he envisions his own role in his people's struggle to define theirs. Swaggering and audacious, Acosta boards a bus for Los Angeles, "the home of the biggest herd of brown buffalos in the entire world." Although he initially arrives with the idea of writing about the "revolution" he has heard is about to break, he ends up thoroughly radicalized by what he sees. Within a few months, he is not only involved in the movement, he is at its vortex.

Ultimately, Acosta discovered that he was unable single-handedly to change the world. He did rise to prominence as a radical attorney, a movement spokesman, and an audacious media figure who garnered widespread attention for the Chicano movement, but, like the movement itself, he could not sustain the energy and commitment required for a long fight. The system proved too solidly entrenched, the assault upon the bastion failed, and little changed. At the end of *The Revolt of the Cockroach People*, Acosta pictures himself as leaving the scene of the battle, disillusioned and very tired of the fighting. His social ideals and his anger, however, remain smoldering beneath the cinders. Driving away, back on the road again, he signals a personal truce, but he recognizes that the historical process does obliterate the personal life after all. The revolt of the cockroach people, all cockroach people, ends to begin somewhere else, perhaps in another city or another time, led by another generation, but inevitably again and again.

TEACHING THE WORK

1. Among Chicanos, the development of personal identity is often linked to the understanding of cultural identity and is often expressed in such bildungsromans as Richard Rodriguez's *Hunger of Memory* (1982) and Oscar Hijuelos' *Our House in the Last World* (1983). How does Acosta relate the personal and the cultural, and what success do his characters have in finding their "place" in America?

2. Racism plays a prominent role in *The Autobiography of a Brown Buffalo*, and at times Acosta pretends he is aligned with a more "acceptable" and exotic minority. This brings up the notion of "passing" among African Americans and of racial shame, which can stem from, or lead to, personal self-hatred. What steps does the Brown Buffalo take to recognize his own self-worth and, by extension, the worth of this community?

3. In Hunter S. Thompson's *Fear and Loathing in Las Vegas*, Acosta is portrayed as "The Samoan." Have students read Thompson's book and compare Thompson's depiction of Acosta with Acosta's own.

NOTES

Page numbers in the text refer to the original edition of *The Autobiography of a Brown Buffalo* (Straight Arrow Books, 1972) and *The Revolt of the Cockroach People* (Straight Arrow Books, 1973).

1. In an article for *Rolling Stone* magazine, written in 1977, Hunter S. Thompson, Acosta's friend, wrote a suitably Gonzo requiem and unfinished memoir on ". . . the Life and Doom of Oscar Zeta Acosta, First and Last of the Savage Brown Buffalos." Titled "The Banshee Screams for Buffalo Meat," the piece chronicles Acosta's last days in Los Angeles and agonizes over the dead-end trails upon which rumors had led him in a personal search for Acosta after his strange disappearance. See *Rolling Stone*, December 1, 1977: 48–59; or, more conveniently, Thompson's *The Great Shark Hunt, Tales from a Strange Time* (New York: Summit Books, 1979), in which the article is reprinted.

2. Roy Pascal, *Design and Truth in Autobiography* (Cambridge, Mass.: Harvard University Press, 1960), 9.

3. Sidonie Ann Smith, "The Song of a Caged Bird: Maya Angelou's Quest After Self-Acceptance," *Southern Humanities Review* 7, no. 4 (Fall 1973): 366.

4. Roger Rosenblatt, "Black Autobiography," in *Autobiography: Essays Theoretical and Critical*, James Olney, ed. Princeton: Princeton University Press (1980): 175–176.

5. Juan Bruce-Novoa, "The Space of Chicano Literature," *De Colores* 1, no. 4 (1975): 27.

REFERENCES AND SUGGESTIONS FOR FURTHER READING

Works by Oscar Acosta

The Autobiography of a Brown Buffalo. San Francisco: Straight Arrow Books, 1972; reprint. New York: Vintage, 1989.

Oscar "Zeta" Acosta, The Uncollected Works, ed. Ilan Stavans. Houston: Arte Público Press, 1996.

The Revolt of the Cockroach People. San Francisco: Straight Arrow Books, 1973; reprint. New York: Vintage Books, 1989.

Other Works

Olivares, Julian, ed. *U.S. Hispanic Autobiography. The Americas Review* 16, no. 3–4 (Fall-Winter 1988).

Padilla, Genaro M. *My History, Not Yours: The Formation of Mexican American Autobiography*. Madison, Wisc.: University of Wisconsin Press, 1993.

Stavans, Ilan. *Bandido: Oscar "Zeta" Acosta & the Chicano Experience*. New York: HarperCollins, 1995.

———. *The Hispanic Condition: Reflections on Culture and Identity in America*. New York: HarperCollins, 1995.

Thompson, Hunter S. *Fear and Loathing in Las Vegas*. New York: Random House, 1971; reprint. New York: Vintage, 1989.

Whitmer, Peter O. *When the Going Gets Weird: The Twisted Life and Times of Hunter S. Thompson: A Very Unauthorized Biography*. New York: Hyperion, 1993.

7

Adapting, Not Assimilating: Edward Rivera's *Family Installments*

Alfredo Villanueva-Collado

EDWARD RIVERA was born in Puerto Rico in 1944. He left the island at the age of seven with his family for New York City where he attended parochial and public schools in East Harlem, also known as *El Barrio*. He received a B.A. from City College and a master's degree from Columbia University in English. Among Rivera's publications are stories and articles in *The Nation, The New York Times, New York* magazine and several story anthologies, and his semifictional "memoir" *Family Installments: Memories of Growing Up Hispanic* (1982). Rivera has been the recipient of a grant from the National Endowment for the Arts and is currently on the faculty of the English Department at the City College of New York, CUNY.

ANALYSIS OF THEMES AND FORMS

An analysis of *Family Installments: Memories of Growing Up Hispanic* reveals a conscious decision to deal with migration's impact on identity in terms of family, education, language, religion, and the workplace through a fictional autobiography. This choice signals a particular type of contract with the reader, through which Rivera creates a distance between himself and the text by adopting a first-person narrator: his protagonist Santos Malanguez (from *malanga*, a native edible root related to yucca), to whom the novel's subtitle would then apply rather than to the book's author himself. It also allows Rivera to generalize from the beginning of his book, and so the subtitle "Growing Up Hispanic" can apply to Rivera, by virtue of his ethnic heritage; to the fictional Malanguez, who shares in that heritage; or to any Hispanic reader who can find, within the pages of the novel, Rivera's definition of what "growing up Hispanic" means at a particular time and in a particular place.

By creating a fictional character such as his protagonist, Rivera removes himself from the kind of authorial privilege that would have allowed him to validate Santos Malanguez's adventures with the "truth" of his own life; the reader has to reach that conclusion by himself. Moreover, the use of a first-person narrator enables Rivera to explore varied types of experience inherent in growing up Hispanic. For him, that response involves the perception and transmission of a particular ideology that shapes and frames the details of growing up Hispanic in the United States.

The first of the novel's thirteen chapters details life for the protagonist's grandparents in Bautabarro, a forgotten barrio in the Puerto Rican highlands in the early 1900s. Rivera paints a grim picture: these are people with no history (14), eking out a living from subsistence farming and finding their only consolation in religion, brought to them by American missionaries (15). One paternal grandfather commits suicide; a paternal grandmother is a raving maniac. The *jíbaro* (country hick) code demands strict adherence to rigid gender roles. Marriages are for life: husbands are all powerful (21); wives and daughters are submissive (23), reared in the code of sacrifice (25). Fathers and brothers guard the family's honor, residing in its unmarried females' virginity. Sexual initiation for males involves bestiality and voyeurism. Education is totally devalued (22); the only way up is also the way out: exile, going to a mythical and much feared place called "Nueva York" (29).

The second chapter's central episode involves the protagonist's father's trip to market with a load of edible roots, *verduras*, which constitutes a parody of one of Puerto Rico's most famous songs, "Lamento Borincano," by Rafael Hernández. In the song, the *jíbarito* leads his mare to market, full of high expectations as to what he will be able to do with the money from prospective sales which do not take place because of the island's dire economic conditions. Hernández launches into a mournful, passionate dirge for his homeland's woes. In Rivera's version, the mare is a run-down female donkey; his future father falls asleep, missing the opportunity to sell advantageously. He wakes up late; the marketplace is empty. He is forced to sell his *viandas* at a loss and, to top it all, the donkey dies on the trip back, getting him deeper into debt with his future father-in-law. Once married, he borrows from him again to set up a bodega or small grocery, which fails miserably, and sets up the action for the only way out: migrating to New York.

The third chapter details both Santos Malanguez's initiation into sex—

his cousin Chuito initiates him into voyeurism and bestiality—and his family's temporary split, since the father migrates first to New York, and then sends for his wife and children. In the meantime, Chuito takes the place of Santos' father. The father's letters are no substitute for his presence, however. Rivera makes it clear that there is a loss of the concept of family lineage as well as a devaluation of written discourse (53), themes that recur throughout the novel. Chuito, considered another brother, goes briefly to San Juan, and returns much changed—pointing yet to another of Rivera's themes: the negative impact of city life in general (66–67). However, the impulse to migrate is almost biological. When we next encounter the Malanguez family, Santos is already enrolled in Catholic primary school in New York.

Edward Rivera's main themes of migration, exile, and change are viewed, for the most part, through a glass darkly. Becoming a Neorican involves a twofold process reminiscent of Matthew Arnold's famous line, "a world dead, another powerless to be born." In Santos' case, it entails both a systematic rejection of his parents' world and values and an implacable analysis of the values and mores of the world he eventually chooses. His initial impulse is outright rejection, a choice that excludes acceptance (and, thus, assimilation), but if he is to survive, he will need to find the proper tools for adaptation. Rivera's answer to this quandary goes beyond an exposure of the new ideology into which he has been thrust, to dealing with aspects of hegemony and ideology as they apply to "growing up Hispanic" and to the values of the pervasive, dominant culture, which embodies the values of a dominant class. In such a way, Rivera is able to depict both the ideology of the dominant culture and the counterculture in which he now lives, with the discourse of the latter serving to point out the limits and flaws of the former.

By developing a pattern of "corrosive irony" of underlying hostility that identifies his text as countercultural, Rivera is able to reveal the fetish character of the dominant culture by inserting depictions of the former into the latter. In other words, since the dominant culture, by its own dominance, seems to believe that its way of being is logical, by counterposing the views of the dominant culture, which surrounds him, to views of the counterculture, now out of context, Rivera is able to show the dominant culture's illogic. Santos Malanguez is able to fight and ultimately resist assimilation by means of this irony, which allows him to examine the dominant culture's ideology by a ruthless analysis of its language, education, family, and religion. He adapts, but he does not assimilate.

In *Family Installments*, religion and education are first seen as working hand in hand to oppress the ethnic minority. Edward Rivera exposes the process of socialization of Hispanic children at the hands of Irish Catholic educators, nuns and brothers, all of whom attempt to force their own ideology on the children. Correctness in the dominant language of the United States—English as opposed to Malanguez's mother language, Spanish—becomes not so much a desirable goal as an instrument with which these characters remind their hapless students of their inferior condition. For example, Sister Felicia, one of the protagonist's elementary schoolteachers, decides who is to receive, as charity, a communion outfit: "Shyness and poor English were an unmistakable sign of someone who needed to have his outfit bought for him" (85). The process of education becomes a process of subordination.

Rivera also shows how, when corrosive irony is applied to language incorrectness, it can be turned into a political counterdiscourse. When Sister Felicia bargains with a merchant at La Marqueta, the Hispanic market in New York's El Barrio, the exchange between her and the Puerto Rican merchant, centered around the words "crucifixion" for "crucifix" and "claps" for "clasp," makes clear that the merchant, in order to survive, must adopt the position of an imperfect manipulator of discourse, while in reality he is playing an elaborate joke on the nun (83). The wink he gives the students establishes a relationship of complicity between the students and the wily merchant, who has just assured himself of a big sale by pretending to be more ignorant than he really is. At the same time, it reveals the sexual pun intended by him as a joke—a dimension of language the nun—supposedly language's champion—ignores.

The means by which socialization takes place also involve the devaluation of the students' ethnic roots and, hence, the mystifying privileging of the dominant culture. Thus, socialization presupposes a rewriting of cultural history. A nun scolds her class, after she catches one of the students picking her nose, by referring to the student's "cannibal ancestors" from South America who were so ignorant they had not even discovered "friction," which they owed to Europeans, along with "True Faith and other forms of Christian civilization" (76). The wordplay here is twofold, containing on the one hand a possible sexual allusion to which the nun remains blissfully unaware and a reference to the Spanish (and English) of "friction" to mean "discontent."

In grammar school, history is used to destroy the students' ethnic identity. In intermediate school, its purpose is subtler: to differentiate between types of Europeans, ultimately privileging the Germanic and Anglo Saxon races over the Mediterranean, Latin races. In an Irish brother's version of the fall of the Roman Empire, God ultimately sides with the "blond *alemanes*" from the North, who eventually had become "true Christians" (128).

Rivera is quite explicit as to the underlying nature of Catholic education and its direct relationship to cultural domination, which reveals itself as power wielded not only through cultural oppression but corporal violence, as well: "The law there seemed to be that if your teacher didn't let you have it good from time to time, there was something morally wrong with him or her" (74). The narrator's manipulation of physical description reinforces this point: " 'What's so funny, Chief?' Brother Lomosney, seventh grade, would ask. He had a powerful neck and shoulders and a regulation crewcut. He had spent four years in the Navy before joining the ACB's and liked to use sailor jargon in class" (108). Two items are worth noticing: the pun on the acrostic letters, which upsets the traditional ABC's, and the reference to sailor jargon. Rivera, by repeating language acquired through Catholic education, exposes its status as a cultural fetish. The nuns do not know slang; moreover, they utilize language as an instrument of cultural oppression, as when Santos Malanguez reports on an overheard conversation two nuns have about a fat boy. One of them suggests that the boy needs a gag on his mouth: " 'Or a zipper,' said the other sister" (94).

The brothers in charge of intermediate school also use language to put down the students but, ironically, their own poor usage reveals their precarious position. They speak incorrectly but get away with it by virtue of the power they hold as the defenders and transmitters of their dominant culture: "Whatsa matter with youse guys today? You're acting like a bunch of fat blue whales. A school of purposes. Either youse got too much spermacity in your heads to understand what I'm driving at, or you haven't been listening" (120).

Once again, the sexual undertone, the fact the audience is composed of male teenagers full of the sexual tensions proper to their age and ironically alluded to in the phrase "spermacity in your heads," eludes the speaker. But he shares an essential identity with all those characters whom Santos has begun identifying as sources of oppression: the brothers are all Irish, as are all the police (118). Something the dominaters carefully try to hide comes to the fore: "The Irish sided with the Irish, the Italians with the Italians and the Latins with the Latins. The law was that you always sided with your own kind" (118). So much for assimilation through the myth of the "melting pot."

Once Rivera has demystified the dominant culture's language of education, he proceeds to give equal treatment to education itself as a medium of assimilation. Bro' Leary gives his students a test on William Shakespeare's *Julius Caesar*, which makes absolutely no sense at all, but which the students are forced to take seriously (it also happens that Bro' Leary is going through a public nervous breakdown). For the students, the material itself is foreign cultural matter. As Rivera/Malanguez gleefully recites the inscrutable questions, one in particular reveals Bro Leary's confused perception of his students' "multicultural" backgrounds: "Could this tragedy have taken place in a Catholic country? E.G. Ireland? Italy? Porto Rico? Poland?" (135). Rivera's protagonist becomes his mouthpiece, pointing out how Shakespeare's language became, to the ears of violent eight graders, "faggot language" (123).

Rivera demystifies religion as well, the key episode being Santos Malanguez's first communion. The reader is powerfully reminded of the connection between religious and educational discourses; Santos calls the small Puerto Ricans "cannibals" waiting to ingest God's flesh (98). The positioning of religious discourse within the dominant has already been exposed as an opportunity for Sister Felicia to assert her charges' linguistic and economic inferiority when she goes to buy them communion suits. But it is turned against her. The ideology she represents is turned by the merchant to his own advantage. While pretending to submit he has, through a corrosive irony, subverted whatever she said.

Joseph Frank (1963), in his seminal essay on spatial form in literature, explains how Gustave Flaubert achieved the texture of space within narrative by juxtaposing events that are supposed to be perceived simultaneously by the reader, each highlighting the other ironically. In *Madame Bovary*, such an effect is achieved in the episode where, at the same time there is a livestock auction on the ground floor of a building and the names of the winners are being called over the roar of the crowd, Rudolph woos Emma on a balcony above. Thus by juxtaposing the lovers' conversation with the language of farming and business, Flaubert emphasizes the former's banality, while revealing their essential sameness (Frank 50).

Rivera's handling of the communion scene, which follows a similar pattern, exposes the relations of subordination and dominance. Santos, frozen with fear, approaches the altar and stumbles. He cannot open his mouth. The priest brings the host down violently and breaks it over the boy's nose. One half of it rolls on the floor; another priest goes on all fours to retrieve it. As if that were not enough, the organ player for the ceremony, a patriotic Puerto Rican having a fight over low wages with his employer, the parish priest, bursts into the Puerto Rican national anthem. Santos, disgraced, returns to his pew and, as he does, pees in his pants out of shame (104–105). This becomes an internalized ethnic shame, as Santos, a seven year old, recites for the reader the dominant culture's view of Puerto Ricans and exposes the dark subtext of what is only superficially a religious ceremony. As he goes up to the altar, the comments he imagines hearing about himself all involve drunkenness (100–101).

The ideological positioning of the characters who represent the dominant culture is exposed through their comments. One priest addresses another: "This whole neighborhood's going to the. . . . ' But Father Rooney cuts him short: 'Not here, Matt. Later, in the rectory' " (105). Sister Felicia's reaction is even more predictable: "She led me back to my pew by the arm she'd pinched, and as she was sitting me down she put her mouth in my ear and said: 'Ssantosss Malanguezzz you are not fit for First Communion and maybe never will be. We have a lot to discuss tomorrow morning' "(105). It is worth mentioning that the Malanguez family not only does not mention the incident, but celebrates the occasion as if communion actually had taken place (105–106).

Rivera has juxtaposed the political, ethnic, religious, educational, and economic ideology as embedded in a religious ceremony, revealing that the ultimate aim of the dominant culture is the preservation of power and the denial of power for those choosing or finding themselves in an adversarial position. This relationship is further explored in the chapter dealing with Santos and his father, in terms of their respective rhetorical modes and, simultaneously, their encounters with police.

Santos' father is fond of oratory (221), poetry readings on the radio (233), and traditional Puerto Rican music (242–43). Santos, meanwhile, who has come into contact with English poetry by means of an anthology given to him by a neighbor, begins to fall in love with poetry as a mirror for his intimate feelings. Here poetic language functions as a private language, in opposition to his father's public language, the language of radio and oratory. Rivera identifies literature, slowly at first and then passionately, as a medium for exposing ideology as well as a vehicle for expressing the inner self. But this process, for Santos, involves a rejection of his father's rhetoric.

Santos is at a crossroads; he must reconcile public and private discourses, each with a version of identity. Assimilation is not possible, for he is constantly reminded of the position assigned him within the dominant culture. One further reminder comes from a member of another minority. Santos follows a friend into Central Park and strays into territory controlled by a black gang whose members steal his money and make him wallow in excrement. He is spared further violence because his friend, who is black and Puerto Rican, pleads his cause, but he is advised to keep to "his" side of the park (159).

This happens to Santos just after he has boasted of his burgeoning assimilation, his ability to dilute his identity. He has been mistaken for a Jew, an Italian, a Greek, even a Hungarian, and he comes away feeling proud for having disguised his accent and his lineage, proof positive that the melting pot theory works (148). Rivera's message is clear: racial and ethnic difference makes any attempt at assimilation a failure. For racially mixed minorities, assimilation means adopting ideology's racist perspectives and abandoning those in one's own group whose skin color does not correspond to one's own. Moreover, it is not the dominant culture's intention to allow minorities to assimilate.

Santos becomes conscious of the disparity between life and literature; to relieve the resulting tension he returns to Central Park. One night he is stopped by the police who, finding a pencil on him, harass him for lack of further evidence, as well as to assert their roles in the power structure. The frisking officer wants to know why Santos is carrying a pencil in the middle of the night; whether he is a graffiti nut, a pervert, or a numbers runner (237). He goes home and throws the anthology away, deciding to simplify his life by taking sides, since he cannot have it both ways (238).

Santos is caught between a dominant discourse, which excludes him, and his father's rhetoric, expressive of values he no longer holds dear. Literature provides an answer. After his encounter with police, he takes his anthology, which his mother has retrieved from the garbage, back to his room, and reads from John Keats: " 'a drowsy numbness pains my sense' was one of the ones I found useful" (238). At this point literature still functions as a private language. It becomes full-fledged counterdiscourse when Santos describes his father's encounter with police. The old man is arrested on a false identity charge during a neighborhood search for a pervert. Santos, who loves his father deeply, states: "Behold, the dreamer cometh. A dreamer of dreams. Let us slay him" (239).

It is crucial to note that poetry is at the same time a critique of ideology and contained in the cultural framework from which ideology originates. Adaptation (not assimilation) implies an acceptance of the former without acceptance of the latter, a systematic analysis of the power relationships. Thus Santos is able to break with his father's culture as manifested in oratory, language, and particularly the "Lamento jíbaro" he is so fond of that, when the record breaks, he asks that the pieces be sent to him (246–47). At the same time, however, he rejects the ideology implicit in the cultural framework where he is now positioned. This double rejection is clearly illustrated in the episode, just prior to his father's death and his mother's return to Puerto Rico, where Santos doesn't return for Christmas, spending it instead in a single room occupancy hotel. When he does come home, he is chided for not having attended Mass. He responds with the truth he has been discovering since primary school: he has chosen to live among enemies (262). His twin defenses are English poetry and isolation.

The novel's last two chapters, appropriately entitled "Ropes of Passage" and "R.I.P.," detail Santos' growing isolation from his family (260), his rejection of higher education discourse (265), the underside of the myths about the workplace and consumption (251), and a rejection of medical discourse (274). Through these, Rivera engages in a systematic disassembling of his cultural surroundings. But a return to Puerto Rico with his moribund father reveals no paradise there either; if anything, the island has become an infernal trap (295). Santos' break with his birthplace is dramatically illustrated by the fact that he cannot find his grandfather's resting place (298). There is nothing left for him but to return to the world of single room occupancy residences and exploitation he calls home: New York (299), to which he must adapt.

This adaptation leads to a challenging of the relationships of power and the adoption of a critical stance by means of available counterdiscourses. Santos Malanguez finds his own in poetry. Edward Rivera has found his in corrosive irony, a systematic critique of ideology, and an exposure of the ways in which the privileged status of dominant groups is preserved and maintained. For him, assimilation is a fiction, an act of bad faith; but adaptation does not necessarily imply a loss of identity or a fragmentation of self.

TEACHING THE WORK

The most direct approach to the teaching of *Family Installments* would be to appeal to the students' own backgrounds as they concentrate on one of the novel's themes.

1. Do a detailed analysis of the roles of family, education, or religion in the novel and compare this to your own experience.

2. Examine how the novel treats sexuality and relationships. How does the novel's view of sexuality correspond to the protagonist's worldview?

3. Analyze the discourse of medicine in the novel and its relationship to medical treatment of minorities.

4. Focus on consumption. What does the Malanguez family buy? How are items paid for? Are these shopping patterns still prevalent among Latino minorities? If you detect changes, what has changed, how and why?

5. Using Santos' experiences, recall your elementary school education. Write about the advantages and disadvantages of public and private education for Latinos.

6. Discuss the role of music in the novel. Compare the significance of music for the novel's family with the role of music in your life, your family's life, your culture.

7. Discuss the role of food in the novel. Students might also compare and contrast this work with others by Latino authors.

8. Compare this novel with a novel written by any other Puerto Rican author, such as Esmeralda Santiago, Nicholasa Mohr, or Piri Thomas, or by a work written by a Chicano or Cuban author. Focus on one theme in both novels. Are there similarities or differences in the treatment of the principal themes?

9. Discuss the effect of the first-person narrative. Does the protagonist's point of view change as he grows up, or is it reaffirmed?

10. Discuss the melting pot theory and its relationship to Santos Malanguez's adaptation to American culture.

11. Discuss the role played by literature in this novel. How does it affect the protagonist?

12. Examine the role of women in the novel. Does it reflect a particular period? Has it changed? If so, describe the changes.

CRITICISM AND WORKS CITED

Foucault, Michel. *The Archeology of Knowledge & the Discourse on Language*, trans. A. M. Sheridan Smith. New York: Pantheon, 1972.

Frank, Joseph. *The Widening Gyre: Crisis and Mastery in Modern Literature*. New Brunswick, N.J.: Rutgers University Press, 1963.

Rivera, Edward. *Family Installments: Memories of Growing Up Hispanic*. New York: William Morrow, 1982.

———. "Stable Manners: Or How the Publication of Family Installments Was Stalled for Three Years and $3,000.00." *Massachusetts Review* 37, no. 3 (Autumn 1996): 377–85.

Sanchez, Marta. "Hispanic- and Anglo-American Discourse in Edward Rivera's *Family Installments*." *American Literary History* 1, no. 4 (Winter 1989): 853–71.

Villanueva-Collado, Alfredo. "Growing Up Hispanic: Discourse and Ideology in *Hunger of Memory* and *Family Installments*. *Americas Review* 16, no. 3–4 (Fall-Winter 1988): 75–90.

Williams, Raymond. *Marxism and Literature*. Oxford: Oxford University Press, 1977.

8

Richard Rodriguez's *Hunger of Memory* and the Rejection of the Private Self

Lizabeth Paravisini-Gebert

RICHARD RODRIGUEZ, the son of Mexican-American immigrants, was born in 1946 in San Francisco, California. Rodriguez graduated in 1967 from Stanford University, received an M.A. from Columbia University in 1969, and attended graduate school at the University of California, Berkeley. His journey through the American educational system, his abrupt decision to leave the academic life, and his alienation from his parents' culture are chronicled in his landmark collection of autobiographical essays, written and published separately between 1973 and 1981: *Hunger of Memory: The Education of Richard Rodriguez* (1982). Controversial when first published, it became one of the most debated texts in U.S. Latino letters. In this aesthetically beautiful book, Rodriguez discusses significant social and political issues, using incidents from his own life to illustrate his points, including the change of language from Spanish to English upon beginning school and a confrontation with affirmative action programs.

Rodriguez's second collection of essays, *Days of Obligation: An Argument with My Mexican Father* (1992), explores a variety of subjects as diverse as the conquest of Mexico, AIDS, and the spiritual and moral landscapes of the United States and Mexico. Rodriguez is considered one of the foremost essayists in the United States, and he is a frequent guest on public television and radio.

ANALYSIS OF THEMES AND FORMS

Richard Rodriguez's *Hunger of Memory: The Education of Richard Rodriguez*, published in 1982 to both critical acclaim and heated controversy, is one of the most elegantly crafted Mexican-American texts. It is also, certainly, one of the most vilified, having gained its notoriety among Chicano critics from its author's apparent rejection of his ancestral Mexican roots. Readers of Rodriguez's complex yet reticent memoir have condemned it as conservative in its decrying of the evils of affirmative action programs, "assimilated" in its apparent lack of sympathy with the Chicano movement's emphasis on *la raza* (a political identification of the Hispanic "race"), and *agringado* (affected by or assimilated into the Anglo community) in its depiction of the heinousness of bilingual programs. Rodriguez's refusal to embrace Chicano politics and identity quickly turned him into a *pocho*, a Mexican American who denied his heritage. He insists that they are not of any particular interest to him. He writes in *Hunger of Memory*, "I do not search Mexican graveyards for ties to unnameable ancestors."[1] Often, he avows, he could barely bring himself to concede that he was "of Mexican ancestry"; not for him a search for identity in the mythical Aztlán, the fabled place of origin that gave the Chicano movement its most powerful symbol of ancestry and roots. As Jeffrey Louis Decker writes in his review of Rodriguez's second book, *Days of Obligation*, "[T]he principal objection Chicano critics raise regarding the work of Richard Rodriguez concerns his failure to engage the reality of the Mexican experience in America."[2]

Yet, upon its publication, *Hunger of Memory* received remarkable praise in the mainstream media. It was the first book written by a Chicano to be widely and enthusiastically reviewed by publications such as the *New York Times Book Review*, *Time*, *Newsweek*, and the *Atlantic Monthly*, which had never before offered such critical consideration to a Hispanic text. Their acclaim stood in stark contrast to the critical backlash from Chicano critics, who perceived that Anglos believed they had found in the book "a key to understanding the Mexican-American and debates related to bilingual education and affirmative action."[3] For Anglos Rodriguez became, in the years immediately following the publication of *Hunger of Memory*, "the voice of 'Hispanic America.'"[4] The ensuing years, and the publication of his second book, *Days of Obligation*,[5] have only solidified his position as the most ubiquitous and recognizable Hispanic public intellectual in the United States. Excerpts from his work are routinely included in the anthologies and "readers" that form the staple of freshman English offerings, and discussions of his work are de rigueur in courses on ethnic literature and multiculturalism in the United States.

The text of *Hunger of Memory* consists of a prologue, "Middle-Class Pastoral," and six loosely connected, chronologically arranged autobiographical essays focusing on Rodriguez's education. The first of these, "Aria," chronicles how the intimate space of Rodriguez's childhood home, where Spanish is the household language, is lost through his determination to learn English and have access to what he calls "public society." The condemnation of bilingual education in "Aria" is developed more fully in the second essay, "The Achievement of Desire," which narrates how his pursuit of education, seen primarily through his love and enjoyment of books, alienates him from his relatively uneducated, Spanish-speaking parents. In "Credo," he links the theme of alienation to his identity as a Mexican Catholic, establishing in the process the basis for the confessional tone of the entire text, which he links to the seminal influence of Saint Augustine's *Confessions*. The fourth essay, "Complexion," explores Rodriguez's unease about his dark skin and what he calls his Indian features. These uncomfortable markers of difference keep reminding him of the ethnicity he seeks to escape through education. In "Profession," Rodriguez focuses on his negative feelings about affirmative action, illustrated by his refusal to accept a teaching position at Yale which he believes has come to him as a result of policies that marginalize him as a less-deserving "ethnic" candidate. "Mr. Secrets," the sixth and last essay, considers the alienating gap that has developed between him and his siblings and their parents as a result of their education and concomitant rise into the middle class.

Hunger of Memory is consistently described as an ethnic autobiography, although its structure as a group of interrelated essays makes that classification somewhat inadequate. The genre of ethnic autobiography requires the articulation of a life from within the bounds of a particular ethnic experience, but Rodriguez seeks to evade the "ethnic literature" label and defines his trajectory toward adulthood as one of disassociation from his ethnic roots. His "metaphor of self" is rooted in his acquisition of a language and a universe of knowledge that can erase the marks of ethnicity that are his undesired ancestral and historical legacy. The "arsenal of literary techniques" he deploys to document this accomplishment seek, not to connect him to his ethnic experience, as is the case in the ethnic autobiography, but to separate himself from a notion of self limited by ethnicity. His position, as Bill Shuter has argued, is that "an authentic ethnic identity cannot survive, and should not be expected to survive, either a public education or the acquisition of a public self."[6]

Rodriguez's repeated allusions to Saint Augustine's *Confessions*, a spiritual autobiography, mark that text as providing a generic example more powerful than the many ethnic autobiographies that precede *Hunger of Memory*. Like the *Confessions*, *Hunger of Memory*, a model of relentless introspection, is written in the confessional mode, as the elaboration of a systematic process of self-inquiry, self-accusation, and acknowledgment of an alienated selfhood. Rodriguez must confess his insistence on learning English as a betrayal of the intimacy of his childhood home; he must recount the progress of his education as a narrative of youthful transgression; he must contextualize his process of maturation as a violation of family life.

Hunger of Memory, as an example of the bildungsroman or chronicle of development, narrates the path followed by a lower-class immigrant child toward success as a middle-class American citizen. As such, it is the very essence of an ethnic autobiography. However, the very success that gives the narrative its coherence—Rodriguez's attainment of a graduate degree in English at one of the country's most prestigious private institutions—is one he repudiates because he finds that it may be perceived as having been achieved through the assistance of the affirmative action programs he deplores. This repudiation of affirmative action programs, which constitutes the most impassioned gesture of disavowal of an ethnically defined experience, is the natural outcome of a text that presents the problem of the Mexican-American child as one made up of endless sets of binary oppositions. Rodriguez insists on seeing the choices available to him as the child of immigrants, not as fluid, multiple, and nuanced, but as rigidly defined as a series of polarities that must be resolved in favor of assimilation: masculine versus feminine, private versus public, Spanish versus English, Catholic versus Protestant, silence versus speech, Mexican versus American. As Rosaura Sánchez has argued, "Rodriguez's metaphysical imaginary [*sic*] is based on a selectively posited grid of categories that allow him to explain differences between American culture and Mexican culture on the basis of dichotomies."[7]

Perhaps the most central of these dichotomies is the one between the public and private spheres. Rodriguez valorizes the "public" over the "private" man, positing the dichotomy as if it were indeed a natural one, as if an individual, when seeking to define his or her identity, were forced to select only one from among many possibilities of development. There is a fundamental fallacy in Rodriguez's positing the need for such a choice, which is most clear to the reader in his arguments concerning the need to embrace an "American" identity (a step that necessitates his relinquishing his Mexican culture) and in his reduction of Spanish to the private sphere.

Rodriguez, as he makes clear in *Hunger of Memory*, "prefers consenting to the myth of a common American identity traceable to New England and the Puritans."[8] His acceptance of this ideological construct, which assumes one single and elementary form of Americanness as a "transcendental truth," leads him to the assumption that in order to become "American" and enter the public sphere, he must cease to be "Mexican"; he must sacrifice all aspects of his identity that can be traced to his parents' ancestry, history, and culture. *Hunger of Memory* does not posit a multicultural America, where immigrants such as Rodriguez's parents can enter "public life" while retaining their language and culture in their private and public lives. Instead, he suggests that the immigrant's only opportunity for integration into American culture depends on his or her willingness to relinquish the markers of his previous identity.

The most salient marker of Rodriguez's Mexicanness (other than his body, which is discussed below) is language. He presents Spanish as the single most powerful obstacle to assimilation (or to entering the public sphere, in the text's construction) for Mexican Americans. Hence the frequent allusions to language and learning, primarily to William Shakespeare's *The Tempest*, in which Caliban seizes the language of Prospero and uses it as a tool to transcend his own limitations. Caliban becomes the model for Rodriguez's own transcendence of the obstacles presented by his Mexicanness—hence the importance given in the text to the process of his education as the path that will lead him from Spanish to English, from Spanish to American culture, and from ignorance to a narrowly defined "culture." In fact, most of the text of *Hunger of Memory* details the discovery of the English language and his mastery of English as a tool. The powerful role of literary allusions in *Hunger of Memory*, allusions rooted in the traditions of English literature, are Rodriguez's textual evidence of the mastery of the dominant culture's tools that he has acquired through his education. Critical praise for Rodriguez as an "exceptional stylist" (Márquez 133) comes in recognition of this mastery.

Hunger of Memory is regarded by many critics as "a eulogy for a lost intimacy embodied in his Spanish-speaking childhood" (Danahay 294). But here, once again, the text demonstrates Rodriguez's narrow perceptions on culture and language—Rodriguez insists on seeing Spanish as a language of the home and intimacy and fails, in the process, to consider its richness and literatures. Tomás Rivera justly chastises Rodriguez for reducing the rich historical and cultural tradition of the Spanish language to a personal voice that "lacks the intelligence and ability to communicate beyond the sensibilities of the personal interactions of personal family life."[9] Of this personal family life, Rodriguez will retain only Catholicism as a part of his identity, although he still will consider the Catholic part of himself (as he regards the Spanish part of himself) as "ancient, cynical, feminine" and childlike, whereas Protestantism will always be depicted as forceful and male.

Hunger of Memory, its uncelebrated ideology and anguished exploration of a self at odds with his ancestry notwithstanding, remains, more than a decade after its publication, "the most sustained and illuminating treatment of the 'problems of assimilation,' " a process poignantly conveyed in the text through the author's alienation from his body, a body whose brownness he has learned to view, not as a proud link to his ancestry, but as a shameful, oppressive symbol: "I am the only one in

the family whose face is severely cut to the line of ancient Indian ancestors. My face is mournfully long, in the classical Indian manner; my profile
suggests one of those beak-nosed Mayan sculptures—the eaglelike face
upturned, open-mouthed, against the deserted, primitive sky" (115).

Rodriguez piercingly describes his growing up ashamed of his body—
"I wanted to forget that I had a body," he writes, "because I had a brown
body" (126). His earliest awareness of his darkness of skin linked it with
hard manual labor, powerful muscles, low intellectual achievement, and
poverty, the very things to which he, as a bookish young boy with
academic ambition, would have been loath to aspire. Rodriguez's "metaphor of self," in the words of one of his critics, "is rooted in his acquisition of language and knowledge,"[10] in the escape from the very
physicality that he has come to identify with brown bodies. As a young
adult attending Stanford, he sought to understand Mexican-American
class oppression through performing physical labor in a construction site.
He learned that the moment of closest identification with *los pobres*—the
poor—came about the moment when the summer sun had made his face
and hands look like those of the Mexican workers; it was also the moment of his greatest awareness of the difference between them. His
education had separated them because it had given him a different "attitude of mind," a different "imagination of himself" (138). The security
that his intellectual development had given him allowed him later to
repossess his body by taking up long-distance running, which he considered a middle-class sport. When he entered his thirties he gained the
body he never had earlier in his youth: "the stomach lipped tight by
muscle; the shoulders rounded by chin-ups; the arms veined." This body
he can clothe in the double-breasted Italian suits and custom-made English shoes that have become the "reassuring reminders of public success" (136–137).

Hunger of Memory is imbued with the "great anxiety" and "precious
sadness" of Rodriguez's rejection of the "duality of his working class
origins" and his embrace of "middle class manners."[11] He emerges from
the text as an individual whose essential goals are privacy and isolation,
"capable of functioning only as an isolated and private individual, deprived of any organic connection with his ethnic group, his social class,
and finally even his own family."[12] His disconnection from his roots and
his family leaves him with a onerous burden of guilt (the guilt of the
private man rather than that of the man committed to the *la raza* movement) which he seeks to exorcise through the emplotting of his narrative
in an archetypal pattern of the tale of confession and redemption. Sin,
purification, and rebirth, the stages of the Christian hagiography, structure Rodriguez's path from his privileging of public over private self,
through the crisis of self-recognition at the British Museum while writing
his dissertation on the metaphysical poets, to the renunciation of all his

ill-gained (because tainted by affirmative action) success, and his self-imposed cloistering in the solitude of a San Francisco apartment and a secretive life: a cloister where the spirit of the "large picture of a sad-eyed Christ, exposing his punctured heart," which hung prominently in his parents' home, continues to preside. The penitent Richard Rodriguez of the conclusion of *Hunger of Memory*, metaphorically flagellated through confession and invoking the mea culpas necessary for absolution, is but an adult version of the child who would "study pictures of martyrs—white-robed virgins fallen in death and the young, almost smiling, St. Sebastian, transfigured in pain" (84)—martyred, but ultimately triumphant.

This aspect of *Hunger of Memory* is highlighted when the text is read against the background of "Late Victorians," an essay Rodriguez included in *Days of Obligation*, in which he again evokes the twin images of confession and the martyred body to describe the ravages of AIDS in San Francisco's gay community. "St. Augustine writes from his cope of dust that we are restless hearts, for earth is not our true home," he reminds us in "Late Victorians," Rodriguez's reticent and guarded public declaration of his own homosexuality. The coda to the meditations on the body in *Hunger of Memory*, it brings a new dimension to Rodriguez's insistence on the rejection of the private self in his earlier book.

Toward the end of the period chronicled in *Hunger of Memory*, Rodriguez describes his mother as having begun to call him Mr. Secrets because he reveals so little of himself and his work to his mother. In "Late Victorians" the secrecy is revealed as that imposed or self-imposed on the homosexual.

The San Francisco of the infinitely moving "Late Victorians" is a city of bodies prey to "tragic conclusions": a young woman steps off the railing of the Golden Gate Bridge "[t]o land like a spilled purse at [the author's] feet" (27); at the Gay Freedom Day parade, "plum-spotted young men" slide by on motorized cable cars; a gay newspaper begins to accept advertisements from funeral parlors and casket makers, another invites homemade obituaries. A city that had had the experience of "watching the civic body burn even as we stood, out of body, on a hillside, in a movie theater" (27), this city is portrayed as joining in true community as AIDS becomes "a disease of the entire city."

The Richard Rodriguez of "Late Victorians," though still self-cast as the quintessential outsider, acknowledges a community, not the community of Chicano ethnicity, but that of life-loving homosexual men forced to grow to confront loss and death. The identification with a community brings forth a rare instance of accusation in Rodriguez's work. Speaking of the disappearance of so many friends and acquaintances, he wonders why it had not "led us to interrogate the landscape."

AIDS, Rodriguez argues, is "a plague of absence . . . condensed into the fluid of passing emotion" (40). It is not a metaphorical disease, but one that underscores the fragility of the body. It was not so in the glory days, the salad days of the Castro District, when "paradise [could be found] at the baths," where a body could float "from body to body, open arms yielding to open arms in an angelic round" (43). The image of the pre-AIDS gay body in "Late Victorians" is predominantly seraphic, built on visions of angels before the fall, bathed in the balmy and merciful halo of the city. For Rodriguez, a writer whose iconography is fundamentally Catholic, AIDS signals the Fall, the recalling to nature of men who "aspired to the mock-angelic settled for the shirt of hair" and are forced to face penance, martyrdom, and death (45).

The collective martyred body, the dead body, is silhouetted against the image of Rodriguez's sculpted body begun in *Hunger of Memory*. The well-exercised body in the earlier text, becomes in "Late Victorians" a body emasculated by the connection between the collective body and death. Bodybuilding becomes "a parody of labor, a useless accumulation of the laborer's bulk and strength" (39). The gym, at once "a closet of privacy and an exhibition gallery," is "nothing if not the occasion for transcendence" where lats can become angelic wings, and the homosexual can move from autosexuality to nonsexuality, the penitence of those guilty of nothing more than being still alive.

For Rodriguez, the martyrdom of the collective, communal body brought about by AIDS confirms a philosophy of life rooted in a Catholic upbringing that taught him not to dream of utopia. The point of Eden, for him, "is not approach but expulsion," and he, a man who had never "learned to love what is corruptible," ends his essay on a note of fruitlessness and penance, a "barren skeptic" uncomfortably shifting his tailbone upon a cold, hard, church pew (47). The overpowering final image is that of the expelled angel, disembodied by the need to eschew a sexuality painfully connected to death, vilified by an ethnic community whose spokesman he refused to be, expelled from paradise, again a penitent, marked by the sin of individuality and yet still blessed with life amidst death. This image of expulsion denies the very possibility of an identity founded on ancestry. Chicano versions of ancestry do not provide comfortable models of identity for a homosexual male; homosexuality, in turn, in its insistence on being "the central fact of identity," through its "covenant against nature" making progeny impossible, sentenced him to the "complaisancies of the barren house" (37).

TEACHING THE WORK

1. There are numerous sources of background information that could prove helpful in approaching *Hunger of Memory*. Perhaps most important are Rodriguez's own autobiographical works, particularly his collection

of essays, *Days of Obligation: An Argument with My Mexican Father* (New York: Viking, 1992) and four of his essays: "An American Writer," in *The Invention of Ethnicity*, ed. Werner Sollors (New York: Oxford University Press, 1989), 3–13; "An Education in Language," in *The State of the Language*, ed. Leonard Michaels and Christopher Ricks (Berkeley: University of California Press, 1980), 129–39; "Going Home Again," *American Scholar* 44 (1974–1975): 15–28; and "Mixed Blood, Columbus's Legacy: A World Made Mestizo," *Harper's* (November 1991): 47–56. For a biographical and critical overview of Rodriguez's career, see Mary E. Teller, "Rodriguez, Richard," in *Contemporary Authors*, ed. Hal May (Detroit: Gale Research, 1985), 429–30; and Richard D. Woods, "Richard Rodriguez," in *Dictionary of Literary Biography: Chicano Series* (Detroit: Gale Research, 1989), 214–16. Although Rodriguez is not fond of granting interviews, readers can find interesting insights into the background to his work in Paul Crowley, "An Ancient Catholic: An Interview with Richard Rodriguez," in *Catholic Lives, Contemporary America*, ed. Thomas J. Ferraro (Durham, N.C.: Duke University Press, 1997), 259–65. Of special interest are two essays on teaching *Hunger of Memory* that offer alternative readings of the text: Martin A. Danahay, "Breaking the Silence: Symbolic Violence and the Teaching of Contemporary 'Ethnic' Autobiography," *College Literature* 18, no. 3 (October 1991): 64–79; and Antonio C. Márquez, "Richard Rodriguez's *Hunger of Memory* and New Perspectives on Ethnic Autobiography," in *Teaching American Ethnic Literatures: Nineteen Essays*, ed. John R. Maitino and David R. Peck (Albuquerque: University of New Mexico Press, 1996), 237–54.

2. *Hunger of Memory*, a richly nuanced text, offers a seemingly inexhaustible list of possible theoretical and thematic approaches, some of which are suggested below. Chief and foremost is perhaps the consideration of genre. Is *Hunger of Memory* an example of an ethnic autobiography or a collection of loosely linked autobiographical essays that lack the narrative structure and personal insight needed for true autobiographical writing? How does the text compare with other examples of ethnic autobiography (see "Other Sources")? Discuss the way the text treats the issue of cultural assimilation and ethnic identity.

3. *Hunger of Memory* locates its emotional center on Rodriguez's rejection of the notions of how to be a Mexican American offered by his parents and relatives. Examine and discuss how the author constructs his own problematic notion of Mexicanness by exploring the text's depiction of the conflicts between generations. Rodriguez approaches the tensions between these relationships across generations from multiple perspectives, beginning from the family's history, as having followed a "natural" trajectory in Mexico, until their migration to the United States. Compare the different constructions of ethnic identity between Rodriguez and his parents' generations.

4. These intergenerational conflicts can also be examined through an analysis of Rodriguez's representation of the body as a marker of ethnicity. Identify the allusions to the Mexican body—his own and those of the Mexicans he comes across: family, relatives, gardeners, and other Mexican laborers. Discuss how these passages indicate Rodriguez's attempts to address the one insurmountable obstacle to his complete assimilation: the body that carries with it distinct aspects of his ethnic ancestry. Such a reading of the text can yield greater understanding of the complexities of Rodriguez's awareness of the links between his body and his belonging to a Mexican population perceived as an underclass.

5. Trace the traumatic impact of this intergenerational separation through Rodriguez's depiction of his problematic relationship with language—the rejection of Spanish, which he regards as necessary to enter American public life. A review of the many allusions to Spanish as the language of home and intimacy, seen against his protestations of English as a public language, could serve as the basis for a revealing examination of the fallacy of language at the center of *Hunger of Memory*, especially as it can serve to mask other reasons behind his desire for separation from his parents. A reading of the text in this light could be linked to a critique of the book as a text that outlines the power of education as an instrument of acculturation.

6. There are in the text numerous references to notions of manhood that could offer substantial material for an examination of gender identity in the light of ethnic identity. These can be highlighted through the contrast between Rodriguez's emphasis on retaining his religious identity as a Catholic and his desire to break the ties between his Mexican childhood and his American manhood. A student interested in this theme could undertake parallel readings of *Hunger of Memory* and Saint Augustine's *Confessions* to ascertain how various concepts of identity are formed and why this seminal Catholic text constitutes such a powerful pre-text for Rodriguez's memoir.

7. An examination of what we could call architectural elements in Rodriguez's work could yield most interesting insights into cross-generational tensions: the contrast between domestic and public spaces (the family home, school, the British Museum Library, and so on); the juxtaposing of the screen doors of his family's working-class home and the sliding doors of the homes of his middle-class Anglo friends; the framing of Mexican men in external spaces (as construction workers, gardeners, and so on) as the means of signaling their contributions to, as well as their exclusion from, middle-class inner spaces. These and other delineations of space in the text can be read as pointers to cross-generational differences, of the separation between the private and public spaces to which Rodriguez attaches such significance in the text.

NOTES

1. Richard Rodriguez, *Hunger of Memory: The Education of Richard Rodriguez* (Boston: David R. Godine, 1982). All references are to this edition and will appear in parentheses in the text.
2. Jeffrey Louis Decker, "Mr. Secrets: Richard Rodriguez Flees the House of Memory," *Transition* 61 (1993): 124–33.
3. Tomás Rivera, "Richard Rodriguez' *Hunger of Memory* as Humanistic Antithesis," *MELUS* 11, no. 4 (Winter 1984): 5.
4. Ramón Saldívar, "Ideologies of the Self: Chicano Autobiography," *Diacritics* 15, no. 3 (1985): 26.
5. Richard Rodriguez, *Days of Obligation: An Argument with My Mexican Father* (New York: Viking, 1992). All references are to this edition and will appear in parentheses in the text.
6. Bill Shuter, "The Confessions of Richard Rodriguez," *Cross Currents* 45, no. 1 (Spring 1995): 95.
7. Rosaura Sánchez, "Calculated Musings: Richard Rodriguez's Metaphysics of Difference." In *The Ethnic Canon: Histories, Institutions, and Interventions*, ed. David Palumbo-Liu. (Minneapolis: University of Minnesota Press, 1995), 160.
8. Ibid. Sánchez is, in her turn, paraphrasing Myra Jehlen's "Introduction: Beyond Transcendence" to *Ideology and Classic American Literature*, ed. Sacvan Bercovitch and Myra Jehlin (Cambridge: Cambridge University Press, 1986), 14.
9. Rivera, "Richard Rodriguez," 8.
10. Antonio C. Márquez, "Richard Rodriguez's *Hunger of Memory* and the Poetics of Experience," *Arizona Quarterly* 40, no. 2 (Summer 1984): 135.
11. Saldívar, "Ideologies," 27.
12. Ibid.

CRITICISM

Alarcón, Norma. "Tropology of Hunger: The 'Miseducation' of Richard Rodriguez." In *The Ethnic Canon: Histories, Institutions, and Interventions*, ed. David Palumbo-Liu. Minneapolis: University of Minnesota Press, 1995, 140–52. Examines the theme of Mexican identity in *Hunger of Memory* from the perspective of its cultural assimilation.

Danahay, Martin A. "Richard Rodriguez's Poetics of Manhood." In *Fictions of Masculinity: Crossing Cultures, Crossing Sexualities*, ed. Peter Murphy. New York: New York University Press, 1994, 290–307. Provides a reading of *Hunger of Memory* as a work that explores the connections between masculinity and ethnicity.

Eakin, Paul John. *Touching the World: Reference in Autobiography*. Princeton, N.J.: Princeton University Press, 1992. In his chapter on *Hunger of Memory*, Eakin calls attention to the presence of two distinct voices in the book—those of the essayist and the storyteller.

Márquez, Antonio C. "Richard Rodriguez's *Hunger of Memory* and the Poetics of Experience." *Arizona Quarterly* 40, no. 2 (Summer 1984): 130–141. This defense of *Hunger of Memory* analyzes the text as "the autobiography of a writer."

Rivera, Tomás. "Richard Rodriguez's *Hunger of Memory* as Humanistic Antithesis." *MELUS* 11, no. 4 (Winter 1984): 5–13. Negative critique of Rodriguez's work by one of the most prominent early critics of Chicano literature.

Romero, Rolando J. "Spanish and English: The Question of Literacy in *Hunger of Memory*." *Confluencia* 6, no. 2 (Spring 1991): 89–100.

Rose, Shirley K. "Metaphors and Myths of Cross-Cultural Literacy: Autobiographical Narratives by Maxine Hong Kingston, Richard Rodriguez, and Malcolm X." *MELUS* 14, no. 1 (Spring 1987): 3–15.

Staten, Henry. "Ethnic Authenticity, Class, and Autobiography: The Case of *Hunger of Memory*." *PMLA* 113, no. 1 (1998): 103–16.

OTHER SOURCES AND SUGGESTED READING

Acuña, Rodolfo. *Occupied America: A History of Chicanos*. New York: Harper, 1981.

Flores, Lauro. "Chicano Autobiography: Culture, Ideology, and the Self." *Americas Review* 18, no. 2 (1980): 80–91.

Galarza, Ernesto. *Barrio Boy: The Story of a Boy's Acculturation*. Notre Dame: University of Notre Dame Press, 1971.

Holte, James Caig. *The Ethnic I: A Sourcebook for Ethnic-American Autobiography*. New York: Greenwood Press, 1988.

Sánchez, George J. *Becoming Mexican American: Ethnicity, Culture, and Identity in Chicano Los Angeles, 1900–1945*. New York: Oxford University Press, 1993.

Sollors, Werner. *Beyond Ethnicity: Consent and Descent in American Culture*. New York: Oxford University Press, 1986.

Sprinker, Michael. "Fictions of the Self: The Form of American Autobiography." In *Autobiography: Essays Theoretical and Critical*, ed. James Olney. Princeton, N.J.: Princeton University Press, 1980.

Suárez-Orozco, Carola, and Marcelo Suárez-Orozco. *Transformations: Immigration, Family Life, and Achievement Among Latino Adolescents*. Stanford: Stanford University Press, 1995.

Wilson, Rob. "Producing American Selves: The Form of American Autobiography." *Boundary 2* (Summer 1991): 104–29.

Villarreal, José Antonio. *Pocho*. New York: Anchor Books, 1959.

9

Teaching Oscar Hijuelos' *Our House in the Last World*

Gustavo Pérez Firmat

OSCAR HIJUELOS, who was born in New York City in 1951, received his bachelor of arts and master's degrees from City College of New York. Hijuelos not only is the best-known Cuban-American writer; he is the first Latino novelist to have been awarded the Pulitzer Prize for fiction. In addition to *Our House in the Last World* (1983), he has published four other novels: *The Mambo Kings Play Songs of Love* (1989), *The Fourteen Sisters of Emilio Montez O'Brien* (1993), *Mr. Ives' Christmas* (1995), and *Empress of the Splendid Season* (1999). All of them have been well received, but *The Mambo Kings Play Songs of Love* (1989), the work that earned Hijuelos the Pulitzer Prize and later became a successful motion picture, has garnered the most critical attention. Reviewers and critics have praised this novel for its vivid and detailed recreation of the mambo craze of the 1950s as well as for its excruciating portrayal of the tragic lives of the two protagonists, César and Nestor Castillo, two Cuban brothers who emigrate to the United States in 1949 and achieve ephemeral fame fronting a mambo orchestra. When it was first published, some reviewers took exception to the novel's "machismo," although Hijuelos himself has pointed out that his intention was to examine rather than endorse the protagonists' obsession with their sexual exploits. Hijuelos' often poetic, sometimes whimsical, style has been linked to the "magical realism" practiced by some contemporary Latin American novelists.

Although perhaps less ambitious than Hijuelos' other novels. *Our House in the Last World* is both a sensitive study of a family's difficult adaptation to life in a new country and an early statement of the themes and procedures that characterize Hijuelos' mature work. The lyrical rendering of urban landscapes, the technique of liberally mixing present and past events, the preoccupation with the connection between cultural and personal identity—all of these recur in his subsequent works.

ANALYSIS OF THEMES AND FORMS

Our House in the Last World, Oscar Hijuelos' first book, is an autobiographical novel that follows the fortunes of the Santinio family over several decades. Beginning with the meeting of Alejo Santinio and Mercedes Sorrea in Cuba in 1939, the novel narrates the couple's marriage, their emigration to the United States, the birth of their children, and the family's difficult life in Spanish Harlem. The central consciousness in the text belongs to Hector, the Santinios' second son who (like Hijuelos) was born in New York in 1951.

A great deal of the narration is given over to detailing the collapse of the Santinio family. Alejo, who arrives in this country with high hopes but can never go farther than the kitchen of a restaurant, is a drunk; Hector's mother, Mercedes, sees visions and talks to spirits. Resentful of her husband and unhappy with her lot, she becomes ill tempered and withdrawn and finally takes refuge in a fantasy world of Cuban ghosts. Although Hector's older brother, Horacio, manages to escape the family's hellish life, Hector continues to live with his parents, and when Alejo drops dead from a heart attack in 1969, the household all but collapses, slipping from poverty to near indigence. Significantly, the last two chapters are entitled "Ghosts" and "Voices from the Last World," as if the family's very materiality required Alejo's physical presence. Once he's gone, Mercedes' fantasies take over the narrative, which ends in a surreal world of dreams and phantasms.

The great theme of Hector's childhood and adolescence is Cuban manhood—what it means, what it costs, how to achieve it. Over and over Hector harps on the fact that he is not as "Cuban" as his father or older brother. He does not speak Spanish; he is blond, frail, and a mama's boy. Unlike Horacio, who follows in his father's footsteps by becoming *muy* macho—a hard-drinking, brawling womanizer—Hector develops into an overweight, shy "American" teenager. As Horacio gloats at one point, "He's just dumb when it comes to being Cuban."[1] Making things worse is his striking physical likeness to his father: "They were like twins, separated by age, with the same eyes, faces, bodies. Except Alejo was from another world—*cubano, cubano*" (145).

As he grows up, Hector develops the sense that he is a defective replica of his father, exact in many outward details but lacking Alejo's Cubanness. Too Cuban to be American but hardly Cuban enough to resemble his father, Hector sees himself as a "freak, a hunchback, a man with a deformed face" (190). He is a "Cuban Quasimodo" (192), a phrase whose hybridity conveys Hector's sense of lacking a suitable cultural habitation.

But Hector is not the only monster in the family. His feelings of inadequacy are complicated by his father's habits of excess. Mercedes' recriminations are not enough to stop Alejo from spending most of his free time away from the house, drinking and womanizing. If Hector thinks of himself as a freak because he is not Cuban enough, he sees his father as a freak for being too Cuban.

Another important theme in this novel, as in other immigrant narratives, is language. When Horacio says that his brother is "dumb," we should not overlook the adjective's linguistic meaning, for Hector's feelings of inferiority have a great deal to do with his poor Spanish, which sets him apart from the "real Cubans" (175). When he tries to speak like his gregarious father, he becomes paralyzed: "His Spanish was unpracticed, practically nonexistent. He had a stutter, and saying a Spanish word made him think of drunkenness. . . . He avoided Spanish even though that was all he heard at home. He read it, understood it, but he grew paralyzed by the prospect of the slightest conversation" (173). For Hector, Spanish is a straight jacket, an iron mask, an artificial skin that defaces him. As a result, Hector views himself as a kind of bicultural mummy: "part Cuban, part American—all wrapped up tightly inside a skin in which he sometimes could not move" (190).

Because for Hector Spanish is the father's tongue, it is a language that he both desires and dreads. Curiously, even though Mercedes writes poetry, it is Alejo who comes to embody the mother tongue. When Hector speaks Spanish, he becomes Alejo; but when he becomes Alejo, he turns into the "monster" who comes home drunk in the middle of the night and abuses his family. Since Spanish focuses his ambivalent feelings toward his father, it is a handicap, a wound, the hump in the hunchback.

This pathological view of the Spanish language was initially shaped by the circumstances in which Hector learned English. Without a doubt the most wrenching scenes in the book are those that describe his prolonged stay in a pediatric hospital when he was only three or four years old (an incident that, like others in the novel, has a parallel in Hijuelos' own life). In 1954, shortly after returning to the United States from a trip to Cuba, Hector becomes seriously ill from a kidney infection and has to spend nearly a year convalescing in a hospital full of terminally ill children. During this period he sees his mother only intermittently and his father not at all. Separated from his parents, he comes under the care of a nurse who takes it upon herself not only to bring him back to health, but also to teach him English. In order to force him to learn the new language, she tries all kinds of scare tactics, even locking him up in a closet from which he's not released until he says, in English, "Let me out!" (103). At first recalcitrant, Hector eventually gives in. The result, however, is that he not only begins speaking English, but also that he develops a distrust of Spanish. In time he believed Spanish was an enemy, and when Mercedes came to visit and told him stories about home, he remained silent, as if the nurse were watching him. Even his dreams were broken up by the static of English, like a number of wasps overcoming the corner of a garden (104).

By the time he goes back home, Hector is a different person. "When we left Cuba," Mercedes says, "Hector was sick but so happy and fat that we didn't know anything. He came back saying *Cuba, Cuba* and spent a lot of time with Alejo. He was a little Cuban, spouting Spanish" (91). A year later, after he is released from the hospital, all of this has changed. Hector is healthy but thin, he no longer speaks Spanish, and he has become distanced from his father, who hardly recognizes him. At the hospital Hector undergoes a death and rebirth. He loses one identity and acquires another. That closet is a womb from which he is delivered by the American nurse, who is both mother and midwife, tender and terrible at the same time.

Immigrant memoirs tend to be conversion narratives. Transculturation, the passage from one culture to another, is a secular conversion whose outward sign is usually the acquisition of a new language. What is striking about *Our House in the Last World* is the location of the scene of cultural passage. For the young immigrant it is typically school that ushers him into the new language, and it is a teacher who replaces the mother or the father. This is the case, for example, in Richard Rodriguez's well-known memoir *Hunger of Memory* (1982). But in Hector's case, the whole experience takes place in a hospital, under the guidance of a nurse. His is not only a conversion, but a cure. This means that Spanish is not only a language, but a disease. For the rest of his life, Hector will view Cuba, its language and its culture, with a mixture of awe and apprehension. In what is perhaps the most striking image in the book, Hector compares the X-rays of his diseased kidneys to the map of Cuba (104). His mysterious illness, which his mother attributes to drinking puddled water, is labeled only a "Cuban infection" (88) carried by everpresent *microbios*, one of the few words in the novel that is almost always written in Spanish.

Hector's contrasting feelings about Spanish and English help to make sense of the novel's narrative point of view. Although *Our House* is ostensibly narrated by an anonymous third-person narrator, the voice that speaks is really Hector's—as indicated by the book's title, given not in the third but in the first person: *our* house. In a monologue toward the end of the book, in which he acknowledges his desire to become a writer, Hector describes the notebooks in which he writes about his family: "When I write in my notebook I feel very close to her [Mercedes] and to the memory of my father. I go back to that certain house. I go back to my beginning" (245). The reference to the title in these sentences further suggests that the narration emerges from a transposition of Hector's notebooks. Moreover, since Hector's description of his journals also echoes the novel's dedication—"To my mother and to the memory of my father"—this passage hints at the autobiographical subtext of the novel. *Our House in the Last World* offers an interesting example of a transposed or third-person autobiography, one which, like other first novels, portrays the artist as a young man.

Because Hector functions as the text's implicit narrator, it is not surprising that the novel evinces a sustained effort of translation. The initial sentence already makes it clear that the "last world" of the title will be recreated according to Hector's peculiar sensibility: "Hector's mother met Alejo Santinio, his Pop, in 1939 when she was twenty-seven years old and working as a ticket girl in the Neptuna movie theater in Holguín, Cuba" (11). Although Hector will not appear as a character for several chapters, from the first word we are made aware that whatever we see will be from his perspective. Even when he is offstage, the story is "Hector's."

It is significant that, in this sentence, his father is labeled, somewhat incongruously, "Pop." From first word to last, this sentence is filled with Cuban sounds—Hector, Alejo Santinio, Neptuna, Holguín, Cuba. Among these words, the colloquial American "Pop" sticks out like a hump. Given Alejo's importance in the novel, this initial act of nomination is crucial. Did Hector, as a child growing up in a Spanish-speaking home, call his father "Pop"? Or was it rather *papá* or *papi*? "I remember my mother and father—'Pop', always 'Pop' " (245). The conversion of *papi* into a *Pop* not only underscores the prevalence of Hector's point of view in the novel; it also entails a decisive act of translation. Turning Alejo into a "Pop" is Hector's way of reducing his father to manageable proportions, of removing or neutralizing some of his terror. The American name fends off the Cuban monster.

Further in the first page we come upon the following description of Hector's mother: "Her name was Mercedes Sorrea, and she was the second of three daughters and not married because her last *prometido*, or 'intended,' who worked in a Cuban sour-milk factory, was a louse" (11). "Louse" functions in this sentence in much the same way as "Pop" does in the other one; it is a monosyllabic epithet that describes a Cuban man, one that almost became Hector's father. The impact of the monosyllable emerges from the clash between the epithet and its context. The Spanish in the first part of the sentence evokes a Cuban world where young women with names like Mercedes are courted by *prometidos* who work in sour-milk factories. But the last word of the sentence sharply revises the cultural context by designating her womanizing fiancé with another American colloquialism, "louse." It is hardly a coincidence that "louse" is a small, disease-bearing organism, for this man is nothing other than another Cuban *microbio* (germ).

As the sentence unfolds, it rattles off one Hispanic marker after another: the girl's name, the Spanish word for "intended," and the reference to the "Cuban sour-milk factory." But this Cuban world so carefully evoked is demolished by that last, monosyllabic barb, *louse*, a word nearly identical to the "house" of the title. It is as if Spanish were the language of posturing, of convention, of unkept promises, and English were the language of revelation. Spanish is illusion, *engaño*; English is truth, *desengaño*. In Spanish, Mercedes' boyfriend is a *prometido*; in plain English, he is just a louse. When Hector was a child in Cuba, his aunt prepared a mysterious, wonderful brew that Hector regarded as a "Cuban magic potion"; years later, he discovers that the concoction was only Hershey's syrup and milk (177). Cuban mystification dissolves in the face of American matter-of-factness.

In one respect, the words Pop and louse are paternal names that bear the son's signature. Hector tames his fear of paternal figures by referring to them in his own words. In the sentences in which they appear, both terms are anomalies, humps of speech. But in this they also resemble Hector, who also does not fit inside the "last world" of his parents. These names convey Hector's ambivalence toward his father as well as his own sense of being a misfit, a "Cuban Quasimodo."

In another respect, these examples illustrate some of the ways in which Hector—and Hijuelos—write *from* Spanish but *toward* English. Even though most of the characters in the book are speakers of Spanish, the narrator makes little attempt to render the foreignness of their speech, and Hector himself drops the written accent from his given name (in Spanish, his name would be spelled Héctor), thus confirming his assimilation into American culture. This drift toward English makes this novel somewhat atypical within Cuban-American literature. By and large, Cuban Americans have so far written for other Cuban Americans, or at most for other Hispanics. This is the case even when they write in English. Only in the last several years, with the appearance of novels by Hijuelos, Virgil Suarez, and Cristina Garcia, have Cuban-American authors sought to reach a broader audience. *Our House in the Last World* is one of the earliest examples of this effort to cross over into the mainstream.

Our House in the Last World is best seen as a valedictory to Cuban culture. The voice that speaks in the novel, a voice that may be close to Hijuelos' itself, is that of someone who retains some ties to Cuban culture but who is no longer Cuban. The novel pays tribute to Cuban culture even as it bids it farewell. As the title makes clear, Cuba is the "last world," a world left behind by the characters. This work is Hector's complex and conflicted elegy to the Spanish language, to his Cuban parents, and to the island's customs and culture.

TEACHING THE WORK

1. "I was born, I have lived, and I have been made over. Is it not time to write my life's story? I am just as much out of the way as if I were dead, for I am absolutely other than the person whose story I have to tell." The classic opening of Mary Antin's *The Promised Land* (1912) captures the movement from birth to rebirth that is central to many ethnic autobiographies. How does this process operate in *Our House in the Last World*? Can Antin's words be applied to Hector? What is the function of Hector's journals in bringing about his makeover? Does he use literature as an instrument of release? Does the novel's conclusion confirm or cast doubt on the protagonist's transformation?

2. One of the themes of *Our House in the Last World* is the harmful impact of exile or emigration on a family. Somber and unsparing, the novel details the miserable existence of the Santinios as they try to adapt to life in a new country. Almost every chapter chronicles a new misfortune—a child's illness, a financial setback, an episode of drunkenness or adultery, or a violent argument between husband and wife or between parents and children. Why is it that the Santinios had such a difficult time adapting to life in the United States? What could they have done differently to improve their situation? To what extent are their problems shared by nonimmigrant families?

3. Formally the novel's most interesting feature is the transposition into the third person of Hector's memoirs. What are the advantages and disadvantages to the use of the third-person omniscient narrator? How would the shape of the narrative have been different if Hector had told the story in his own voice? As an exercise, recreate entries from Hector's journals based on episodes in the novel. (For a useful discussion of third-person autobiography, see the chapter written by Philippe Lejeune cited in the list of suggested readings.)

4. Hijuelos' novel can be usefully contrasted with Richard Rodriguez's *Hunger of Memory*. The following extract is the scene in Rodriguez's autobiography where the protagonist describes the crucial moment in his transition from Spanish to English.

The nun said, in a friendly but oddly impersonal voice, "Boys and girls, this is Richard Rodriguez." (I heard her sound out: *Rich-heard Road-ree-guess*.) It was the first time I had heard anyone name me in English. "Richard," the nun repeated more slowly, writing my name down in her black leather book. Quickly I turned to see my mother's face dissolve in a watery blur behind the pebbled glass door. (*Hunger of Memory* [New York: Bantam, 1983], 11)

Compare this episode of cultural passage with the hospital scene in *Our House in the Last World*. How do the school and hospital function similarly? Differently? Compare the role of the teacher and the nurse. Does Hector also become distanced from his mother? And what is the significance in the change of the protagonists' names from Ricardo to Richard and from Héctor to Hector? Ask the students to think about their own names as markers of identity. How important is it to have a comfortable relationship with your name?

5. Contemplating his father's corpse, Hector thinks: "The problem was that his body, stretched out in the coffin, was so imposing" (210). Why is this a problem? A problem for whom? To judge by this passage, it seems that, even in death, Alejo remains a fearsome presence in his son's life. Is this an indication that Hector never manages to distance himself from his father, to exorcise his ghost? Relevant here are the last words of the novel, where Alejo (from beyond the grave) says to Mercedes: "Do not be afraid" (253). Does Hector ever overcome his fear of his father? Is the composition of the novel itself an act of courage? Can it be seen as Hector's (and Hijuelos') way of solving the "problem" of lingering paternal oppression?

NOTE

1. *Our House in the Last World* (New York: Washington Square Press, 1983), 178. Other page references will be given in the text.

FURTHER READING

Lejeune, Philippe. "Autobiography in the Third Person." In *On Autobiography*, ed. Paul John Eakin. Minneapolis: University of Minnesota Press, 1989.
Luis, William. *Dance Between Two Cultures: Latino-Caribbean Literature Written in the United States*. Nashville, Tenn.: Vanderbilt University Press, 1997.
Pérez Firmat, Gustavo. *Life on the Hyphen: The Cuban-American Way*. Austin: University of Texas Press, 1994.

Female Voices in Sandra Cisneros' *The House on Mango Street*

Myrna-Yamil González

SANDRA CISNEROS was born in 1954 in Chicago, Illinois. The daughter of a Mexican father and a Mexican-American mother, Cisneros was the only girl among six brothers in a family that frequently traveled between Chicago and Mexico to visit her father's family. Since new living quarters had to be found after each trip to Mexico, Cisneros' childhood was spent in a variety of run-down Hispanic neighborhoods until 1966 when her parents purchased a small, two-story bungalow in a Puerto Rican neighborhood on Chicago's north side. These experiences inspired her first book, *The House on Mango Street* (1983), which received the Before Columbus American Book Award in 1985.

Cisneros is also a poet. At Loyola University and later at the University of Iowa's Writer's Workshop in the late 1970s she began searching for her creative Latina voice and published her first poems in journals and later in several collections: *Bad Boys* (1980), *The Rodrigo Poems* (1985), *My Wicked, Wicked Ways* (1987), and *Loose Woman* (1994). In 1991, in a then rare example of a work by a Hispanic woman recognized by a mainstream U.S. press, Random House published *Woman Hollering Creek and Other Stories*, twenty-two diverse tales narrated from a female perspective. The work was awarded the P.E.N. Center West Award for best fiction in 1992. *Woman Hollering Creek*, a powerful work of fiction writing, has a heightened gender and cultural consciousness that is true to Cisneros' stated creative goals, according to a 1991 interview: "[I]n my stories and life I am trying to show that U.S. Latinas have to reinvent, to remythologize, ourselves. A myth believed by almost everyone, even Latina women, is that they are passive, submissive, long-suffering, either a spit-fire or a Madonna. Yet those of us who are their daughters, mothers, sisters know that some of the fiercest women on this planet are Latina women." Cisneros' works have earned her an international reputation and a secure niche in American letters.

ANALYSIS OF THEMES AND FORMS

Poet, essayist, and short story writer, Sandra Cisneros is one of the most celebrated contemporary Chicana writers, with a number of acclaimed publications; her most famous work to date, however, is her first fictional work, *The House on Mango Street*, which presents the life of the young narrator Esperanza through her own experiences and those of her neighbors and her community. The work is dedicated "A las Mujeres—To the Women," all the female characters whose lives have enriched that of the protagonist and who represent a diversity of challenges and perspectives. As the protagonist, Esperanza revises and reclaims her cultural inheritance; Cisneros, the author, proposes a reconsideration of contemporary Chicana inheritance, evident in the voices of her female characters.

A short book comprising 44 brief, finely crafted tales, *Mango Street* is narrated by a Chicana girl named Esperanza Cordero who is presented to the reader over the course of a few years as she moves from childhood to adolescence. Her stories give voice to the people who live in the barrio, the inhabitants of Mango Street in urban Chicago, who have not traditionally been heard in the mainstream culture. They are the experiences of a diverse community that is mainly, although not exclusively, Latino: *Mango Street*'s occupants include emigrants from the southern United States, African Americans, and Hispanics from diverse cultures. Some characters are limited to one chapter; others span several. We observe them change—for better or worse—from Esperanza's insightful perspective. The book combines humorous observations with touching scenes that reflect the protagonist's process of maturation.

Esperanza's neighbors are often colorful—her girlish playmates from Texas, a hefty neighbor who refuses to speak English—as are some incidents of her life, particularly those that occur during her first job. Other events are sadder—her experiences with death and sexual assault, for example. As the work develops, Esperanza's youthful voice and her naïve, halting language gradually mature into the graceful expression of a poised and articulate young woman, increasingly more resolute in her female identity. Through it all, however, we are reminded of the protagonist's lament: she desperately desires to leave the small and crumbling house she inhabits with her family and live in a proper house of her own.

In *Mango Street* Cisneros creates a protagonist that is a storyteller and a mythmaker who draws upon old tales and new experiences to create an impressionistic poetics of a culturally diverse Chicago neighborhood; the structure of the narrative suggests the influence of oral traditions and the blending of cultural identities (March 183). The young narrator has internalized the worldview and experiences of her parents, her friends, and the society of which she is a part as she strives to locate her identity. In this regard, her name itself is significant, as Julian Olivares has observed:

Her surname [Cordero], meaning "lamb", operates symbolically in the text. . . . She refuses to sacrifice her gender to a patriarchic society . . . Esperanza depicts the lonely and imprisoned, the physically and psychologically abused Latinas; and in this way she displays her collective identity with her sisters. But in the endeavor to establish her identity, to fit into her name, Esperanza also undertakes a personal quest to liberate herself from the gender constraints of her culture. ("Entering the House on Mango Street" 213)

Esperanza's name, which means "hope" in Spanish, can also mean a wait (*espera*). She has inherited her great-grandmother's name but must deconstruct it; Esperanza's great-grandmother is a subjugated Mexican woman who had been taken away from her family by force. She therefore embodies a submissive female model that the young Esperanza must reject. But Esperanza would like to go even farther: she would change her name completely to redirect her life away from a possible repetition of her ancestor's sad history. "I would like to baptize myself under a new name, a name like the real me, the one nobody sees. Esperanza as Lisandra or Maritza or Zeze the X. Yes. Something like Zeze the X will do" (11).

Indications of Esperanza's formation as a writer and a hint of her eventual departure from home and Mango Street are found in several stories related to death, among them "Born Bad" in which is found the idea that creativity is not only a means of escaping the confines of Mango Street but also an affirmation of life and rebirth (Olivares, "Sandra Cisneros' " 166). In "Born Bad," the protagonist's long-suffering Aunt Guadalupe dies. Esperanza believes that she will go to hell with her friends Lucy and Rachel because they have done something to cause the tragedy. The girls had been playing a guessing game imitating people, among them Aunt Guadalupe, the aunt who liked to listen to the children's stories: "You must remember to keep writing, Esperanza. You must keep writing. It will keep you free" (60–61). On the day of the game, the aunt who had encouraged Esperanza's creativity dies. Writing, her aunt had told her, will lead to her liberation, which, indeed will prove to be true. "It is through writing, through the aesthetic perception of her reality, that Esperanza discovers who she is, affirms her identity, and finds her house.... Puzzled once about where to find a house and thinking that freedom could only be encountered outside the physical and cultural space of her barrio, Esperanza is now astonished that freedom can be found in writing" (Olivares, "Entering" 223).

Through her creativity, Esperanza inhabits the house of storytelling. Consequently, the house is a book to be written, blank pages to be filled with her voice and with the voices of women trapped by their economic and cultural restriction. It represents the attainment of identity and the realization of freedom through the space of writing, as expressed in the last story, "Mango Says Goodbye Sometimes."

Alternative Female Voices

Curanderas/Seers

Women's lives are circumscribed by cultural values and norms that dictate their behavior and roles; female authors often suggest new roles or imbue existing models with more accessible and more affirming traits and characteristics. Among Chicana writers, many have been inspired by the representation of power and control of such Aztec goddesses as Coatlicue, and the nurturing tradition of the Christian Virgin of Guadalupe, the patron saint of Mexico. The traditional figure of the *curandera/bruja* or healer/witch has also emerged as a powerful female symbol. The *curandera* has two attributes: a positive one as a healer and a negative one as a *bruja* or witch/seer. The *curandera* possesses intuitive and cognitive skills; her connection to and interrelation with the natural world is part of her ancient knowledge. The fact that the *curandera* has emerged as a powerful figure in the writing of both women and men demonstrates not only her enduring representational qualities as myth and symbol but also the close identification of the culture with her mystic and spiritual qualities (Rebolledo 83–84). Cisneros' *curanderas* in *Mango Street* are of the affirming variety.

In "The Three Sisters," for example, Esperanza comes in contact with *curanderas* on two different occasions. Her first experience is with Elenita, the seer first mentioned in "Elenita, Cards, Palm, Water." Elenita's deeds are performed in the kitchen, the section of the house containing all the implements required for her craft. Among the tasks required of Esperanza is to fill a cup with water in order to attempt to see what Elenita perceives, particularly peoples' faces, but Esperanza sees nothing. Elenita then proceeds to read the tarot cards: "now my fortune begins. My whole

life on that kitchen table: past, present and future" (63). Finally Elenita
reads her palms, where she sees jealousy, sorrow, a pillar of bees, and a
"mattress of luxury" (63). Esperanza wants to know only about a house,
but the only home Elenita sees is in the heart: "a new house, a house
made of heart. I'll light a candle for you. Thank you and goodbye and
be careful of the evil eye" (64). Esperanza pays her five dollars and
leaves, left puzzled by the oracle.

Esperanza then encounters three mysterious sisters, describing them
as "one with laughter like tin and one with eyes of a cat and one with
hands like porcelain. . . . They had the power and could sense what was
what" (103–4). One of them, "the old blue-veined" sister, asks her name.
When Esperanza replies, she is told it is a good name. The one with cat
eyes tells the others to look at Esperanza's hands, and they inform her
that she is special and foretell a future in which she will go very far.
Esperanza is told to make a wish, and when she does so they assure her
it will come true. The sister with the porcelain hands calls Esperanza
aside and remarks, "When you leave you must remember to come back
for the others. A circle, understand? You will always be Esperanza. You
will always be Mango Street. You can't erase what you know. You can't
forget who you are" (106).

Critics have had various responses to the visit by the "three sisters."
Jayne March regards it as the catalyst that finally impels Esperanza to
find a house of her own (184). Leslie Gutiérrez-Jones considers the fact
that the sisters recognize Esperanza's special qualities; the idea that "that
she'll go very far" is a recognition of her responsibility to herself and
her talent, a responsibility that will necessitate her packing "her bags of
book and paper." Esperanza finally realizes the implications of her talents and acknowledges in her final vignette that she will indeed go far
(Gutiérrez-Jones 302). Olivares adds,

[T]hese women appear at critical junctures to advance the narrative and assist
the heroine in her quest . . . the sisters' intervention is related in the combination
of the characteristic prose-poem form with an extended dialogue sequence. On
the level of the plot, the elderly sisters, who appear like fairy godmothers, bring
revelation and the gift of self to Esperanza. Esperanza begins to assume her name
and identity. The three sisters now appear on the symbolic level as the Three
Fates who determine the heroine's destiny and leave her with the prophecy of
self-knowledge. . . . Three mysterious women embed in Esperanza's psyche a cultural and political determination that will find expression in her vocation as a
writer. ("Entering" 223–25)

For Tey Diana Rebolledo, the *curandera* is a compelling figure in Chicano literature precisely because she is a woman who has control over
her own life and destiny as well as that of others. The *curandera* has a

special relationship to the earth and nature—she understands the cycles of creation, development, and destruction, unifying the past, present, and future. Incorporating intuition and rationality, the *curandera* bends or harnesses power; she takes an active role in her environment. She listens carefully and thus understands collective as well as individual psychology embedded in ethnic beliefs and practices and can be perceived as a cultural psychologist or psychiatrist. Individual human behavior is always weighed against communal good. The *curandera* intimately understands community (Rebolledo 87–88).

Mujeres malas/"Bad" Women

Mujeres andariegas (wandering women) and *mujeres callejeras* (street women) are terms that imply both restlessness and wickedness. These are women who do not stay at home tending to their husbands, children, and parents. Unbound by socially construed morals or cultural practices, they must therefore be, by implication, wicked: *putas*, or loose women. The negative cultural stereotypes placed on *mujeres andariegas* result from a patriarchal culture that wills women to be passive, self-denying, and nurturing.

Another perspective, however, is to view these literary and real women as *mujeres de fuerza*—strong, independent women, who are self-sufficient; they thrive and prosper in spite of the possible consequences of their actions (Rebolledo 183). The cultural ideal of the self-sacrificing girl who stays at home and lets others control her body—the Virgin of Guadalupe ideal—and its opposite, the woman who controls her own sexuality and destiny—the powerful pre-Columbian Aztec goddess ideal—are both elements of the Chicana cultural and literary heritage. So too are the women who dare to speak out on public issues, often defined as troublemakers for actively seeking change and seeking justice, a common theme throughout Chicana literature (Rebolledo 189–90). The "bad girl" image, another common theme, is associated with the female awareness of sexuality, the desire to understand the erotic self and sensual capabilities that clash with the cultural norms of a strong traditional family, and the limitations imposed by the Church and a male-oriented society (Rebolledo 192).

In *Mango Street*, Esperanza risks censure by defying convention. "I have begun my own quiet war. Simple. Sure. I am one who leaves the table like a man, without putting back the chair or picking up the plate" (89). In her fantasy, when she is grown, she will be like the woman who is "beautiful and cruel . . . the one who drives men crazy and laughs at them all the way. Her power is her own. She will not give it away" (89). This, however, is an idealized desire; it ignores the possibility that being wicked or defiant does not exempt women from suffering.

For many female characters in *Mango Street*, an awareness of sexual desire is accompanied with violence. In the chapter "Sally," for example, the girl must deal with her father's abuse and restrictions. She is precluded from dancing and staying out after school. According to her father, being beautiful is trouble (81). Sally is physically abused by a father who fears that she will run away like her sisters did. She rationalizes his actions by claiming that he never hit her that hard. Eventually Sally frees herself from the abusive situation only to discover yet another: she marries a controlling husband who prohibits her from using the phone or looking outside the window or receiving visitors. In "Marin," the young girl is also prohibited from leaving the house. She stands by the doorway and dreams of meeting someone who will marry her and take her away. "What matters is for the boys to see us and for us to see them" (26). Alicia in "Alicia Who Sees Mice" is afraid of mice and of fathers; Rafaela, the protagonist of another vignette, "gets locked indoors because her husband is afraid Rafaela will run away since she is too beautiful to look at" (79).

Sire's girlfriend, Lois, in "Sire," on the other hand, does things that Esperanza's mother does not approve of: "those girls are the ones that go into alleys" (73). Esperanza wishes she could follow Lois' example: "I want to sit out bad at night, a boy around my neck and the wind under my skirt" (73). Lois is an example of wicked girls, *malcriadas*, girls brought up in the wrong way. The responsibility for being *malcriada* rests on parents and the immediate family, an attitude that places pressure on families who, in turn, pressure their daughters not to transgress (Rebolledo 192). Bad girls grow up to be wicked women. To be wicked, then, is to have sinned against the Church and society's norms. To sin is to expose your body, to have unsanctioned sexual relations, to expose your private self in a public way. To sin is to penetrate male space, the transgression of public spaces as opposed to the space of the house (Rebolledo 193). The women in *Mango Street* believe they have only one solution to their dilemma: await the arrival of the prince who will hopefully take them away, "lay their necks on the threshold waiting for the ball and chain" (88).

Defining *Mango Street*'s genre has been problematic because the work incorporates a generic diversity. Described as a novel, novella, collection of prose poems, vignettes or literary sketches, *historia, testimonio,* lyrical narration, *cuentos del corazón,* or stories from the barrio, *Mango Street,* according to Sonia Saldívar-Hull, is both lyrical and realistic with the rhythms of poetry and the narrative power of fiction. The difficulty critics have faced in categorizing *Mango Street* may be due to the fact that it represents *un género nuevo,* a new genre (Saldívar-Hull 93).

The image of the house is essential to the work; it is an extension of Esperanza Cordero's identity. As her character develops and she becomes more aware of gender constraints, the wish for a pretty house becomes a desire for unfettered female space which she ultimately creates for herself through her writing (Olivares, "Entering" 214). By the work's end, Esperanza has created a home in the heart (Gutiérrez-Jones 296). Cisneros herself describes the house as metaphor from a very personal perspective:

My consciousness of growing up, the consciousness of myself, the subjects that I write about, the voice that I write in. . . . The madeleine—to use Proust's term— was Bachelard's poetics of space. The house. The house! Everyone was talking about the house the way they'd always been talking about everything. It was that moment that I realized. "I don't have a house—these things don't matter to me!" I don't have a house, how could I talk about a house! With people from my neighborhood, you'd be talking about a very different house than the one Bachelard was talking about—the wonderful house of memory. My house was a prison for me; I don't want to talk about house. (Jussawalla and Dasenbrock 301–2)

But she does write about it, and in so doing arrives at the realization of the possibility of escape through the space of writing, as well as a determination to move away from Mango Street. "On the higher plane of art, then, Esperanza transcends her condition, finding another house which is the space of literature. Yet what she writes about reinforces her solidarity with the people, the women, of Mango Street" (Olivares, "Sandra Cisneros' " 167). Esperanza creates new stories, new myths, that will free herself and possibly others as well. By the end of the book, she has become an assertive yet tolerant figure who consciously accepts the difficulties of her life as part of her development as a writer. Esperanza's experiences suggest that, despite the forces of discrimination and class difference that continue to operate, she can create a sense of herself that, in its integration and ambivalence, is different. In a way, Esperanza discovers that her "homeland" is mythical, and spiritual, not necessarily tied to one locality (March 184).

Mango Street also explores a world where women are betrayed by the ideology of "home," a world where girls are raised to believe that marriage to the "right man" can liberate them from poverty and the rule of fathers, and a world where young girls learn to fear sexuality because the realities of rape and incest further complicate the fact of living in poverty (Saldívar-Hull 103). Esperanza, the storyteller, speaks from and for the marginalized. She creates and chronicles her developing identity not through self-absorbed introspection, but by noting, recording, and responding to the lives around her—those lives about which almost half of the collection's 44 stories are named, such characters as Lucy and Rachel, Esperanza's friends, or Marin, who hopes to find someone who will change her life. The character of Esperanza moves from early dissatisfaction with her identity and life situation through a series of experiences that reveal the nexus of pressures on her, including sex-role expectations, race and class discrimination, and the blending of the spiritual and the material worlds. These factors underlie the main stresses in Esperanza's development: the desire for a satisfying home, the questioning of personal identity and gender roles, and especially the search for a good friend who can provide acceptance and understanding (March 179).

In many ways Cisneros' work reflects the concern of contemporary Chicana feminism which combines the question of gender and sexuality with issues of race, culture, and class. As Yvonne Yarbro-Bejarano explains in "Chicana Literature from a Chicana Feminist Perspective," Chicana feminists have spearheaded a critique of the destructive aspects of the Chicano culture's definition of gender roles which targets heterosexist as well as patriarchal prejudices. But perhaps the most important principle of Chicana feminist criticism is the realization that the Chicana's experience as a woman is inextricable from her experience as a member of an oppressed working-class racial minority and an ethnic subculture. "The Chicana confronts the damaging fragmentation of their identity into component parts at war with each other. To speak about being women in distinction from speaking about being Hispana, Black, Jewish, or any other is an invitation to silence" (Yarbo-Bejarano 733). The fact that Chicanas tell stories about themselves and other Chicanas/Latinas challenges the dominant male concepts of cultural ownership and literary authority and rejects the dominant culture's definition of what a Chicana is. In writing, they refuse the objectification imposed by gender roles and racial and economic limitations. The Chicana writer finds that the self she seeks to define is not an individual self but a collective one. In other words, the power, the permission, the authority to tell stories about herself and other Chicanas come from her cultural, racial/ethnic, and linguistic community, a community with a literary tradition. The Chicana writer derives literary authority from the oral tradition of her community, which in turn empowers her to commit her stories to writing (734).

Esperanza is aware of the racial and economic oppression her community suffers, but it is the fate of the women in her barrio that has the most profound impact on her. Besides finding her path to self-definition through careful observation of the victimized women around her, Esperanza also encounters positive models who encourage her interest in studying and her creativity (the university student Alicia, for example). As Jayne E. March observes, writing is essential in connecting Esperanza with female power; her promise to share that power with other women is fulfilled by the text itself.

In *The House on Mango Street*, therefore, Sandra Cisneros presents a diversity of female voices from the marginalized perspective of the Chicana/Latina experience. Her house and its environment symbolize women's spaces and afford the protagonist an identity with her immediate and extended barrio family. Ultimately, however, Esperanza's true identity and freedom will be found in her writing; there she discovers the recipe for achieving her goals while never forgetting her origins. Her writing helps her—and us—make sense of the world around her and the women who are a part of that world. It is offered to "the ones I left behind . . . the ones who cannot out" (110) and it offers the possibility that a woman can achieve anything in life if she can locate the strength and courage to leave confining situations and discover who she truly is.

TEACHING THE WORK

1. Numerous studies on Chicana literature would be helpful in contextualizing the text. Comparisons could also be made to Latina writers from other Hispanic cultures, such as Esmeralda Santiago, Cristina Garcia, and Julia Alvarez. Students could examine how themes and experiences may vary according to one's cultural group (Mexican American, Puerto Rican, Cuban, or Dominican) or by region of the United States. Issues of social class should be included in this analysis, especially when comparing such authors as Cisneros and Santiago to Alvarez and Garcia. Is one's cultural group as significant as one's social class in forming one's identity?

2. Compare male authors who have written in this coming-of-age genre. How significant is gender in creating the tensions faced by a young girl in our society? How does ethnicity complicate the issue? Are Esperanza's experiences similar to those of other young people in the larger U.S. society? The female bildungsroman has been studied by such authors as Esther Klein Labovitz in *The Myth of the Heroine: The Female Bildungsroman in the Twentieth Century* (1986); other critics have examined the writings of the genre by women of U.S. ethnic and racial minorities. How do their female expressions of this genre differ?

3. Use the text to discuss literary genres given the style and the various approaches used by Cisneros. What makes the work difficult to define? How might each of the categories critics have assigned to it be validated?

4. Compare Cisneros' poetic work to her prose. Are themes similar to those found in *Mango Street* found in her collections of poetry?

5. Explain why Esperanza wants to have a house but not the one on Mango Street. Compare it with the one you lived in while growing up. How does the neigborhood compare to your own in terms of the ethnic makeup of the inhabitants? Did any of your neighbors have a strong impact on your life?

6. Identify the nationality of some of the characters in the textbook, relate their historical experiences, and prepare a brief essay comparing

Chicano history in the United States with that of other Latino communities, for example, Puerto Rican, Cuban, or Dominican.

CRITICISM AND FURTHER READING

Castillo, Debra A. "Toward a Latin American Feminist Literary Practice." In *Talking Back: Toward a Latin American Feminist Literary Theory Criticism*, ed. Debra A. Castillo. Ithaca: Cornell University Press, 1992, 1–70.

Cisneros, Sandra. *The House on Mango Street*. New York: Vintage Contemporaries, 1991. All references in the text are to this edition.

Corson Carter, Nancy. "Claiming the Bittersweet Matrix: Alice Walker, Sandra Cisneros, and Adrienne Rich." *Critique: Studies in Modern Fiction* 35, no. 4 (Summer 1994): 195–204.

Doyle, Jacqueline. "More Room of Her Own: Sandra Cisnero's *The House on Mango Street*." MELUS 19, no. 4 (Winter 1994): 5–35. This analysis explores the similarities, connections, and transformations of *A Room of One's Own* by Virginia Woolf and *The House on Mango Street*.

Gutiérrez-Jones, Leslie S. "Different Voices: The Re-Bildung of the Barrio in Sandra Cisnero's *The House on Mango Street*." In *Anxious Power: Reading, Writing, and Ambivalence in Narrative by Women*, eds. Carol J. Singley and Susan Elizabeth Sweeney. Albany: State University of New York Press, 1993, 295–312.

Jussawalla, Feroza, and Reed Way Dasenbrock. "Sandra Cisneros." In *Interviews with Writers of the Post-Colonial World*, eds. Feroza Jussawalla and Reed Way Dasenbrock. Jackson: University Press of Mississippi, 1992, 286–306.

March, Jayne E. "Difference, Identity, and Sandra Cisneros' *The House on Mango Street*." *Hungarian Journal of English and American Studies* 2, no. 1 (1996): 173–87.

Olivares, Julian. "Entering the House on Mango Street." In *Teaching American Ethnic Literatures: Nineteen Essays*, eds. John R. Maitino and David R. Peck. Albuquerque: University of New Mexico Press, 1996, 209–35. An excellent essay that compares *Mango Street* with . . . *y no se lo tragó la tierra* by Tomás Rivera and explores the literary tradition of Chicanas. Olivares suggests topics for teaching the work.

———. "Sandra Cisneros' *The House on Mango Street* and the Poetics of Space." In *Beyond Stereotypes: The Critical Analysis of Chicana Literature*, ed. María Herrera-Sobek. Binghamton, N.Y.: Bilingual Press, 1985, 160–70.

Rebolledo, Tey Diana. *Women Singing in the Snow*. Tucson: University of Arizona Press, 1995.

Saldívar-Hull, Sonia. "Mujeres en lucha: Women in Struggle in Sandra Cisnero's *The House on Mango Street*." In *Feminism on the Border: From Gender Politics to Geopolitics*. Ph.D. diss., University of Texas at Austin, 1990, 84–127.

Sloboda, Nicholas. "A Home in the Heart: Sandra Cisnero's *The House on Mango Street*" *Aztlán* 22 (Fall 1997): 89–106.

Yarbro-Bejarano, Yvonne. "Chicana Literature from a Chicana Feminist Perspective." In *Feminisms: An Anthology of Literary Theory and Criticism*, eds. Robyn R. Warhol and Diane Price Herndl. New Brunswick, N.J.: Rutgers University Press, 1993, 732–37.

11

The Dominican-American Bildungsroman: Julia Alvarez's *How the Garcia Girls Lost Their Accents*

Heather Rosario-Sievert

JULIA ALVAREZ was born in 1950 in New York City. She was raised, however, in the Dominican Republic in an extended Dominican family that was highly influenced by North American attitudes: "Mine was an American childhood." Her father, a medical doctor, was forced to emigrate with his wife and daughters to the United States in 1960 due to his opposition to the regime of the Dominican dictator, Rafael Leonidas Trujillo. The homesickness and alienation Alvarez experienced in the United States, her struggle to find a place for herself in a new environment, are the foundation of much of her writing, particularly in her first novel, *How the Garcia Girls Lost Their Accents* (1991). Alvarez has also published several collections of poetry including *Homecoming* (1984) and *The Other Side: El Otro Lado* (1996). A graduate of Middlebury College and Syracuse University (M.F.A. 1975), Alvarez became an English professor at Middlebury in 1988.

Her highly autobiographical and successful first novel was followed in 1995 by another work of fiction, *In the Time of the Butterflies*, a novel that follows the lives of the Mirabel sisters, three of whom were murdered for their political activism by the brutal Trujillo regime, and in 1997 by *Yo!*, a novel that revisits the Garcia girls from her first work. Julia Alvarez's most recent work, *Something to Declare* (1998), is a collection of essays that trace the diverse lessons she has learned on the way to becoming a writer.

ANALYSIS OF THEMES AND FORMS

How the Garcia Girls Lost Their Accents, by Julia Alvarez, is a female bildungsroman, a relatively recent evolution of the traditional genre that
deals with the education and youthful development—as well as such
early life choices as career, love, and marriage—of a young man and his
plans for his future, which often include a spiritual or philosophical im-
petus. The bildung that Julia Alvarez presents in *How the Garcia Girls
Lost Their Accents* follows some of the traditional patterns but has unique
features as well. To begin with, *Garcia Girls* is the first novel written in
English by a writer from the Dominican Republic, and as such, it breaks
new ground. It is, as well as being a female bildungsroman, a novel of
culture, bringing the Dominican cultural experience and cultural iconography to the English-speaking world. *Garcia Girls* reviews the odyssey of
a family, particularly of its four sisters, born in the Dominican Republic,
and traces their lives in a reverse direction. Through episodic and often
amusing stories it demonstrates a life viewed in retrospect. The work is
concerned with origins, in this case Dominican women's beginnings. The
great storytellers in Alvarez's life and in her culture were women. It
stands to reason that in establishing her own voice she would also provide one for them.

The *Garcia Girls* comprises fifteen stories divided into three sections of
five stories each. They are narrated alternately in first and third person
and in reverse chronological order. The first group of stories is dated
"1989–1972," for example, with a beginning story that appears rather to
be an ending. It is Yolanda's tale (Yolanda's character, which opens and
closes the novel, is the author's alter ego) of her disappointing return to
the country of her birth, the Dominican Republic, as an adult. She believes she might return to stay, but the trip makes her realize that she is
no longer the *dominicana* she was before she left. Her life experiences in
between, the stories that fill the rest of the chapters, have made her an
outsider in her own land.

Subsequent stories focus on the changes wrought on all the Garcias as
a result of their transplantation. In the second section, "1970–1960," the
girls are younger, still finding their tone, adjusting to a new space and
culture. The final section, "1960–1956," sends the family back to the island and explains the political reasons for their exile. In danger from the
repressive secret police, the Garcias must flee their homeland. Pleasant
childhood memories of life in the de la Torre family compound, an extended upper-class family life of servants and emotional security, are
brought into sharp relief when contrasted with the anxieties and traumas
the reader knows will await them in the future. The reader has already
encountered their future losses and gains.

In addition to being a novel of development, *How the Garcia Girls Lost*

Their Accents is a picaresque novel. The *pícaras* or picaresque protagonists of this work, as in the case of their earlier literary counterparts, are concerned with freedom and survival, as their emigration from the Dominican Republic to the United States clearly demonstrates. Their survival is not the basic kind of filling the belly, though, although that too enters the picture in their new homeland. Following the picaresque tradition, the survival that they seek is moral, spiritual, and affective; the Garcia girls move from adventure to adventure, delineating both the internal and the external voyage. *How the Garcia Girls Lost Their Accents* spans the distance between literal birth in one language and culture, and rebirth in the language and customs of a new culture. The picaresque is reshaped and updated by Alvarez.

The principal narrative voice in *Garcia Girls* is Yo's—Yolanda's. She is the sister and daughter who becomes a writer. It is her point of view that sets the novel in motion, so that in the initial segment it is Yolanda who returns to the Dominican Republic. It is the writer returning to place, to family, to customs and language—the point of origin—after having experienced the crucible of separation and socialization. Return is a prevalent theme in all of Alvarez's work, but in this case, in addition to establishing the groundwork for the bildung of the female members of the family, Alvarez is, simultaneously, through the character of Yolanda, articulating the *Kunstlerroman* of the artist. In other words, portraits of growing up and growing up *as an artist* are achieved simultaneously.

The *Garcia Girls* is about finding a voice, uncovering the unconscious, and recovering the essential meaning of language, albeit in an idiom not one's own. It is about growing up in an alien world. But as in the case of other female novels of this genre, as Esther Kleinbord Labovitz reminds us in her groundbreaking study, *The Myth of the Heroine: The Female Bildungsroman in the Twentieth Century*, "underlying every other assumption of a definition . . . of the female Bildungsroman is the overt and subtle presence of patriarchy" (249). The Garcia girls map their Bildung in large measure by overturning the personal family patriarchal hierarchy, ruled over by their father, Carlos Garcia, to the cultural and societal rituals of dress, dating, and the proper areas of interest and involvement for "young ladies," to ultimately the larger patriarchal dictatorship of the state, which caused them to flee from the Dominican Republic and set them on their quest of self-realization and self-definition.

In the second chapter, "Sofia," which deals with Yolanda's youngest sister, Alvarez shows the dilemma of a young woman trying to become her self and battling, in a very pragmatic sense, not only the societal basis of patriarchy, but the actual patriarch, her father, Carlos Garcia. As in the traditional bildungsroman—and in the picaresque—the heroine (this time Sofia) packs her bags and leaves her family to make her own way. This challenge to the patriarchal limits placed on women in the family and in society is met with estrangement and resistance by the patriarch; no matter how hard the daughter later attempts to make amends, no matter how much the other women in the Garcia family (the three remaining sisters and Mami) coax and cajole Papi into reconciliation with Sofia, he refuses. It is only when a male child is born to the prodigal daughter that she redeems herself in her father's eyes. Sofia then insists on expressing her female sensual self, the part of her evolving self that her father had tried to repress, and call her father's attention to her triumphant sensuality and independence. In her variation on the game blindman's bluff played by the Garcia family at each of their father's birthday parties, Sofia kisses her father sensuously (39). Sexual awareness represents a kind of knowledge that was formerly the province of patriarchy alone. It is a powerful statement when acted upon by a young Dominican woman in her struggle against the father and in support of her own realization.

The bridge between bildung and patriarchy in the *Garcia Girls* is the mother, Laura Garcia. She is the traditional Dominican wife and mother, yet she is also quite unique; her transplantation to the United States has not left her intact either. Laura is an ideal example of what Labovitz would call the necessary "shedding," the leaving off of the elements of the past. She is continuously confronted by the new. Her frequent forays to the housewares section of a large department store assault her mind and her senses with countless examples of the potential of human capability, designs that are essentially for women whose province is the home. If *for* women, however, then why not *by* women? In the United States, Laura discovers her spirit of invention. She is always aspiring to innovation, and with each new invention she moves ever closer to reinventing her self yet again. Her schemes begin to take shape when all the burdens that the unexamined life have to bear are put to bed: household tasks, children, women's traditional obligations.

Laura Garcia also challenges the rules for language usage at home by resisting—instinctively—the patriarchal edict that women, like children, should remain silent. Thus when her husband encourages her to use Spanish with the girls, she snaps, " 'When in Rome, do unto the Romans' " (135). Above all else Laura Garcia desires success for her daughters, especially for her daughter Yo ("I" in Spanish) for whom she would want fame as well as success. When Yoyo (as Yolanda is also called) is chosen by the nuns at her school to give the Teacher's Day address, her Mami appreciates on an unconscious level the dramatic possibilities of the honor. Language, she knows, is the vehicle for redefinition and reformation. Her own command of the new language is "a mishmash of malapropisms," but Yo's command of English is already beginning to emerge as elegant, a genuine tool in the articulation and formulation of her self. Yolanda might not have to delay her development as women have generally had to do. An undistinguished student in her native country, and a displaced and uncomfortable child in her new one, Yoyo "needed to settle somewhere and since the natives were unfriendly and the country inhospitable, she took root in the language" (141).

Yolanda's school speech—the creation of it, the agonizing over it, her inability to write it, and her father's ultimate destruction of the speech she finally writes—is one of the focal points of the novel and of Yolanda's bildung. After having spent days trying to write the piece, isolating herself from her family and particularly from her parents, Yo begins reading poetry for inspiration. She encounters Walt Whitman's *Song of Myself* and this becomes her catalyst. Yo is unleashed. Words become for her, as for Whitman, akin to her actual self. She burns as she writes. When she finally finishes the piece, she reads her writing to her mother who catches Yo's fervor and identifies with it; Laura is also in the process of creating a new self.

When Yolanda reads it to her father, however, the response is entirely different. He is horrified that she had not observed the conventions of class and society as he knew them to be and is terrified that, by flouting the nuns' authority, she may be placing herself and the family in jeopardy. Coming from a culture of dictatorship and repression, and perhaps unconscious of the effect those conditions have had upon him, he applies his old Dominican values to the new. To add insult to injury, his wife sides with his daughter. "Soon he would be surrounded by a houseful of independent women" (145–46). The speech, not to be tolerated, is grabbed from Yolanda's hands and he tears it to pieces (146). It is through language that Yolanda has attempted to create herself and through language that patriarchy intrudes itself, attempting to thwart a young woman's effort at pursuing her own bildung. But Yolanda's path is already determined. In her pain, through her rage, she gathers her words along with the fragments of the speech that her father had scattered. They become her weapons. On her knees, undaunted, Yoyo thinks of the worst thing she can say to her father. Gathering a handful of scraps, she stands up and hurls them in his face pronouncing the dictator Trujillo's hated nickname: "Chapita! You're just another Chapita" (147).

Ultimately it is Laura and her spirit for renovation that saves the day. She and her daughter invent a less fervent, more prosaic paean to the teachers on their day, one that is successful in a traditional sense. When Carlos Garcia finally capitulates a day or so later, he offers Yoyo a gift—an electric typewriter. In the final analysis her words had power; they had facilitated her individuation away from her parents, out on her own. Yolanda leaves for boarding school, a traditional step in the male-centered bildungsroman. There she explores her own growing sexual awareness, a fundamental requirement of the female bildungsroman. Although aware of her sexuality, Yo delays acting on her desires. A "lapsed" Catholic, she admits that she and her sisters had become "pretty well Americanized" since their arrival in the States so she "didn't have a good excuse." In spite of being on her own, Yolanda still carried the prohibitions learned at home within her.

For women who come from a place other than where they find themselves, the bildung is vastly complicated. Not only are place and language factors in their ultimate education, but elements that native-born women may take for granted can be at once terrifying and thrilling for the uninitiated. In Yolanda's childhood, for example, her understanding of the English language is limited. It becomes more specialized within its limitations, however, as the greater world of such important events as the war in Vietnam impinge on her immediate one. It is a language born out of context, however, without real reference. Such words learned in school as "nuclear bomb, radioactive fallout and bomb shelter," for example, demonstrated on a blackboard with "a flurry of chalkmarks for the dusty fallout that would kill us all" (67), convert snow into a threatening danger for a new immigrant girl from a tropical Caribbean country. While Alvarez may be using her own family as a model for the fictive Garcias (see Rosario-Sievert, "Conversation with Julia Alvarez"), the Dominican female bildungsroman as an expression of writing from "a minority culture" in the United States also encompasses society and culture. This bears out the contentions of Annie O. Esturoy in *Daughters of Self Creation: The Contemporary Chicana Novel* and Geta LeSeur in her book about the black bildungsroman, *Ten Is the Age of Darkness: The Black Bildungsroman*: among women and men who have been marginalized by the dominant social group, the bildung of the individual must take place within the context of community, chronicling culture, race, history, and place. It must provide its own referentiality since, for the Chicana, for blacks, and certainly for Dominicans, the white Eurocentric, English-speaking world holds few points of common experience.

Actual dangers, beyond the implied ones, based on language arise in the protagonists' lives as well. As often the case in female bildungsromans, the girl who is striving to become must ward off seduction and other attempts to invalidate her efforts by men who seem to or pretend to care about her. A real woman, girls are told, is one who stays with her man. She is someone for whom love is enough, someone who does not strive to capture and retain her own complexity. In not caving in to the idea that "love" is "enough" expressed by the monolingual man in her life—her husband—in his unconscious effort to prevent her from "being her own person," Yolanda exemplifies women who typically face this obstacle in their quest for selfhood. Yolanda's marriage fails, and despite all her efforts to the contrary, in spite of all her training and self-awareness, the failure fragments her personality and causes its ultimate disintegration. Yolanda experiences a crisis of identity: "She didn't want to divide herself any more, three persons in one Yo" (78). She talks but cannot be understood, nor can she understand. Yolanda is ensnared in yet another cultural, psychological, linguistic trap. The change into "Joe" demonstrates that madness is the bridge between bildung and personality: the fact of metamorphosing "Yo" into "Joe," masculinizing and Americanizing the character, is a comment on gender and linguistic ambiguity. In this character Alvarez recognizes all of the literary female characters and their creators, as well as the other women in history who have been relegated to secondary, sacrificial positions, driven to madness or death.

The *Garcia Girls* takes up the cudgel against patriarchy on several fronts. The girls wage their war in the United States and in the Dominican Republic, for example. When Fifi (Sofia) is remanded to the island for having stashed some marijuana in her room in New York, the sisters view this as a fall from freedom, back into the stultifying yoke of patriarchy. What will she or won't she be permitted to do? They plot to save their baby sister from the strictures by which she is bound in the patriarchal structure and ensnare Manuel, her super macho boyfriend, who will certainly not permit Fifi to become her self. "It was a regular revolution: constant skirmishes. Until the time we took open aim and won, and our summers—if not lives—became our own" (111).

The world of learning is also a battlefield. If the bildungsroman is the novel of the education of a young person, then the education of the Garcia girls, like other elements of their lives, tends to the extreme. This is the traditional bildung gone awry. Sandra, for example, while away at school, also has what is referred to as "a small breakdown": all she does is read. In the female bildungsroman, a woman's education, or a woman's attempt to educate herself, is regarded as an act tantamount to madness. While Sandra may indeed have actually been having a small breakdown, her emotional trauma serves Alvarez as a vehicle for commentary, a social mirror set up to reflect the risks and dangers that exist when women try to "read all the great works of man." Doubtless, books can "drive her crazy."

If the female bildungsroman requires, as Labovitz contends, a "shedding," a leaving off of the trappings of the old self in order for the bildung to commence, in the *Garcia Girls* it is only in the last 100 pages that we see what this collective shedding has actually entailed. In the section that moves farthest back temporally, setting, culture, political reality, and language change and shift as we are taken back to witness all that the Garcias—particularly, although not exclusively, the women—have had to shed before embarking on their arduous education. We sense where they had all been and what psychic, psychological, and physical space they have had to travel; we begin to understand how all-encompassing their education has been. The Garcias have had to shed all those elements that customarily define cultural and personal stability; the character of Chucha, "the old lady" who had "forever" worked for the de la Torre clan (Laura Garcia's family), is the personification of all of those primal elements that were a part of them. An old Haitian servant, she casts spells, mixes potions, invokes spirits; Chucha is the basic repository of deeply rooted, foundational folk customs that bind the Garcia girls to their land more than any of the more superficial elements of culture. Chucha is a woman who truly understands the significance of being forced to leave one's land. Through Chucha, through her belief system, her talismans, and her icons, the girls are at once bound and freed.

"When I was a girl, I left my country too and never went back. Never saw father or mother or sisters or brothers. I brought only this along." She held the bundle up and finished unwrapping it from its white sheet. It was a statue carved out of wood like the kind I saw years later in the anthro textbooks I used to pore over, as if staring at those little talismanic wooden carvings would somehow be my madeleine, bringing back my past to me like they say tasting that cookie did for Proust. But the textbook gods never triggered any four-volume memory in my head. Just this little moment I'm recalling here. . . . Chucha held each of our heads in her hands and wailed a prayer over us. We were used to some of the strange stuff from daily contact with her, but maybe it was because today we could feel an ending in the air, anyhow, we all started to cry as if Chucha had finally released her own tears in each of us. (221)

The ending of this bildung/Kunstlerroman pays homage, albeit indirectly, to Maxine Hong Kingston whose inspired and revealing personal talk stories actually gave Alvarez artistic permission to write her own (see Rosario-Sievert, "Conversation," 34). Alvarez remains haunted, however, by the past she had seemed to resolve. Having offered us Yolanda's story in slow motion, at the end she collapses time, speeding things up, seeming to tie up loose ends—but not really. The story, and the Garcias, will be revisited yet again in another work, Alvarez's subsequent novel, Yo!

TEACHING THE WORK

1. A recent book, *The Dominican Americans* by Silvio Torres-Saillant and Ramona Hernandez (Greenwood Press, 1998), offers a good overview of the Dominican population in the United States in terms of their history, their culture, and their struggle to become Dominican Americans. Annie O. Esturoy examines the Chicana bildungsroman, and Geta LeSeur discusses the black bildungsroman. Discuss the ways women of their respective racial and ethnic groups have handled their emergence into the public sphere. Compare the ways that women of Mexican, Indian, Af-

rican, and, by extension, Dominican ancestry have had to adapt their culture and their language to a new language and culture in order to realize their human potential.

2. *How the Garcia Girls Lost Their Accents* may also be read as a cultural novel and may be interpreted as an attempt by Alvarez to validate and authenticate her Dominican heritage in a North American context. Compare how each sister deals with her own personal struggle.

3. Discuss how the *Garcia Girls* can also be read as a novel of the immigrant experience. Compare Alvarez's depiction with other authors such as Paule Marshall, Anzia Yezierska, Jamaica Kincaid, and Maxine Hong Kingston.

4. Choose one of the characters in the novel, identify with that character, and write a short essay entitled "Through the Eyes of . . . ," describing how he or she, as the character, perceives the dilemma of one of the other characters.

5. Read Maxine Hong Kingston's *Woman Warrior* (1976) to determine why that novel was so inspiring to Alvarez. Compare and contrast the two works with regard to culture, language, and ethnicity.

CRITICISM

Barak, Julie. " 'Turning and Turning in the Widening Gyre': A Second Coming into Language in Julia Alvarez's *How the Garcia Girls Lost Their Accents*." *MELUS* 23, no. 1 (Spring 1998): 159–76.

Castellucci Cox, Karen. "A Particular Blessing: Storytelling as Healing in the Novels of Julia Alvarez." In *Healing Cultures: Art and Religion as Curative Practices in the Caribbean and Its Diaspora*, ed. Margarite Fernández Olmos and Lizabeth Paravisini-Gebert. New York: St. Martin's Press, forthcoming.

Hoffman, Joan M. " 'She Wants to Be Called Yolanda Now': Identity, Language, and the Third Sister in *How the Garcia Girls Lost Their Accents*." *Bilingual Review/La Revista Bilingue* 23, no. 1 (January-April 1998): 21–27.

"Julia Alvarez: Author, Poet." *Notable Hispanic American Women, Book II*. Detroit: Gale Research, 1998, 20–22. Bio-bibliographical essay.

Rosario-Sievert, Heather. "Anxiety, Repression, and Return: The Language of Julia Alvarez." *Readerly/Writerly Texts: Essays on Literature, Literary/Textual Criticism, and Pedagogy* 4, no. 2 (Spring-Summer 1997): 125–39.

———. "Conversation with Julia Alvarez." *Review: Latin American Literature and Arts* 54 (Spring 1997): 31–37. A discussion of the function of biography and literature, and how Alvarez gained the artistic freedom to speak through her own experience.

SUGGESTED READINGS

Coco de Filippis, Daisy. *Tertuliando/Hanging Out*. Santo Domingo, Dominican Republic: Comisión Publicación de la Feria Nacional del Libro, 1997. A compendium of writings primarily by Dominican women writers living in the United States.

Sención, Viriato. *They Forged the Signature of God.* Willimantic, Conn.: Curbstone Press, 1995. A fictionalized account of the recent political history of the Dominican Republic.

Torres-Saillant, Silvio, and Ramona Hernandez. *The Dominican Americans.* Westport, Conn.: Greenwood Press, 1998. Historical and sociological perspective of the Dominican migration from the homeland to the United States.

OTHER SOURCES

Alvarez, Julia. *Homecoming.* New York: Grove Press, 1994.

———. *How the Garcia Girls Lost Their Accents.* New York: Plume, 1992.

———. *In the Time of the Butterflies.* Chapel Hill, N.C.: Algonquin Books of Chapel Hill, 1994.

———. *The Other Side (El Otro Lado).* Poems. New York: Dutton, 1995.

———. *Yo!* Chapel Hill, N.C.: Algonquin Books of Chapel Hill, 1997.

Brathwaite, Edward Kamau. *History of the Voice.* London: Beacon, 1984.

Esturoy, Annie O. *Daughters of Self Creation: The Contemporary Chicana Novel.* Albuquerque: University of New Mexico Press, 1996.

Hakuta, Kenji. *Mirror of Language: The Debate on Bilingualism.* New York: Basic Books, 1986.

Labovitz, Esther Kleinbord. *The Myth of the Heroine: The Female Bildungsroman in the Twentieth Century.* New York: Peter Lang, 1986.

LeSeur, Geta. *Ten Is the Age of Darkness: The Black Bildungsroman.* Columbia: University of Missouri Press, 1995.

Said, Edward. *Culture and Imperialism.* New York: Knopf, 1993.

Vigil, Evangelina. *Woman of Her Word: Hispanic Women Write.* 2d ed. Houston: Arte Público, 1987.

12

In Context: Gloria Anzaldúa's *Borderlands/La Frontera: The New Mestiza*

Hector A. Torres

GLORIA ANZALDÚA is a poet, fiction writer, essayist, and lecturer whose work has greatly influenced feminist, lesbian, and Chicano writing style. Born in Jesus Maria of the Valley, in South Texas, in 1942, she later moved with her family to the small town of Hargill, Texas. After her father's death when she was fifteen, Anzaldúa and her family became migrant farmworkers. Despite the obstacles she faced in obtaining a formal education, Anzaldúa managed to complete her undergraduate studies at Pan American University in Texas and receive an M.A. from the University of Texas at Austin. Prior to writing her major work, *Borderlands/La Frontera: The New Mestiza* in 1987, Anzaldúa had coedited, with Cherríe Moraga, *This Bridge Called My Back: Radical Writings by Women of Color* in 1981, which received the Before Columbus Foundation's American Book Award. She has also edited *Making Face, Making Soul/Haciendo Caras: Creative and Critical Perspectives by Women of Color* (1990).

Borderlands/La Frontera, a bilingual book combining several genres, is a sort of literary mestizaje (racial mixing); the structure itself represents Anzaldúa's ideas of mixing historiography with poetry in a broad thematic range, from philosophy to poetry. She has stated that the most descriptive term for those of Hispanic descent in the United States is neither Hispanic nor Latino but Mestizo, since all Latinos are of mixed blood. In *Borderlands* she adds a new dimension to the discussion of border consciousness—a theme that includes the ideas of displacement, fragmentation, and estrangement produced by the straddling of borders—with the inclusion of gender, "mestiza consciousness." Perhaps her most important goal is one she has worked toward from an early age: to overturn Chicano patriarchal family traditions. Feminism, lesbianism, an intense ethnic identity, and a highly personal emphasis (including the use of her own family in her writing) characterize her work. Anzaldúa has been heralded by many critics as the foremost example of the successful mixing of literary genres and a stylistic reflection of the varied cultural influences experienced by Latinos in the United States.

ANALYSIS OF THEMES AND FORMS

In an unpublished interview, Gloria Anzaldúa outlined one of the major differences separating mainstream from marginalized writers: "a minority writer . . . when he or she writes, a lot of times it is with the desire, the imperative, the urge, or the need to explain, interpret and present his or her culture against the silencing, the repression, the erasure by the dominant culture" (Torres, "Gloria Anzaldúa" 11). This imperative leads to a very different type of theory construction in Anzaldúa's view. Under this imperative the minority writer produces a theory that is much more readable but not any less rigorous, precisely because the "fit" between fact and theory, description and explanation, life and text is more immediate in terms of the political context in which that theory or explanation is written. By contrast, continues Anzaldúa, the theory that proceeds from the academy, which she calls "high theory," is done in abstract language from a very "objective" perspective, excluding autobiographical references. In this mode, a fledgling writer must put his or her experience aside, master a canon of abstract ideas, and write in a fixed genre that goes against Anzaldúa's approach, which is to produce writing that is at once personal and accessible. Hence, for Anzaldúa, in the construction of a theoretical framework that would articulate the experience of the minority writer, anything is allowed; what characterizes this path for women of color is a continual struggle to go against the mainstream and just be oneself. Having taken this road herself, Anzaldúa recognizes the toll she has had to pay because of her commitment to write in a different mode, to speak in the voice of a woman of color.

To date, Gloria Anzaldúa's *Borderlands* stands as her *obra maestra* (masterpiece). Full of passion, energy, and innovation, *Borderlands* is a far-reaching work, shifting in and out of the traditional literary and expository genres, blending poetry and prose, switching between English and Spanish, all in order to weave an autobiography resonating with the many voices of Anzaldúa's lived, imagined, and "read" experience. The result is an autobiographical work that speaks in poetic, epic, and tragic voices. As referential text it designates the historical, sociolinguistic, and political realities that constitutes the U.S.–Mexican border area from Brownsville, Texas, to San Diego, California.

Borderlands is divided into two major sections: the first is a long essay entitled "Atravesando Fronteras/Crossing Borders," and the second is a collection of poems, "Un Agitado Viento/Ehécatl, the Wind." The essay is subdivided into seven constituent essays, each of which explores the theme of border crossing from distinct perspectives. The opening part, for example, sets the historical and political stage from which Anzaldúa will articulate what it means to live on the border, both literally and figuratively. Entitled "The Homeland, Aztlán/El Otro México," this short essay provides a sweeping view of the major historical events that have gone into producing the present-day border between the United States and Mexico. The first part of the title is derived from available historical scholarship; the second part, "El Otro México," she got from conversations with her family, who see the South Valley of Texas as becoming "un otro México" (another Mexico) because, as an uncle of hers says, "it's full of wetbacks." Thus the slash in the title itself represents a border between scholarly writing and the everyday experience of people who live in the valley. As Anzaldúa says about this text: "I don't feel that I, Gloria, produced *Borderlands* all by myself. I just happen to be the mouth-piece . . . the channel. While I do feel that the images and words . . . the way that I speak . . . the structure and style are mine, I found the raw material out there in the world, in other people's experiences, and in books" (Torres, "Gloria Anzaldúa" 13).

It is precisely this merger of scholarship and experience that makes Anzaldúa's "low" mode of theory construction so compelling. For instance, in the last subsection of the opening essay—"*El cruzar del mojado/* Illegal Crossing"—Anzaldúa, in a sense, replies to her uncle, agreeing that the valley is another Mexico—an *other* of Mexico: "We have a tradition of migration, a tradition of long walks. Today we are witnessing *la migración de los pueblos mexicanos*, the return odyssey to the historical/ mythological Aztlán. This time the traffic is from south to north"[1] (11). This other Mexico is part of Aztlán, with a division (the U.S. border) running through it.

The historical outline she provides starts from the earliest migrations from north to south of the Gochise people circa 1000 B.C., through the conquest of Mexico in 1521, through the signing of the Treaty of Gua-dalupe Hidalgo in 1848, and into the present. From personal experience Anzaldúa tells of her family's "ancestral lands" which were taken away. Out of such individual experience, the history of the American South-west was formed.

In the metaphorical figure of the *mujer indocumentada* (undocumented woman), Anzaldúa exploits the full referential power of that history. She, as the undocumented woman, not only represents the dividing line but also occupies it as a matter of ongoing, personal history: "This is her home/this thin edge of/barbwire" (13). As such, she is the perfect model for a theory of "the Borderlands," with a capital B, which Anzaldúa intends to symbolize the thin line between different beliefs and cultures.

Anzaldúa's language, linguistic codes, and ethnic identity also play key roles in her theory of the borderlands. "How to Tame a Wild Tongue," a brief expository essay, deals with the negative social attitudes toward Chicano ways of speaking, and the effects of these negative attitudes on the linguistic and ethnic self. The description of Chicano Spanish offered by Anzaldúa is concise and informative; it approaches the descriptive requirements of linguistic theory. The analysis of attitudes toward language that she presents rigorously exposes the many ways in which language can be used as an oppressive tool—in attitudes that prohibit Chicano school kids from speaking Spanish at recess, make the accent of Chicano English an impediment to economic advancement, and look down on Chicano Spanish as "mutilation of Spanish." Anzaldúa digs deeply into the political roots of these attitudes with her radical equation between language and identity: "So if you really want to hurt me, talk badly about my language. Ethnic identity is twin to linguistic identity—I am my language" (59).

The final short essay, "*La conciencia de la mestiza*/Towards a New Consciousness," is perhaps the most speculative and theoretically rich of the seven essays that make up "*Atravesando Fronteras*/Crossing Borders." The essay begins by boldly announcing that, like *la mujer indocumentada*, humanity is about to cross into an alien land: "From this radical, ideological, cultural and biological cross-pollination, an 'alien' consciousness is presently in the making—a new mestiza consciousness, *una conciencia de mujer*. It is a consciousness of the Borderlands" (77). The capital B indicates that Anzaldúa is talking about the symbolic borderlands, and, as a consequence, the dialectic that will be responsible for the formation of the mestiza consciousness, according to her, will be spiritual in nature. This does not mean, however, that the dialectic is ahistorical; on the contrary, like all her theories, the dialectic derives its power from the experience of daily life. Nor does the spiritual nature of the dialectic mean that it is moving toward absolute synthesis and unity; on the contrary, the dialectic moves toward *mestizaje* (racial mixture). In the end, the dialectic of the mestiza is spiritual in nature only because it works over, through, and on human consciousness, a phenomenon that cannot be reduced to a single, stable category. Consciousness cannot be just a subject, nor can it be just an object. For Anzaldúa, it is both—the subject studies, the object *is* studied—and more, a third element: a new consciousness—a mestiza consciousness—and though it is a source of intense pain, its energy comes from continual creative motion that keeps breaking down the unitary aspects of each new paradigm" (79–80). The process of breaking down unities amounts to the daily work of resisting Anglo-American political hegemonies, while, at the same time, allowing for political alliances; resisting the oppressive elements of Chicano culture, while understanding their roots in oppression. Above all, mestiza consciousness designates what Anzaldúa calls "a tolerance for ambiguity," a concept that is clearly linked to her experience with language. Like the phenomenon of linguistic ambiguity, which requires that one strive to see through the surface structure of an utterance to understand how other potential meanings also reside in the deep structure, Anzaldúa points to the many meanings with which one can invest reality. In this task it is once again the mestiza who is already in advance of others.

Borderlands exemplifies the political potential of postmodern aesthetics; the rich blend of narrative genres and styles extends the range of *Borderlands* into such topics and themes as history, philosophy, linguistics, and psychology. Thus, *Borderlands* is as much a multicultural epic as an autobiography. It is also however an engaged piece of literature, which is to say that it confronts U.S. society and critiques its oppressive institutional structures and policies. Gloria Anzaldúa describes herself as a woman writer who has gone against the grain of the Anglo-American tradition of literature. As a Chicana and a lesbian writer, Anzaldúa embodies several fronts marginalized by Anglo-American literary tradition. By writing *Borderlands* in a code-switching style, by drawing from a variety of generic social codes, and by disrupting the norms of cohesion and coherence in the textual composition of *Borderlands*, Anzaldúa challenges the cultural authorities of the United States and the literary canon of the Anglo-American academy. Against a tradition that has its roots in a Puritan history and its centers of authority in the American university, Anzaldúa indeed seems to be clearing a much needed space for herself and other minority writers who seek literary self-representation. Despite these challenges, *Borderlands* is widely taught in a variety of humanities courses on U.S. campuses in such areas as Women's Studies, Ethnic Studies, Gay and Lesbian Studies, and Chicano/a and American Literature. The fact that an essay such as this one is now needed to facilitate the teaching of the work is evidence that Gloria Anzaldúa's *Borderlands* is making a difference in the way U.S. society and culture perceives itself; indeed, *Borderlands* can be read profitably with this general concern in mind.

Any critical evaluation of *Borderlands* would be remiss if it did not situate the work within the current postmodern condition. In *Retrospace: Collected Essays on Chicano Literature*, one of the most highly influential critical essays written on Chicano/a literary discourse, Juan Bruce-Novoa asserts that Chicano/a literature is a response to the chaos of modern life. Certainly, in its structural composition, *Borderlands* represents the chaos of contemporary modern society. But, because *Borderlands* is an engaged text of literature, the way it represents chaos involves a questioning of the social underpinnings of that chaos. When Gloria Anzaldúa picks up the pen in the social act of writing, the scope of her creativity is broader than the life of a single self, and the chaos of modern society is not merely a philosophical abstraction but the concrete effect of social and economic forces. The manner in which Anzaldúa engages life with literature in *Borderlands* gives the text its unique authority to speak with such forthrightness, and while Anzaldúa speaks with a strong didactic voice in *Borderlands*, she does not do so at the expense of literary aesthetics. Art and politics merge for Anzaldúa in her notion of "mestiza consciousness." To her, mestiza consciousness, to some extent, composes the text and its relationship to Anglo-American literary history can provide ways to understand and teach the work.

Mestiza consciousness represents a challenge and a contribution to Western metaphysics in that it posits that life is not one thing and logic another, with different rules governing the two. Instead, as a basic modus operandi, Anzaldúa rejects that assumption in favor of the view that both life and logic are always changing through their interaction with each other; a person's identity is not static, nor is the logic of the surrounding world. Anzaldúa takes to heart the Heraclitean proposition that one can never step twice into the same river, and she gives it her own borderlands bent. Many students of *Borderlands* quickly become attuned to this shifting notion of identity, and they often quote the following passage: "That focal point or fulcrum, that juncture where the mestiza stands, is where phenomena tend to collide. It is where the possibility of uniting all that is separate occurs" (79). In philosophical terms, Anzaldúa describes the reason why mestiza consciousness cannot begin with a comfortable definition of identity: the mestiza, bombarded from every sector of U.S. society, often cannot decide who or what she is in a way that satisfies institutional ideologies.

Mestiza consciousness, then, is necessary if the mestiza is to keep U.S. society from having the last word on her identity. Anzaldúa locates this effort in the body, describing it as "a source of intense pain, its energy comes from continual creative motion that keeps breaking down the unitary aspect of each new paradigm" (80). This aspect of mestiza consciousness does not totally negate the idea of identity per se but seeks instead to keep identity an open question, a possibility. In other words, for the mestiza of which Anzaldúa speaks, identity is not a given but a matter of daily crafting from the experience of everyday life.

From the intense focus on the experience of everyday life, Anzaldúa draws the authority to contest the assumption that the categories of Western logic are in any way unaffected by such experience. Anzaldúa wants her writing to matter to the culture and society of the United States in a concrete political and aesthetic way. Her idea of mestiza consciousness exposes the complicity of Western idea of logic and political oppression. Anzaldúa is very explicit about demonstrating the oppressive effects of the subject-object dichotomy on the body of the mestiza. The author allows her mestiza consciousness to take speculative flight in the desire to change the world: "The answer to the problems between the white race and the colored, between males and females, lies in healing the split that originates in the very foundation of our lives, our culture, our languages, our thoughts" (80). From this point of view, the subject-object dichotomy is not simply an innocent abstraction away from everyday life experience, but a rigid imposition on the mind and body of the mestiza. Anzaldúa's literary discourse at such points in her text appears as an incisive piece of critical philosophy, a dialectic that mixes life experience with abstract logic creating a *mestizaje*, a mixture, blending, hybridity of critical categories with a theoretical vision of her everyday life. Thus, the social act of writing *Borderlands* is a political act of resistance against the tendency in Western culture and its educational curriculum to reduce the complexity of human life to simple dichotomies.

As a postmodern text, *Borderlands* is not linear and hence can be opened and read beginning with any chapter, a trait that resembles the epic characteristic of beginning a story line in medias res. This is a great advantage when teaching *Borderlands* not only because it justifies referring to the text as a multicultural epic but also because this characteristic is intimately related to the logic of postmodernism which relies on a notion of identity that is supple, flexible, and pliant, and thus goes against the grain of the Western prescription that identity must be defined by a set of necessary and sufficient traits. Anzaldúa's view of identity does not imply unilaterally that the postmodern condition is an "anything goes" situation. As a *mestizaje* of art and politics, *Borderlands* appeals to a particular social, linguistic, and ethnic identity aware that these categories are in constant flux. Postmodern logic thus conceived is a logic of inclusion, of "both" rather than "either-or." *Borderlands'* mestiza consciousness mirrors and practices this logic of inclusion.

The concept of mestiza consciousness gives the seven narrative autobiographical chapters of *Borderlands* an underlying unity. (Undoubtedly a study of Anzaldúa's poetry in *Borderlands* can be carried out through the lens of mestiza consciousness, but such a focus merits its own space). Chapter one, "The Homeland, Aztlán/*El otro México,*" immediately introduces readers to the dynamic of double logic in *Borderlands*: the American Southwest is at once the home of Chicanas and Chicanos and a foreign place. This situation creates for the Mexican-descended population of this geographical region a double consciousness. On the one hand, everything about the borderlands looks quite familiar to the Chicano/a population because, prior to 1848, this geographical zone was under the sovereign rule of Mexico. The Treaty of Guadalupe Hidalgo is thus a key document for understanding not only *Borderlands* but also the entire literary production of Chicano/a writers. Anzaldúa's impassioned and ironic version of that history merits close inspection not only for what she says about it but also for what she leaves unstated. Anzaldúa does not lead the reader toward her conclusions in linear form step by step. Rather, she prefers that her historical account be effective not only because of the sheer weight of the history of the U.S. Southwest, but also by the manner in which she dramatizes it in both lyric and prose.

In chapter two, Anzaldúa turns her mestiza dialectics in the direction of Chicano culture and levels a devastating critique of its own oppressive ways toward Chicanas. Herein the reader becomes aware of Anzaldúa's total resistance to the oppression of her female body from any and all quarters. What is especially intriguing about this chapter is the image of the Shadow Beast, a source of strength for Anzaldúa to resist Chicano culture's insistence that she behave like a traditional Mexican woman. The Shadow Beast image is also a disruptive sexual force, much like Sigmund Freud's concept of the libido as sexual energy. Regarding mestiza consciousness, the Shadow Beast additionally offers the promise of a spiritual unification of Anzaldúa's male and female selves in what she calls the *hieros gamos*, a Greek expression meaning "divine marriage." A rich storehouse of multileveled meanings is opened up, particularly for those readers who are acquainted with Carl Jung's version of psychoanalysis. Anzaldúa's open declaration of her lesbianism is an example of resistance to what could be called "compulsory heterosexuality." Her declaration that she chose her lesbian sexuality thus places *Borderlands* squarely within the maelstrom of the multicultural debates marking the politics of representation in contemporary American society.

Anzaldúa links chapters three and four closely with the image of the Aztec goddess Coatlicue, an image she uses to represent the unconscious processes of the mind—dreams, uncanny sensations, defense mechanisms, compulsions, and so on. No simple literary device, the image of Coatlicue in Anzaldúa's hands is first and foremost a way to heal the effects of oppressive Western institutions and their ideologies—the Catholic and Protestant religions, Western anthropology and psychology; in sum, the subject-object dichotomy. The detailed account of the image of Coatlicue and the syncretism that ensues when the Virgin of Guadalupe appears to Juan Diego in 1531 establish an analogy with the opening anecdote from the author's own life and her poem. Just as the appearance of the Virgin of Guadalupe on Tepeyac Hill in the Mexican colonial capital—the site of Coatlicue's temple—proved to be a form of indigenous resistance to the authority of Spanish Catholicism, so Anzaldúa now exercises the right to theorize the wounds on her body and use that theory—the Coatlicue state—to contest the oppression of institutionalized religion and institutional Western education.

Chapters five and six, "How to Tame a Wild Tongue" and *"Tlilli, Tla-palli*: The Path of the Red and Black Ink," introduce the role of language and the social act of writing. Chapter five, for instance, affirms the importance for the new mestiza of writing in her home dialect. The affirmation of one's dialect reflects a practical reality; if the new mestiza/o delays creativity until attaining accomplishment in the Western literary and critical canon, she/he might by default give up on it altogether. Of course, *Borderlands* is itself a major example of a piece of writing that affirms the home dialect, and with effective results. It is also proof that a "homely" dialect can be used to express the "high" theoretical concepts of the Western academy.

A key example of this is seen in the Mexican-Spanish proverb An-zaldúa poses as an epigraph to her description of the linguistic codes of the U.S.–Mexico borderlands: *"Quien tiene boca se equivoca"* (Whoever speaks may err in doing so [my translation], 55). This piece of Mexican folk wisdom encapsulates the necessity to maintain a continual critique of one's own point of view by sheer dint of the fact that the act of speaking contains perils. Thus, mestiza consciousness requires that, on the one hand, the position one takes on a subject should carry a substantial degree of authority while, on the other, it should question the full impact of that position. A good example of the process of cross-referencing is elucidated in Anzaldúa's categorical proposition: "Language is a male discourse" (54). By itself this declarative statement imputes a negative essence to language in the sense that language is a hostile site for the new mestiza. While Anzaldúa contests the erasure of female identity in language, nothing about her mestiza consciousness sanctions an argument against men.

In fact, in chapter seven, Anzaldúa shows that the scope of her dialectics of *mestizaje* must include the male presence. Her discourse entitled, *"Que no se nos olvide los hombres"* (Let us not forget the men [my translation], 83), is in effect a compassionate one, for it historicizes the way men, Chicano and non-Chicano alike, internalize a false machismo. Nothing could be more profitable for male students that to expose the negative effects that patriarchy has on their own ideological consciousness. The generosity of this point of view should provide ample material for critical discussion and debate.

TEACHING THE WORK

1. Any one of the dramatic scenes that make up chapter one can be studied for the levels of meaning Anzaldúa seeks to connote regarding history and borders. The scene concerning Pedro, a relative who is deported by the immigration authorities, for example, is especially gripping

as it is tinged with a touch of humor. How does this episode document the shame and injustice Pedro experiences? Have students analyze the significance of borders in people's lives.

2. The spiritual element Anzaldúa adds to her mestiza dialectics can be discussed at length with respect to her daring self-analysis in which she proposes that she chose to be a lesbian. This topic provides an opportunity for students to discuss issues around sexuality, personal identity, and social pressures to conform.

3. Discuss the image of the Aztec female deity and its rich meaning, keeping in mind when teaching chapters three and four that Anzaldúa does not employ it in her text as a purely formal literary device.

4. Teachers can direct students to consider the juxtaposition of personal experience with history. Discuss the appearance of snakes in chapter three and what they signify. Anzaldúa's poem *ella tiene su tono* dramatizes the way early childhood experiences can have a determinative character throughout one's life, as the experience of being bitten by a snake had on her. This could lead to a fascinating discussion of personal events in the students' lives of a similarly important nature.

5. The teacher of *Borderlands* can use chapters five and six to address the issue of authority and language. Within *Borderlands* the teacher can move throughout the text paying attention to just how Anzaldúa observes the profound knowledge of folk language and wisdom in the composition of her own text.

NOTE

1. All page numbers in parentheses refer to the 1987 edition of *Borderlands: The New Mestiza/La frontera* (San Francisco: Aunt Lute Foundation Books).

RELATED WORKS AND SUGGESTIONS FOR FURTHER READING

Anzaldúa, Gloria. *Making Face, Making Soul/Haciendo Caras: Creative and Critical Perspectives by Feminists of Color,* ed. Gloria Anzaldúa. San Francisco: Spinsters/Aunt Lute Foundation Books, 1990. Strengthens Anzaldúa's position as a committed writer, here working to give space to a cross-spectrum of women writers.

———. "Speaking in Tongues: A Letter to Third World Women Writers." In *This Bridge Called My Back: Writings by Radical Women of Color,* ed. Cherríe Moraga and Gloria Anzaldúa. New York: Kitchen Table: Women of Color Press, 1981, 163–73.

Bruce-Novoa, Juan. *Retrospace: Collected Essays on Chicano Literature.* Houston: Arte Público Press, 1990. Contains update of his classic essay, "The Space of Chicano Literature."

Castillo, Ana. *The Mixquiahuala Letters.* New York: Anchor Books Doubleday,

1986. Works well in conjunction with *Borderlands* because it focuses on the experience of Chicanas in Anglo and Mexican cultures.

Islas, Arturo. *The Rain God*. New York: Avon Books, 1984. Thinly disguised autobiography.

JanMohamed, Abdul, R., and David Lloyd. "Introduction: Toward a Theory of Minority Discourse: What Is to Be Done?" In *The Nature and Context of Minority Discourse*, ed. R. Jan Mohamed Abdul and David Lloyd. New York: Oxford University Press, 1990, 1–16. Situates politics of the social act of writing in a global context.

Mora, Pat. *The House of Houses*. Boston: Beacon Press, 1997. Winner of the 1998 Premio Aztlán, instituted by Rudolfo and Patricia Anaya, concerns U.S.–Mexico borderlands.

Saldívar, Ramón. *Chicano Narrative: The Dialectics of Difference*. Madison, Wisc.: University of Wisconsin Press, 1990.

Torres, Hector A. "Gloria Anzaldúa." In *Dictionary of Literary Biography*. ed. Francisco A. Lomelí and Carl R. Shirley. Vol. 122. Detroit: Gale Research, 1992, 1–16. A biography based on a lengthy ethnographic interview.

13

Writing a Life: *When I Was Puerto Rican* by Esmeralda Santiago

Aileen Schmidt

ESMERALDA SANTIAGO was born in Puerto Rico in 1948, the eldest of eleven children raised by a single mother. Her early years on the island were divided between a life in a small village among the *jíbaros*, or country people, and the suburbs of the capital city of San Juan. As a young teenager Santiago moved with her family to Brooklyn, New York, where she began a new phase of her life. Her varied experiences as a young girl in these diverse cultural settings, the life of a cultural go-between, would become the basis of her memoir, *When I Was Puerto Rican*, which appeared in 1993, first in English and later in a Spanish version by the author herself. Santiago remained in the United States, graduated from Harvard University in 1976, and later earned an MFA in fiction writing from Sarah Lawrence College.

In 1996 Esmeralda Santiago published her first novel, *America's Dream*, a work that explores a determined woman's search for autonomy and, in 1998, a follow-up to her memoir, *Almost a Woman*, which traces the young adolescent protagonist of *When I Was Puerto Rican* from the barrios of New York to Harvard and a life of writing. In addition to her fictional work and her memoirs, Santiago has published a collection of "holiday memories" of Latino authors, *Las Christmas* (1998), which preserves cherished cultural recollections. With her husband, Frank Cantor, Santiago has founded a film and production company, Cantomedia, that has produced award-winning documentaries.

ANALYSIS OF THEMES AND FORMS

When I Was Puerto Rican (1993), a poignant autobiographical narrative, is Esmeralda Santiago's first book. The memoir tells the story of her childhood in Puerto Rico and her adolescent years in New York City, where the family lived after they left the island in search of a better life. Negi, as the author-narrator is affectionately called, is an alert, inquisitive, and sensitive girl. She experiences frequent relocations in rural and urban Puerto Rico during the 1950s, and later in New York, for a variety of reasons: arguments between her parents that always end in their separation and eventual reconciliation, economic hardship, new siblings, and an extended family. As the oldest child, she is constantly being given too many responsibilities for her age and she sometimes resents it. Her sense of duty and obedience, however, quells any hint of rebellion. She grows to be a passionate reader, and education turns her life around. She gains admission to the prestigious High School of Performing Arts and later becomes a scholarship student at Harvard University.

The book's structure consists of 13 chapters, a prologue, an epilogue, and a glossary of Puerto Rican words and phrases. Most titles display a combination of Spanish and English, an element that will be discussed later. Each chapter is introduced by a typical Puerto Rican adage or aphorism, a *refrán*, in Spanish, with the English translation included. Students should pay attention to these *refranes*, for they reveal much about Puerto Rican culture—its values, mores, and practices—and showcase relevant themes and experiences of the narrator.

The "Prologue: How to Eat a Guava" aims to establish a difference between the adult woman shopping at a New York supermarket and the young girl who last ate a guava on the day she left Puerto Rico. This section, strikingly emotional and gracefully written, is about memory and remembrance, the essence of all autobiographical writing. It also introduces in a metaphorical sense the main theme of this memoir: identity. The problem of identity is the cornerstone of the narration. The prologue anticipates the duality that is central to the whole story and partly explains the book's ironical title: the young *jíbara* who becomes another New York City person. Yet the author-narrator validates both realities. Although there has been a rupture with her past and she is no longer completely Puerto Rican, the guavas of her childhood still attract and tempt her, summoning her to an identity she cannot ignore.

The first chapter is appropriately titled "Jíbara." We meet the four-year-old Negi, whose parents have moved to rural Macún, a barrio in the northern town of Toa Baja. All the emblems of the Puerto Rican *jíbaro* are present: an exuberant and rich countryside, very modest wood and metal houses, large families, traditional Puerto Rican music, and strong family ties. Negi's small house is poor and overcrowded, but the parents are devoted to their children and there is a sense of pride in their family life.

The little girl feels content in this environment, but she is confused about her identity. Negi is proud of being a *jíbara* despite the fact that her mother belittles *jíbaros* for their backwardness and traditional ways. She wants her children to be something better.

I wanted to be a *jíbara* more than anything in the world. . . . If we were not *jíbaros*, why did we live like them? . . . Even at the tender age when I didn't yet know my real name, I was puzzled by the hypocrisy of celebrating a people everyone looked down on. (12, 13)[1]

The first two chapters depict Negi's private ambience and the larger social world. The traditional values of a patriarchal society are bestowed upon her at birth. Her "education sentimentale" begins with her parents' conflictive relationship and the advice of female relatives. She will learn not to trust men, yet to accept their foibles. Gender roles are clearly defined early in the narration: men are natural flirts whose freedom is not to be challenged; women stay at home to raise the children and do not question their subordination.

Her mother dares to leave Negi's father because of his unfaithfulness (although she takes him back several times before she leaves for good and takes her children to New York City), and they move to the city. Life in urban Santurce, a very hectic commercial center, represents an encounter with otherness, a confrontation with difference. A new dimension of Negi's identity is assigned by her classmates, teachers, and neighbors. In the city she is denigrated for being a *jíbara*.

I knew they were different, or rather, I was different. Already I'd been singled out in school for my wildness, my loud voice, and large gestures better suited to the expansive countryside but out of place in concrete rooms. . . . What a *jíbara*. . . . In Santurce I had become what I wasn't in Macún. In Santurce a *jíbara* was something no one wanted to be. (39)

Back in Macún after her parents reconcile, Negi experiences for the first time the influence of political opportunism and demagoguery, and she develops a political consciousness of sorts. A visit by U.S. "experts" in nutrition and hygiene ("the American Invasion of Macún") is a significant cultural shock that has an impact on Macún's residents and introduces a new element into Negi's identity. The *Americanos* would "teach our mothers all about proper nutrition and hygiene, so that we would grow up as tall and strong as Dick, Jane, and Sally, the *Americanitos* in our primers" (64).

The patronizing and sometimes ludicrous talks given by the experts ignore the distinctiveness of Puerto Rican culture and the economical and cultural realities of rural life. Negi learns about the complexities of power relations in society when her father explains the colonial situation of Puerto Rico and the politics of assimilation. She proudly states her refusal to learn English at school so as not to become an American (73).

Negi feels a strong attachment to her father, Pablo. They share a common sensibility and love of knowledge, poetry, and education. Learning about his womanizing hurts her more than anything. Feeling neglected, she busies herself with household chores and tending too many children leaving little time for dreaming, poetry, or thought. The bond between mother and daughter, however, is stronger—a female empathy and solidarity that nourishes Negi's admiration and respect for her mother. The work is, in fact, a tribute to the author's mother, Monin (it is dedicated to her), the most important figure in Negi's life and undoubtedly a role model. Monin is a true fighter: strong, determined, responsible, intelligent, and resourceful. Her dignity and strength empower her in the never-ending struggle for the well-being of her children. Working outside the house and receiving a salary have made her independent and content, although she must confront the bias of a traditional society when she sets out to work in a factory.

Monin leaves Pablo when he refuses to marry her after living together for many years and bringing seven children into the world. She boldly decides to move to New York City alone with the children, without any formal education, money, or knowledge of English. This is a turning point in Monin's life as well as that of her daughter, who clearly understands the disruption that their journey represents: "the Puerto Rican *jíbara* . . . was to become a hybrid who would never forgive the uprooting" (209).

In the United States Negi encounters a hostile milieu toward her Puerto Ricanness. Her identity as a Puerto Rican is co-opted by a comprehensive "Hispanic" categorization imposed by Anglos. New and complex factors, such as race, ethnicity, class, and gender, qualify identity in New York and lead to a kind of discrimination and oppression she had never experienced in Puerto Rico. The conditions and limits imposed by ethnic and racial diversity overwhelm Negi, and she develops a sharp consciousness of the impact of intolerance and racism in daily life.

School becomes a personal challenge. Negi is an intelligent girl whose talents bring notable achievements. She quickly learns English (it is significant that her very capable English teacher is a black woman) and is recognized by the school's authorities. Negi is unwavering in her decision to overcome the marginality of the typical immigrant through education. She decides to take control of her life and to change it by using her best asset—her intelligence. Education is her only hope for independence, self-respect, and social acceptance. As always, her mother is an inspiration and a strong force behind Negi's determination:

"I'm not working this hard so that you kids can end up working in factories all your lives. You study, get good grades, and graduate from high school so that you can have a profession, not just a job." (246)

In "A Shot at It," the last chapter of the book, we come upon a crucial moment in Negi's adolescence. Aware of her capabilities, her guidance counselor arranges for an audition at the prestigious High School of Performing Arts. He selects a speech from a play about a New York drawing room at the turn of the century for Negi to perform, a selection that is totally inappropriate for a Puerto Rican girl from Brooklyn. She learns the monologue phonetically, having been coached "on how to behave like a lady," but the audition is a disaster nevertheless. She leaves distraught, fearing the worst:

[A]shamed that, after all the hours of practice . . . after the expense of new clothes and shoes, after Mami had to take a day off from work to take me into Manhattan, after all that. I had failed the audition and would never, ever, get out of Brooklyn. (266)

The reader is taken by surprise in "Epilogue: One of These Days," the last section of the memoir, whose first lines explain the uncertain ending of the previous chapter. "A decade after my graduation from Performing Arts, I visited the school. I was by then living in Boston, a scholarship student at Harvard University" (269). One of the teachers who was present at the audition and had become her high school mentor admiringly remarks "how far" she has come. Negi is now a twenty-seven-year-old woman who has "forgotten the skinny brown girl with the curled hair, wool jumper, and lively hands." Yet she still yearns for recognition and silently but convincingly anticipates that "one of these days" she will have a place on Performing Arts' bulletin board where newspaper clippings about famous former students are posted.

One possible critical approach to this text is a gender study critique. Gender studies have been part of academic life for the last three decades when gender became understood as the social, cultural, and psychological meanings that constitute the identities of men and women. This approach analyzes the differences between men and women that are determined by society and not by biology. It refers to what society establishes as feminine and masculine. Gender also signifies power. Gender relations are power relations, asymmetrical and defined by inequality and male domination.

Gender, therefore, influences our perception of literature. Given that women's reality is seen as inferior and limited, women's writing will also be devalued. Writing by women is underestimated and considered less important than men's, whose experiences are deemed universal. Incorporating gender into our analysis will allow us to understand why men's life stories are considered exemplary and representative, important enough to be read as models and paradigms, and why women who write autobiographically are challenging that tradition and, in so doing, are overturning society's view of women.

Thus, *When I Was Puerto Rican* is not merely an inspiring narrative about Negi's coming of age but a story about the various cultural repertoires that influence the articulation of the identity of the Latina woman. To fully appreciate this well-written text, it should be seen as a successful example of autobiographical writing by women, the literary self-expression of women's lives. Through the narration of their life experiences, women transcend the literary and social marginality in which patriarchy has situated them. By writing about themselves, they become producers and creators of knowledge and meaning, and in so doing they validate the historical experiences of women. Autobiographical writing is an act of empowerment, a discourse of self-awareness and assertiveness. By writing this memoir Esmeralda Santiago not only validates her identity as a woman, but she also legitimizes several instances of *otherness*: Puerto Rican, immigrant, mulatta, and poor. Identity is thus a site of multiple possibilities, all compounded by her feelings of separation, her marginality. As all the other women in this story, Negi must stand up to the power structure of a male-dominated society. They consistently and creatively strive to overcome the limits of their subordination and make a conscious endeavor to improve their lives and protect their children.

Another asset of this book is the naturalness of its language. The narrative discourse is a brilliant display of wit, liveliness, and agility. The author, a first-rate narrator, is always in control of the subject matter. Her style is remarkably expressive, the language is natural and unaffected; it immediately captures the reader's attention and makes the reading accessible and easy to follow. The use of Spanish words and aphorisms is unquestionably inherent to the essence of the life being narrated. Esmeralda Santiago's poetic imagination gives rein to a literary discourse as passionate and urgent as the immediacy of her life experience.

A Spanish translation by the author, *Cuando yo era puertorriqueña*, was published in 1994. This version, as well as the original edition, has been very successful, although some reviewers have criticized the awkwardness of some of the Spanish usage. It is relevant to note that the Spanish edition begins with an "Introduction" in which Santiago discusses her intense and apparently contradictory connection to both languages. She distinguishes between a life "lived" in Spanish but narrated in English. Her identity is defined by her life/linguistic experience: she lives and writes in both languages. As a Puerto Rican living in the United States, she positions herself as a "hybrid between one world and the other." Living in two worlds, one American and one Puerto Rican, is at times painful and she resents having been "brought" to the States. Yet, as an author, she values the feelings that inspired her writing about being two things at the same time: "a North American *jíbara.*" Her memoir teaches us that there are many modes of Puerto Ricanness; her life urges us to accept and value diversity. Puerto Ricanness is not a fixed or monolithic instance; it is anchored in the multiple circumstances that inform it.

Most reviewers have acclaimed this memoir for its sincerity, warmth, and impeccable writing skills. However, several Puerto Rican critics have pointed out the flaws of what they consider a conscious effort by Santiago to construct a typical "success story" tailored to satisfy the demands of the American publishing market, always eager for inspirational stories about the opportunities of the American dream. For these critics, Santiago has bowed to the preconceived notions and clichés of the Anglo-Saxon culture about Puerto Rican immigration. They criticize the stereotyping of characters and situations which fosters intolerance and bigotry.

Although these elements can be taken into account when teaching *When I Was Puerto Rican,* an analysis of the book must primarily validate the author's creative freedom and respect her life experiences. It must acknowledge that autobiographical writing is fundamentally a story about the author's unique perception of her life. Santiago's honesty should not be doubted; her narration should be seen as a process of self-understanding. Her own words about the particular situation of Puerto Ricans in the United States are very revealing in this context.

These degrees of Puerto Ricanism have to be addressed. It is causing a lot of pain because it's so easy to go back and forth, from one place to the other. I think that's why so many of our children are so confused and have such low self-esteem. They don't have a sense of belonging to one or the other culture. You feel guilty for becoming Americanized, and you feel guilty because you're not Puerto Rican enough.[2]

A discussion regarding her idealistic and at times naïve portrayal of the countryside, as well as a debate about the pathos and isolation of growing up in a racist society, would help to understand the complex cultural contexts of Puerto Rico and the United States that sustain her writing.

Seen within the context of a growing corpus of immigration narratives, all of them significant accounts of the conflicts and negotiations of identity in a foreign culture, those written by women are particularly relevant: *Borderlands/La Frontera* (Gloria Anzaldúa, Chicana, 1987), *The House on Mango Street* (Sandra Cisneros, Chicana, 1989), *Silent Dancing* (Judith Ortiz Cofer, Puerto Rican, 1990), *How the Garcia Girls Lost Their Accents* (Julia Alvarez, Dominican, 1991), and *Dreaming in Cuban* (Cristina Garcia, Cuban, 1992), among many others.

Finally, it should be noted that, in her 1998 sequel to her first memoir, *Almost a Woman,* an engaging work of complexity and psychological intuition in which Santiago accounts for her teenage years in Brooklyn, her diverse work experiences in Manhattan, and her struggle for independence from her mother, the author reveals her evolving mastery as a narrator.

TEACHING THE WORK

1. Since this book is an autobiographical narrative, discussion should emphasize the personal. Students should be encouraged to reflect upon their own experiences and feelings as a way to develop an understanding of their own lives. The discussion must aim to make them insightful and sensitive to their personal reality. A short self-narrative could be assigned for building up a sense of pride in their heritage, an awareness of their history and culture. The goal of this exercise is to make them conscious of the historical value of personal experience.

2. The history of the United States is anchored in multiple immigrations. Ask students to do historical research on the immigration of a particular ethnic group. The objective is for them to understand the economical, political, and social causes of emigration. Discuss how gender, race, ethnicity, and class can influence and frequently distort our perception of immigrants.

3. Identity assumes diverse meanings for the characters in the book and is experienced differently in Puerto Rico and in the United States. How do students conceptualize their identity? As a fixed set of values and beliefs, an abstraction, a changing condition? Discussion should emphasize the contrasts in the perception of identity within several generations of the same family and should analyze the reasons for this disparity.

4. The presence of the community is of paramount importance in the characters' lives. Discussion should emphasize the role of communal life, the rituals, beliefs, solidarity, and bonds between the members of the students' communities and the influences on the quality of their lives.

5. A debate about the importance of education should consider the contributions of the so-called minorities and their role as agents in the creation of knowledge. While emphasizing respect and tolerance for diversity, students should be led to examine how discrimination and other forms of oppression hinder the development of racial and ethnic minorities.

6. Special attention should be given to the literary values of Santiago's rich and vibrant language. An analysis of certain fragments (especially the Prologue, "Why Women Remain *jamona*," and "Angels on the Ceiling") should note the beauty and expressiveness of her narrative discourse.

7. A noteworthy project could be a comparative analysis of *When I Was Puerto Rican* and its sequel, *Almost a Woman*. Students should focus on the technical aspects of a memoir, as well as its subject matter. Is there a difference in the narrative style in these two works? How has the author-protagonist changed? What could be the reasons for this? Are the issues and themes exposed in the sequel relevant to the students' lives? What might be expected of a third Santiago memoir?

NOTES

1. All page references from *When I Was Puerto Rican* (New York: Vintage Books, 1993).

2. Carmen Dolores Trelles, *Puerto Rican Voices in English. Interviews with Writers.* (Westport, Conn.: Praeger, 1997), 165.

CRITICISM AND FURTHER READING

The Americas Review 16, no. 3–4 (Fall-Winter 1988). Useful special issue of the journal, titled *A Review of Hispanic Literature and Art of the U.S.A.*

Benmayor, Rina, Ana L. Juarbe, and Rosa M. Torruellas. *Responses to Poverty Among Puerto Rican Women: Identity, Community, and Cultural Citizenship.* New York: Center for Puerto Rican Studies, 1992.

Brodzki, Bella, and Celeste Schenck, eds. *Life/Lines: Theorizing Women's Autobiography.* Ithaca: N.Y.: Cornell University Press, 1988.

Cahill, Susan, ed. *Growing Up Female: Stories by Women Writers from the American Mosaic.* New York: Mentor, 1993.

Colón, Jesús. *A Puerto Rican in New York and Other Sketches.* New York: International Publishers, 1991 (first ed., 1961).

"Esmeralda Santiago (1948–)." In *Notable Hispanic American Women, Book II.* Detroit: Gale Research, 1998, 293–94.

Flores, Juan. *Divided Borders: Essays on Puerto Rican Identity.* Houston: Arte Público Press, 1993.

Hernández, Carmen Dolores. *Puerto Rican Voices in English: Interviews with Writers.* Westport, Conn.: Praeger, 1997.

The "Oral History Project," at the Center for Puerto Rican studies, Hunter College, CUNY, New York City, is an excellent source. It would be helpful to consult several of their publications, in which different scholars strive to "document, analyze and make available . . . a comprehensive portrait of the Puerto Rican migration to the United States from the early 1900's to the present."

Santiago, Roberto, ed. *Boricuas: Influential Puerto Rican Writings, An Anthology.* New York: Ballantine, 1995.

14

Judith Ortiz Cofer's
The Latin Deli

Rafael Ocasio

JUDITH ORTIZ COFER was born in 1952 in Hormigueros, Puerto Rico. Because of her father's job with the U.S. Navy, she was brought to live at a young age to Paterson, New Jersey, while her father was assigned to duty in Brooklyn, New York. Her early years were divided between her home in Paterson and her maternal family's home in Puerto Rico. Ortiz Cofer has described her experience of bilingualism as a challenge. Her ultimate goal was to master English sufficiently to write poetry. She indeed did master the language and received a degree in English from Augusta College in 1973 and an M.A. from Florida Atlantic University in 1977. She has taught on the faculty of a number of institutions, including the University of Miami and the University of Georgia, and has published several books of poetry: *Peregrina* (1986), *Terms of Survival* and *Reaching for the Mainland*, both in 1987.

In 1989 Ortiz Cofer published her first novel, *The Line of the Sun*. The book includes the autobiographical elements usually found in a first novel; it traces three generations of a Puerto Rican family from an island village to their new home in Paterson, New Jersey. The balance that the protagonist of the novel strives to achieve is also a theme of Ortiz Cofer's volume of poetry and personal essays, *Silent Dancing*, published in 1990. Ortiz Cofer's acclaimed collection of poems, stories, and essays, *The Latin Deli*, published in 1993, won the Anisfield-Wolf Book Award. A collection of stories based on the lives of teenagers in a New Jersey barrio, *An Island Like You: Stories of the Barrio*, was published in 1995. Her most recent work, *The Year of Our Revolution: New and Selected Stories and Poems*, was published in 1998.

ANALYSIS OF THEMES AND FORMS

Judith Ortiz Cofer's *The Latin Deli* (1993) presents distinctive voices of numerous Puerto Rican female characters in essays, short story narratives, and poetry, which stress the plight of their lives in a Puerto Rican barrio in an urban North American city. Ortiz Cofer's characters voice a strong feminist awareness that sets them apart from counterpart male characters. Until recent years, Puerto Rican literature was dominated by male writers who had centered Puerto Rican culture within male-oriented sociodynamics. As a result, although their production represents a fairly comprehensive history of Puerto Rican immigration, it understates the contributions of women to the creation of a multicultural, gender-based concept of Puerto Ricanness in the United States.

Constant shifts from one language to another during her stays in Paterson and Hormigueros produced in Ortiz Cofer a strong interest in languages: "I decided that my main weapon in life was communication. I had to learn the language of the place where I was living in order to survive" (Ocasio, "Puerto Rican Literature in Georgia" 44). This arrangement of constantly moving between the United States and Puerto Rico has made Ortiz Cofer a poignant observer of Puerto Rican culture. She is also a strong critic of mainstream America's racist and sexist opinions about the Puerto Rican community, and of Puerto Rican culture's rigid views of sexual relationships.

Ortiz Cofer's adolescent years are marked with personal experiences as a member of a marginalized cultural group. When she was fourteen, her family moved to Augusta, Georgia, an event that marks Ortiz Cofer's rupture with Puerto Rican–American urban culture and exposes her to new forms of racial discrimination. She married John Cofer at nineteen, worked on a master's degree in English literature while taking care of their baby daughter, and established a home in Louisville, Georgia, a rural community where she and her husband have a farm. When asked about the reason for her self-imposed exile from Puerto Rican cultural centers, she has insisted that her decision was not a calculated one.

If I look around me I see hundreds of acres of trees and they are my community as far as a physical community. However, if I look around my cabin I have shelves and shelves of books by writers who are present here as if they were in my presence. I am not out of touch. I do not need to be in New York City or in Puerto Rico to write about being a Puerto Rican. I am not making a political stand by being geographically where I am. This is my life and I work where I find myself. (Ocasio, "Puerto Rican Literature" 46).

In fact, readers of *The Latin Deli* are struck by the importance of Puerto Rican–oriented locales as graphic representatives of Puerto Rican culture.

Two significant cultural groupings, lush Puerto Rican nature and urban American settings related to inner-city life, are set up as elements of conflict in maintaining either a pure island-oriented Puerto Ricanness or a hyphenated Puerto Rican–Americanness. The predominantly Spanish-speaking barrio with its distinctive cultural icons (for example, the bodegas, or neighborhood markets that carry a variety of island products) creates of "el Building" (a tenement of recent immigrants) a territoriality equivalent to that of the island of Puerto Rico. The clash between the self-imposed island of el Building and the remembered images of Puerto Rico provides *The Latin Deli* with a recurring theme of civilization versus the uncivilized:

The city here represents decadence. El Building was an attempt by these people to give form and meaning to their lives. The building itself was a trap. They were in an artificial environment, a vertical barrio. There is no such thing. It's not so much that the city was evil, but it was an environment that fostered evil. The people in el Building did not understand the dual nature. They wanted the island in the city. They never resolved this dichotomy. The island is Eden, and hell is in the city. (Ocasio, "Puerto Rican Literature" 48)

The Latin Deli is notable for its combination of poems and short narratives that develop similar literary themes or address socio-gendered issues. Ortiz Cofer, essentially a poet, has recognized the influence of poetry on her literary production as a whole:

I consider poetry my primary genre and greatest discipline. Poetry is what connects me to my memory, to my imagination, to my subconscious life, and to my original language. In fact, I cannot think of anything that I have done in fiction or nonfiction that has not found expression in either a successful or unsuccessful poem. (Ocasio, "Puerto Rican Literature" 49)

The poetic memory draws heavily from specific incidents and "character figures" that are representatives of island or urban Puerto Rican socio-cultural constructions. These prominent figures are also related to specific associations that either offer comfort or ease the pain of cultural adaptation in the United States. They also stand against each other with solid views of city or rural values; their clash and the ways in which a solution to these differences is achieved create the hybrid culture of el barrio.

The 38 poems can be divided into well-developed, cohesive themes assembled in chronological order to correspond to the developmental personality phases of the character who inspires the poem. Key family members, such as the grandmother who lives on the island, appear with special prominence. A woman of strong will, unlike the traditional submissive Puerto Rican wife, the grandmother becomes a prototype of a rural feminist who is in personal control of her family affairs in spite of the social restrictions imposed upon women by Puerto Rican culture. The grandmother is also a rich repository of folklore and of enigmatic stories of family and national characters who achieve literary status in Ortiz Cofer's writing. Ortiz Cofer has pointed out that her grandmother's impact—literary and personal—has been profound. In her stories she attempts to recreate for her readers the teachings that she learned from her:

I remember that, at certain times of my life, she said things that affected me. I don't remember exactly what those words were. In my stories, in order to make them art and in order to make them connect with other people, I put words into this woman's mouth that are roughly equivalent to what I think her messages were. (Ocasio, "An Interview with Judith Ortiz Cofer" 735)

Other female figures, such as the mother who must face life in the United States, make use of some of the grandmother's traits in order to survive the cultural and gender clash experienced by Puerto Rican women on their arrival in the United States. The father, although less visible, is presented as a domineering figure; his excessive control over his family is attributed to his overzealous desire to protect them from the urban dangers present in el barrio. These views are presented by a female character who remembers her childhood from an adult perspective. Her experiences as a first-generation Puerto Rican–American illustrate the socio-gendered dynamics of negotiating between modernity and dated cultural values.

The dichotomy of the city as civilized but evil, full of dangers for women, is in strong contrast to the beauty of Puerto Rican nature. The island's lush, exotic, and erotic background is opposed to the impoverished el Building. The tension, which takes on subtle undertones of protest against the low economic conditions typical of the Puerto Rican community in the United States, is also central to the existentialist anguish experienced by the poetic voices caught between life in an urban city and their memories or family's memories of life in Puerto Rico. Puerto Rico is romanticized into a benevolent and generous world. The most vivid image of the island is that of a mother-earth that symbolically provides all characters with the strength to survive the hardships and the dangers in el barrio.

The sociocultural clash experienced by the Puerto Rican immigrant ends, however, with the first-generation Puerto Rican–American characters who have become associated with the creation of a new Puerto Rican identity. If Ortiz Cofer's poetry reflects a strong association with metaphorical representations of Puerto Rican identity, her short stories deal with a more concrete view of Puerto Ricanness from either perspective: island or city. These stories, unlike the poems, document cultural confrontations—due to social, economic, or gender factors—experienced by immigrant Puerto Rican female characters. The stories illustrate how women deal with the gender-based society forced on them by Puerto Rican men who try to defend both the women and themselves against the urban dangers of el barrio.

Like the poems, the stories are set up as vignettes in chronological order beginning with an adolescent Puerto Rican girl who shares a small apartment with her parents in a tenement building located in a Spanish barrio in Paterson, New Jersey. The representation of the apartment as small, and therefore restrictive, provides the tone for the short stories. Puerto Rico's island culture—encapsulated in the neighborhood activities that take place in el Building—contrasts sharply with popular teenage cultures and interests which are marked by an inclination toward mainstream activities. These stories demonstrate why Puerto Rican culture might seem chauvinistic to outsiders.

The short stories gravitate toward ethnic issues related to the domestic and international diversities present in el Building and its surrounding areas. "American Lesson," for instance, begins when children are dismissed from school because of the assassination of President John F. Kennedy. Most of the children are delighted to get out of school, but the story's protagonist is upset that her plans to meet a fellow student after school for a study session may be derailed by this unexpected incident. The young adolescent girl is so self-absorbed in her expectation that her study session may turn out to be a romantic date that she is not struck by the open grief expressed by members of the barrio, many of whom greatly admired President Kennedy. Just when the reader begins to believe that she has missed an important lesson in American history, the young girl experiences her own lesson in race relations. In spite of her mother's complaints, she goes to her study date, but she is sharply turned away by the boy's mother, a white woman from Georgia, who hints to the girl that she objects to her son's interracial relationship with people who inhabit el Building.

Other teenage girl protagonists are faced with their parents' zealous observance of proper behavior for a young Puerto Rican woman. In the face of strong parental restrictions, which are closely related to the parents' attempts to resist cultural assimilation, these girls become interpreters of the conflicting points of view of Puerto Rican and American sexual relationships. As agents of change, Puerto Rican–American teenage girls must confront their parents' views on social and personal interaction, which are determined in part by their island's conception of gender dynamics.

Friendship bonds by cultural and gender association serve as an important theme in "Nada" (Nothing). This short story highlights political issues with regard to contemporary Puerto Rican identity vis-à-vis the colonial association with the United States. Confrontation with American political institutions takes place when Doña Ernestina, a recent widow, refuses to accept from the Army a U.S. flag and a medal in honor of the death of her only son, who was killed while fighting in Vietnam. Doña Ernestina's political statement is clear: she finds herself lonely and forgotten in a foreign country that does not appreciate the sacrifice of her only child. The feeling of emptiness, obvious in the title, is also reflected by Doña Ernestina's neighbors in el Building. They are puzzled by her cold reaction to her son's death, as pointed out by one of her close friends: "Doesn't Doña Ernestina feel anything?" (51). The tragic end, Doña Ernestina's suicide shortly after giving away her meager possessions to friends and strangers, confirms the feeling of abuse experienced by some of the characters, who see themselves as mere peons in a dehumanizing industrial system.

The relationship between memory and testimony, character and author, insinuated in the poems and the short stories, is pivotal in understanding a third genre, essays that address the themes and subjects dealt with in the poems and short stories. Ortiz Cofer has labeled these essays "creative non-fiction": "[It] goes back to my comments about recollections and memories being partly fiction" (Ocasio, "An Interview" 735). Although the essays do not serve as critical analyses of either the poems or the short narratives, they do offer insight into Ortiz Cofer's feminist stand on Puerto Ricanness and its clash with mainstream American culture.

The essays are outstanding in their handling of autobiographical data—mostly the author's analysis of her own experiences as a member of an immigrant Puerto Rican family with a higher income than that of most of the other Puerto Rican families in urban Paterson. In chronological order, these essays concentrate on specific time frames that describe Ortiz Cofer's coming of age as a woman of color and as a writer interested in exploring gender and racial issues. It can be argued that the major contribution of these essays is their openly political nature, which is also present in some of the poems and stories. The gendered-political discourse of the essays is supported by key personal experiences in a testimonial account that is meant to affect the reader as Ortiz Cofer's grandmother affected her and changed her life:

Yet I am one of the lucky ones. My parents made it possible for me to acquire a stronger footing in the mainstream culture by giving me the chance at an education. And books and art have saved me from the harsher forms of ethnic and racial prejudice that many of my Hispanic compañeras have had to endure. I travel a lot around the United States, reading from my books of poetry and my novel, and the reception I most often receive is one of positive interest by people who want to know more about my culture. ("The Myth of the Latin Woman," *The Latin Deli* 154)

The Latin Deli has received several distinguished awards, including the Anisfield-Wolf Book Award in 1994, selected by Rita Dove, Ashley Montague, and Henry Louis Gates, Jr. "Nada" received the O. Henry Prize in 1994, and "Advanced Biology" took Special Mention, *Best American Essays* anthology in 1992. In addition, HBO has purchased the rights for a film based on the short story "Corazón's Café."

TEACHING THE WORK

1. Issues relating to Puerto Rican immigration after World War II and the settling of that population in northern American cities such as New York City, Chicago, and Paterson, New Jersey, have not raised much academic interest until recent times. Two field research projects for students interested in the socioeconomic dynamics of Puerto Rican communities are suggested: (1) interview Puerto Rican immigrants with varying numbers of years of residence in the United States, making sure to include questions specific to an immigrant's initial experience, such as language barriers and religious and racial confrontations with mainstream groups and with other ethnic groups outside the barrio; and (2) travel to Spanish-speaking barrios and visit culturally specific locales, such as bodegas, *botánicas*, and Salsa music halls, to gain exposure to the Spanish language and witness the bilingualism that characterizes Puerto Rican and other Latino communities.

2. Debate the fact that, 100 years after the Spanish American War of 1898 in which Puerto Rico became an American territory, U.S. and Puerto Rican voters now face important choices about granting the island independence or statehood. Discuss the possible role of language and culture in the treatment of this issue.

3. Ask students to compile a list of stereotypes of social, religious, or ethnic groups (e.g., Latinos, African Americans, women of color, gays and lesbians, Muslims, or Jews) based on popular views presented in art or in the media, including Hollywood films. Discuss how the various stereotypes change according to historic and economic factors.

4. Puerto Rican and other Latino groups have often expressed their concern about the negative representation of Latino characters in plays and films. Ortiz Cofer's essay "The Myth of the Latin Woman: I Just Met a Girl Named María" touches on the mainstream's stereotypes based on Hollywood's depictions of Latina women. A controversial Broadway show, *The Capeman*, is based on the social conversion of a former teenage Puerto Rican gang member who killed two Anglo teenagers in cold blood. Have students listen to such songs as those of the Broadway show

and react to their content. Areas of possible conflict include the creation of a Puerto Rican barrio discourse as imagined by a white composer (Paul Simon), the cultural icons or symbols used in this so-called barrio discourse, and its final goal or intent. More advanced analysis may include the comparison of songs from *The Capeman* and those from an equally controversial play along the same lines: Leonard Bernstein's *West Side Story*.

CRITICISM AND FURTHER READING

Ocasio, Rafael. "American History." *Masterplots II: Short Story, Supplement*, ed. Frank N. Magill. Pasadena, Calif.: Salem Press, 1996, 2789–91. Critical analysis of Ortiz Cofer's short story "American History."

———. "A Feminist View of Puerto Rican Identity." *Latino Review of Books* 1, no. 2 (Fall 1995): 29–31. Critical overview of *The Latin Deli*.

———. "The Infinite Variety of the Puerto Rican Reality: An Interview with Judith Ortiz Cofer." *Callaloo* 17, no. 3 (1994): 730–42. In this interview Judith Ortiz Cofer reacts to other critics' views of so-called ethnic literature.

———. "An Interview with Judith Ortiz Cofer." *The Americas Review* 22, no. 3–4 (Fall-Winter 1994): 84–90.

———. "Puerto Rican Literature in Georgia? An Interview with Judith Ortiz Cofer." *Kenyon Review* 14, no. 4 (Fall 1992): 43–50.

———. "Speaking in Puerto Rican: An Interview with Judith Ortiz Cofer." *Bilingual Review/Revista Bilingüe* 17, no. 2 (May-August 1992): 143–46. Ortiz Cofer talks about her passion for poetry and her reason for writing narrative.

Some further readings on the immigration experience as viewed by Puerto Rican women writers include the following authors, who draw from their autobiographical memories related to growing up in New York City: Nicholasa Mohr, *Nilda* (1973), and Esmeralda Santiago, *When I Was Puerto Rican* (1993). In *Nilda*, a first-generation Puerto Rican adolescent girl growing up in New York in the 1940s provides a strong historical background to the formation of the Puerto Rican barrios during that decade. Ortiz Cofer's novel *The Line of the Sun* (1989) recreates a similar scenario updated to include the socioeconomic issues faced by the Puerto Rican communities in the 1970s.

15

Cristina Garcia's *Dreaming in Cuban*: The Contested Domains of Politics, Family, and History

Iraida H. López

CRISTINA GARCIA was born in Havana, Cuba, in 1958; in 1960, during the first major wave of Cuban immigration following the 1959 Cuban Revolution, she immigrated with her family to the United States. Garcia studied political science at Barnard College and international studies at Johns Hopkins University (M.A. 1981); she later worked as a reporter and correspondent for *Time* magazine. Frustrated, as she has claimed, "with the constraints of journalism," she began to work on the novel that became her first, *Dreaming in Cuban* (1992), an original and compelling work inspired by her Cuban heritage. *Dreaming in Cuban* has won critical and popular acclaim, including a nomination for a National Book Award. In a *New York Times* book review, Thulani Davis described it as "Fierce, visionary, and at the same time oddly beguiling and funny." A lyrical work that blends realism with dreamlike sequences, the story chronicles three generations of the del Pino family from the 1930s to the early 1980s. After publishing a nonfiction work in 1995 about Cuban automobiles, *Cars of Cuba*, Garcia published a second novel, *The Agüero Sisters*, in 1997, which is similar in theme to her first in that it too describes a Cuban family divided by personal and political passions.

ANALYSIS OF THEMES AND FORMS

Although the Cuban presence in the United States, particularly in New York and in the Florida cities of Tampa and Key West, dates back to the late nineteenth century, Cuban mass migration began in 1959, after the triumph of the Cuban revolution. This political event—the takeover of the government by Fidel Castro and socialist revolutionaries backed by a popular majority—drove nearly one million disaffected Cubans to abandon the island and led to the emergence of an ethnic community on the U.S. side of the Florida Straits. Although the resettlement meant economic prosperity for many, it brought a certain kind of hardship to most, as exiles came under a siege of politics. Often exile comes wrapped in a fiercely nationalist discourse that makes no concessions.

Almost 40 years after the initial exodus, the fiery, one-sided, public rhetoric has not changed much. Close observers of the Cuban ethnic enclave in Miami have attested to an unrelenting, uncompromising nationalism (Pérez, "Cubans in the United States"). Culturally, however, a noticeable evolution, best exemplified in literature and popular culture, has taken place with the coming of age of younger generations. The exile sensibility that marked the initial works of Cuban writers on American soil has been replaced with a hybrid identity that straddles two cultures. While the older exiled writers lived spiritually and emotionally on the island and wrote in Spanish, the younger generations have exhibited their biculturalism in standard English, often sprinkled with an array of Spanish words.

While it seems that the Cuban exile community required only one word for its definition, Cuban, the younger generation of writers is more aware of the intersection of nationalism and ethnicity with gender, sexuality, and race. Cuban American may be a sufficient designator for some, but others claim more than an ethnic identity. Fiction and nonfiction writing by Cuban Americans suggests that the construction of gender and sexual identities is as important an endeavor as the forging of an ethnic identity. For a sector of the Cuban-American community, this is a reflection of their postsecondary education in a given time and place (since the 1970s, in the United States).

With her choice of title and themes in Dreaming in Cuban (1992), Cristina Garcia claims a place within the politically charged field of Cuban-American studies. Politics play an important, albeit subdued, role in Dreaming in Cuban. The pervasiveness of politics and of the deep divisions it entails, along with an awareness of gender-related themes, is one of the noteworthy features of Garcia's autobiographical novel, a finalist for the 1992 National Book Award. Dreaming in Cuban concerns women's perspectives of historical events and the impact they have on an extended family. Although the writer is committed to the theme of politics, her novel offers guarded hope for building bridges across ideological divides.

By shifting the scene back and forth between Cuba and the United States, Garcia portrays the historically abysmal gap between Communists and anti-Communists through a cast of women characters who belong to three generations of the del Pino family. Although background information is provided by way of letters woven into the text, the narrative focuses on these women over an eight-year period starting in 1972. The novel narrates their trials and tribulations as they attempt to make sense of their lives on the island and in the Cuban diaspora, or mass exile. Celia, the island-based matriarch, is the glue that holds together, however tenuously, this divided and complicated family. With a flair for short-lived relationships, Felicia is assisted by Celia, her mother, in ministering to the needs of her three children. Lourdes, Felicia's sister, who left Cuba with her family, is incapable of coming to terms with the troubled relationship between her and Celia. The young Pilar, Lourdes' daughter, was separated from Celia at an early age, but she communicates with her grandmother in their dreams. Toward the end of the novel, at Pilar's urging, Pilar and Lourdes return briefly to Cuba for a family visit. While in Cuba, Lourdes manages to lure Ivanito, Felicia's son, into the Peruvian embassy where the Cubans who leave the country via the Cuban port of Mariel in 1980 have assembled. Celia, unable to bear the pain of a dissolved family (her husband, Jorge, and her children, Felicia and Javier, have died over the course of the story), commits suicide by drowning in the sea.

The events are narrated through the eyes of the women. Celia, Lourdes, Felicia, and Pilar are fully developed characters capable of both deceiving and being deceived. Unlike her kin, Celia stands out as an unwitting Ariadne-like figure for some of the other characters. The reader may find one of them more attractive, but each character has her own personality and her own reasons for praising or despising the revolution. Through her authentically expressed experiences and motivations, each character evaluates this historical event. By offering their colliding views, Garcia's novel presents a nuanced vision of Cuban reality. Some critics have been quick to notice this: "*Dreaming in Cuban*'s unique contribution lies in its opening up the ideological, literary, and political forum to reflect the complexity and diversity of perspectives articulated by three generations of Cubans" (Marrero 153).

Within the spectrum of perspectives provided by the characters, the reader comes face to face with the conflicting political issues on the island and in exile. This polarization confers a certain appeal to the search for spaces in between the extremes of political ideologies. The intent to complicate the political space mirrors the yearning of the writer, whose family split up after the revolution. Garcia remarked in an interview, "Half of my family came here, half stayed there, and most of them didn't speak to each other for twenty years. There was very little shading, very little room for gray or for interpretation" (López 607). Garcia's own experience, then, brings about the exploration of gray areas. Not surprisingly, Pilar, the writer's alter ego, is the character who, by dint of her hybrid identity, tries to bridge the divide.

The marked polarization among the characters does not always have to do with high policy—the most commonly accepted meaning of politics—and its play in the public arena. Garcia's characters and their struggles reflect the politics of a different, semiprivate domain: family alliances, both within and across generations. The expansive impulse that occurs in the strictly political dimension resonates here as well. The family's diverse conflicts and hierarchies are mediated by love and individual obsessions. That its conflicts cut across gender lines only adds to the complexity of *Dreaming in Cuban*. Family politics, in fact, stretch the historical framework, taking the reader back to the 1930s when Celia falls victim to the charms of Gustavo, a Spanish Don Juan.

The family's political polarization is embodied by Celia, who supports the revolution, and Lourdes, who resettles with her family in New York. The divide, however, is not only ideological; it includes a class dimension, for the Puente family, the owners of casinos and estates, is among the wealthiest on the island and accept Lourdes only reluctantly. Furthermore, individual responses to the unresolved emotional crisis between Celia, Jorge, and Lourdes crisscross the political and social chasm. Leaving behind the scene of her rape at the hands of government soldiers, Lourdes, a resolute and independent woman, is now the proud owner of the Yankee Doodle Bakery in Brooklyn. She is a fierce anti-Communist whose views, according to Pilar, "are strictly black-and-white" (26). Meanwhile Celia, of humble rural origins, has found a renewed sense of purpose within the revolution, especially after she is appointed a civilian judge.

Within these two poles, the extremes in the Cuban political continuum, other characters make their way, each contributing details that complicate the broader picture. Felicia is nudged to follow the revolutionary path but, caught in upheavals of her own and driven by spiritual restlessness, she feels alienated by the emptiness of belligerent slogans. Pilar, the aspiring artist, who rebels against her mother's politics, offers a counterweight to Lourdes' admiration for the American political and social system.

Family alliances do not fare any better. Bowing to the pronouncement that "families are essentially political" (86), the characters are forced to choose sides. In addition to political issues, the family is divided on personal issues. The distressing relationship between Lourdes and Celia originates in the lack of passion that Celia, infatuated with Gustavo, brings to her marriage with Jorge del Pino. Because of Celia's unremitting commitment to the memory of her former lover, Jorge and his family drive her insane. Celia gives birth to Lourdes and, shortly afterward, is confined to a mental institution. Lourdes is never able to forgive her mother for abandoning her. While pregnant, Celia dreams about escaping to Spain, but only if she has a son. If she has a girl, she will stay and "train her to read the columns of blood and numbers in men's eyes, to understand the morphology of survival" (42). However, Celia later develops a close bond with her youngest and most vulnerable child, Javier. This alliance is reproduced in Felicia's own family with the disturbing relationship between her and her son, Ivanito, and between her twin daughters and Hugo, their father. Yet another alliance is forged between Pilar and her father until she discovers that he is unfaithful to Lourdes. Although the characters maintain strong, if selective, attachments with one another, no real family nucleus exists, and the extended family becomes a site of interrogation for multiple layers of tension.

Divergent versions of official history result in yet another area of contention. Historical events are salient causes of dislocation and fragmentation, and the women characters evaluate these events harshly and try to settle scores. One way they do this is to express outright resentment toward the selection process by which some events become standard history and others are bypassed. Some of the younger characters bitterly denounce historical records that exclude what is meaningful to marginal groups, such as women and blacks. Instead of "one damn battle after another" (28), the rebellious Pilar would "record other things. Like the time there was a freak hailstorm in the Congo and the women took it as a sign that they should rule. Or the life stories of prostitutes in Bombay. Why don't I know anything about them? Who chooses what we should know or what's important?" (28).

The partiality of historical accounts is another source of anger. Felicia's friend Herminia, who is black and the daughter of a *babalao* (a high priest of Santería, a religion practiced in Cuba), finds fault with the conventional depiction of the 1912 armed uprising in Cuba staged by the Movimiento de los Independientes de Color which pitted blacks against whites: "The war that killed my grandfather and great-uncles and thousands of other blacks is only a footnote in our history books. Why, then, should I trust anything I read?" (185). In this passage, Pilar and Herminia clearly articulate what Garcia had in mind while she was writing *Dreaming in Cuban*: "Traditional history, the way it has been written, interpreted and recorded, obviates women and the evolution of home, family and society, and basically becomes a recording of battles and wars and dubious accomplishments of men. You learn where politics really lie at home" (López 107).

In order to level the power relations between ordinary women and male historical figures, Fidel Castro is placed in circumstances far removed from the usual military settings. In a telling episode, Felicia must enroll in a rehabilitation program in the mountains that presumably will correct her "antisocial behavior." There she fantasizes about a sexual encounter with *el Líder* Fidel Castro. In this scene, the larger-than-life public figure of Castro is possibly disarmed and undressed and made to perform sexually in a private act. He is placed in a different battlefield, one in which he is called upon to give sexual pleasure. It is Felicia who, through her imagination, assumes control of the situation. Simultaneously, she avoids the trap of idolizing Castro (as Celia does) and of demonizing him (as Lourdes does).

Similarly, to counteract the powerful political forces that dwarf meaningful individual and family events, Pilar takes it upon herself to write a personal diary. The reader does not have access to this diary, which Pilar is forced to hide from her mother, Lourdes. However, the letters Celia writes the eleventh of every month to the Spanish businessman who seduced and abandoned her are a vehicle through which personal and family events get recorded. They are the most lyrical writings in the book. These letters, never mailed, covering a period of 25 years, are Celia's legacy to Pilar, who then becomes the repository of the family history in exile. The written testimony, together with the magic realist oral exchanges sustained by the characters despite the distance and the divide, will preserve the family's history, even if in exile. Indeed, the last letter Celia writes, dated January 11, 1959, 10 days into the revolution, on the day of Pilar's birth, puts closure to the monthly reporting: "I will no longer write to you, *mi amor*. She [Pilar] will remember everything" (245). The text, then, underscores the strategic significance of memory and mnemonic selection in the transmission of legacies and the construction of identities. As Celia writes in one of her letters, "Memory is a skilled seducer" (97). Thus, *Dreaming in Cuban* echoes the characters' concerns and offers, through the microcosm of the del Pino family, its own rewriting of the effects of recent historical events, along with conflicting interpretations.

The structure of the novel reinforces the decentralizing spirit that animates the text. Narrative techniques are deployed parallel to the themes to show the range of perceptions and interpretations constructed by these women about the forces—historical, political, patriarchal, cultural, and personal—that shape their lives. First and third-person narratives alternate throughout the novel. Since first-person narratives give an illusion of autonomy, they diminish the power of the omniscient narrator who seems to always "intrude" into the characters' thoughts. The first-person narrative are centered on Pilar, Luz (one of Felicia's twin daughters), Ivanito, Herminia, and Celia (through her letters). Even in the more frequent third-person sections, however, the narrator stays close to the characters' field of view. Thus, the narrator is kept busy moving back and forth among the characters. For example, in the chapter titled "The Fire Between Them," the focus shifts from Felicia to Ivanito and then to Celia.

The various chapters encompass multiple points of view which offer the reader different interpretations of the same incident (the wandering away of Pilar at the airport viewed through the eyes of both Pilar and Lourdes), the same object (the artistic rendition of the Statue of Liberty depicted through Pilar and Lourdes), and even the same character (the contrasting opinions about Hugo Villaverde, Felicia's first husband).

Because the novel presents a variety of discourses, Mikhail Bakhtin's insights on dialogism are particularly relevant to *Dreaming in Cuban*. In this literary genre, multiple and contradictory languages confront one another and help delineate their boundaries. Even the plot of the novel, in Bakhtin's words, "is subordinated to the task of coordinating and exposing languages to each other" (365). This thesis is clearly demonstrated in Garcia's novel. Several passages illustrate the "alienness" or "foreignness" of another person's language as perceived by a speaker of the same national language. In some cases, the difference results from the ideological clash between the characters. For instance, Lourdes utterly fails when, back in Santa Teresa del Mar, she attempts to convert passersby to a capitalist way of life by pointing out how much better American cars are than Soviet ones.

Pilar concludes that the language Lourdes speaks "is lost to them. It's another idiom entirely" (221). Similarly, Lourdes tries to recruit Ivanito's help for the bakeries she dreams of opening from coast to coast, but she fails to hear what he has to say: "I tell her I want to be a translator for world leaders, that I speak good Russian, but I don't think she hears me. Instead, Tía looks right through me and describes a Christmas show at Rockefeller Center with an indoor parade of camels" (230). In other cases, the foreignness is brought about not by political duality, but by the inability of personal encounters to break down barriers and transcend the isolation of the characters. This break in communication occurs even between Felicia and her beloved Ivanito: "What is he saying? Each word is a code she must decipher, a foreign language, a streak of gunshot" (81).

Even as the doomed characters sometimes speak past rather than with each other, the text constitutes the space where they "meet" and where the reader engages in communication. The reader has full access to the gamut of discourses and strategies employed to decentralize the narrative and offer alternative points of view. This narrative scheme by itself does not produce a happy ending, as confirmed by the adverse fate of the novel's characters. At another level, however, it offers the distinct possibility of dreaming, in Cuban as in any dialect, of the fragile coexistence of ideologies, languages, and discourses in a single space. This potential represents an innovative and inspiring approach within the emerging field of Cuban-American fiction.

TEACHING THE WORK

Background Information

Due to its recent publication, there is little written criticism of *Dreaming in Cuban*. See Mary S. Vázquez, "Cuba as Text and Context in Cristina Garcia's *Dreaming in Cuban*," which examines the unifying role of Cuba as metaphor for the novel's estranged characters. For an analysis of the meaning of Santería in three Cuban-American works, including *Dreaming in Cuban*, see María Teresa Marrero, "Historical and Literary *Santería*: Unveiling Gender and Identity in U.S. Cuban Literature." One article that dwells on the expression of sexuality as a tool for social and cultural critique in several works written by Latinas, including *Dreaming in Cuban*, is Margarite Fernández Olmos, "Sexual Politics and the Latina Writer." Among the best book reviews are those by Thulani Davis, "Fidel Came Between Them," and Suzanne Ruta, "Hyphenated Americans," *Women's Review of Books* 9, no. 9 (June 1992): 11–12.

For an interview with the writer, see Iraida H. López, " 'And There Is Only My Imagination Where Our History Should Be': An Interview with Cristina Garcia." See also Marifeli Pérez-Stable, "Culture Maker: Cristina Garcia. Marifeli Pérez-Stable Interviews the Author of *Dreaming in Cuban*," *culturefront* 2, no. 1 (1993): 9–11; and Allan Vorda, "A Fish Swims in My Lung: An Interview with Cristina Garcia," *Face to Face: Interviews with Contemporary Novelists*, ed. Allan Vorda (Houston: Rice University Press, 1993): 63–76.

Other Approaches

This chapter stresses broad political issues in the novel through an examination of politics, family, and history, and literary strategies. The text lends itself to other readings.

1. Direct students to identify and discuss the use of magic realism in the book. Compare this work and the work of other Latin American writers associated with this technique, such as Isabel Allende and Gabriel Garcia Márquez. Magic realism is one of the reasons why Garcia's work has been seen as "the latest sign that American literature has its own hybrid offspring of the Latin American school" (Davis). By its mix of real and unreal elements in a straightforward manner, this technique blurs the boundaries between the real and the magic.

2. Given the relevance of cultural markers in ethnic literature, analyze the Cuban syncretic religion Santería as reflected in *Dreaming in Cuban*. Marrero examines the role of Santería, in her essay, as a sign of cultural retention in the development of a Cuban-American cultural identity.

3. Compare the portrayal of the family unit in various Latino/a works.

Other autobiographical narratives that explore this theme are *The House on Mango Street* (1984) by Sandra Cisneros, *Silent Dancing. A Partial Remembrance of a Puerto Rican Childhood* (1990) by Judith Ortiz Cofer, *Our House in the Last World* (1983) by Oscar Hijuelos, *Nilda* (1973) by Nicholasa Mohr, and *Crazy Love* (1989) by Elías Miguel Muñoz. Have students discuss the role played within the family of individuals, usually young, who mediate between the culture of the immigrant group and the dominant Anglo culture. Among works that deal with this topic are *How the Garcia Girls Lost Their Accents* (1991) by Julia Alvarez and *Botánica* (1990) by Dolores Prida.

4. Review the literature available on Cuban-American fiction and place *Dreaming in Cuban* in this context. Articles by Eliana Rivero examine the evolution from Cuban to Cuban-American identity through the study of literature, especially poetry, taking into account generational, gender, and political perspectives. *Life on the Hyphen: The Cuban-American Way* (1994) by Gustavo Pérez Firmat incorporates popular music and television programs into the study of Cuban-American expressions. In addition, the following anthologies of Cuban-American literature may be consulted: Carolina Hospital, ed., *Cuban-American Writers. Los Atrevidos* (1988) and Virgil Suárez and Delia Poey, eds., *Little Havana Blues. A Cuban-American Literature Anthology* (1996). Suárez and Poey's anthology includes a short story by Cristina Garcia.

5. *Dreaming in Cuban* may serve as a point of departure for a rich discussion on the implications of colliding visions and perceptions. Locate and compare those episodes in the novel where differing points of view are reflected. Find contrasting views of the Cuban revolution in the eyes of the characters, and find other instances that give rise to different interpretations. One example is Pilar's description of her painting of the Statue of Liberty (141) versus Lourdes' interpretation (171): Lourdes sees the bugs surrounding the symbol of liberty, but Pilar sees thorns that look like barbed wire. Explain the different interpretations. As a related activity, compare several versions of another story to determine commonality and difference. Additional suggestions for similar tasks that help students deal with other people's beliefs, views, perceptions, and interpretations are included in John Chafee, *Thinking Critically*, 3d ed. (Boston: Houghton Mifflin, 1991).

CRITICISM AND RELATED WORKS

Bakhtin, M. M. *The Dialogic Imagination: Four Essays*, trans. Caryl Emerson, ed. Michael Holquist. Austin: University of Texas Press, 1981.

Davis, Thulani. "Fidel Came Between Them." *New York Times Book Review* 97 (17 May 1992): 14.

Fernández Olmos, Margarite. "Sexual Politics and the Latina Writer." *Bendíceme,*

América. Latino Writers of the United States, ed. Harold Augenbraum, Terry Quinn, and Ilan Stavans. New York: Mercantile Library, 1993, 44–52.

García, Cristina. *Dreaming in Cuban*. New York: Alfred A. Knopf, 1992.

Hospital, Carolina, ed. *Cuban American Writers: Los Atrevidos*. Princeton, N.J.: Ediciones Ellas/Linden Lane Press, 1988.

López, Iraida H. " ' . . . And There Is Only My Imagination Where Our History Should Be': An Interview with Cristina Garcia." *Michigan Quarterly Review* 33, no. 3 (1994): 605–17. Reprinted in *Bridges to Cuba/Puentes a Cuba*, ed. Ruth Behar. Ann Arbor: University of Michigan Press, 1995, 102–14.

Luis, William. "Reading the Master Codes of Cuban Culture in Cristina Garcia's *Dreaming in Cuban*." *Cuban Studies/Estudios Cubanos* 26 (1996): 201–23. Luis includes these ideas in his study *Dance Between Two Cultures: Latino Caribbean Literature Written in the United States*. Nashville, Tenn.: Vanderbilt University Press, 1997.

Marrero, María Teresa. "Historical and Literary *Santería*: Unveiling Gender and Identity in U.S. Cuban Literature." In *Tropicalizations. Transcultural Representations of Latinidad*, ed. Frances R. Aparicio and Susana Chávez-Silverman. Hanover, N.H.: University Press of New England, 1997, 139–59.

Pérez, Lisandro. "Cubans in the United States: The Paradoxes of Exile Culture." *culturefront* 2, no. 1 (1993): 12–16.

Pérez Firmat, Gustavo. *Life on the Hyphen. The Cuban-American Way*. Austin: University of Texas Press, 1994.

Rivero, Eliana. "From Immigrants to Ethnics: Cuban American Women Writers in the U.S." In *Breaking Boundaries: Latina Writing and Critical Readings*, ed. Asunción Horno-Delgado et al. Amherst: University of Massachusetts Press, 1989, 189–200.

———. "Hispanic Literature in the United States: Self-Image and Conflict." *Revista Chicano-Riqueña* 13, no. 3–4 (1985): 173–92.

———. "(Re) Writing Sugarcane Memories: Cuban Americans and Literature." In *Paradise Lost or Gained?: The Literature of Hispanic Exile*, ed. Fernando Alegría and Jorge Rufinelli. Houston: Arte Público Press, 1991, 164–82.

Said, Edward. "Reflections on Exile. In *Out There: Marginalization and Contemporary Cultures*, ed. Russell Ferguson, Martha Gever, Trinh T. Minh-ha, and Cornel West. New York: Museum of Contemporary Arts/MIT Press, 1990, 357–66.

Sommer, Doris. "Rigoberta's Secrets." *Latin American Perspectives* 18, no. 3 (1991): 32–50.

Suárez, Virgil, and Delia Poey, eds. *Little Havana Blues: A Cuban-American Literature Anthology*. Houston: Arte Público Press, 1996.

Vázquez, Mary S. "Cuba as Text and Context in Cristina Garcia's *Dreaming in Cuban*." *Bilingual Review/Revista Bilingüe* 20, no. 1 (1995): 22–27.

16

Junot Díaz's *Drown*: Revisiting "Those Mean Streets"

Lizabeth Paravisini-Gebert

JUNOT DÍAZ was born in 1968 in a poor section of the city of Santo Domingo, the capital of the Dominican Republic, and moved to the United States as a child of seven. In the United States Díaz's family moved to a Latino neighborhood in New Jersey where he attended Kean College in Union before transferring to Rutgers University in New Brunswick. Rutgers' offerings in Latino and African-American history and literature opened new possibilities for creativity and political awareness, and Díaz came "to see himself—and assert himself—as a Dominican, an American, and a writer."[1] After his graduation from Rutgers, Díaz enrolled in the graduate writing program at Cornell University, from which he received a master's degree in Fine Arts. In 1996 he published a collection of short stories, *Drown*, which has made him one of the most promising members of the younger generation of Latino authors.

ANALYSIS OF THEMES AND FORMS

Since the publication in 1996 of his first collection of short stories, *Drown*, Dominican-born author Junot Díaz has been acclaimed by critics as "one of the most original, vibrant and engrossing voices to come along in many years."[2] Chosen by *Newsweek* as one of their "new faces of '96"— "A Deserving Dark Horse"—the young writer quickly became "the most highly trumpeted talent of the season."[3]

Díaz's memories of his home island, of both urban and rural spaces, are faint, "like the fixed image of photographs . . . [t]here is a snapshot of his childhood house, or a kung fu movie he once saw dubbed in Spanish, or a visit to Haiti,"[4] but they reverberate in his autobiographical stories as sparse but eloquent elements of a landscape of memory and experience.

Díaz's narrative space, however, is dominated not by nostalgic recreations of idealized childhood landscapes, but by the bleak, barren, and decayed margins of New Jersey's inner cities. Díaz, whom critics have praised for his acute powers of observation, has a sharp eye for the social and human blight that has resulted from urban neglect. The trajectory of his characters' lives mirrors Díaz's own observations and experiences in this setting. The New Jersey he writes about, as he told one interviewer, "is the one he knows: a place of blue-collar towns of Latino immigrants, of tostones (mashed fried plantains) and malls and roads where 'beer bottles grow out of the weeds like squashes.' "[5] His own family was not immune to the destructive aspects of this new environment—his father, somewhat of a womanizer, abandoned the family for another woman when Díaz was an adolescent, and his mother, with her insufficient knowledge of English, could find only substandard employment.

Díaz learned early to escape his unpromising circumstances through writing. He began to write in earnest as a high school sophomore when his older brother, Rafael, was diagnosed with leukemia and was hospitalized. Díaz "spent his days scribbling long letters to Rafa."[6] He found another avenue of escape through education by attending Kean College and later transferring to Rutgers University in New Brunswick. After graduation from Rutgers, Díaz enrolled in the graduate writing program at Cornell University.

The marketing of Díaz's stories reads like a cautionary tale about the commodification of Latino literature, its literary merit notwithstanding. He erupted into the public notice quite dramatically with a blitz of publicity following the announcement of his having received "gobs of money" for his first collection of short stories and a novel he had not yet started. The story of the feeding frenzy that led to his receiving "six figures" from Riverhead Books has the fascination of the proverbial train wreck. If the tale of his discovery by Rosenthal recalls that of Lana Turner's own discovery at Schwab's Drugstore in its serendipity and improbability, that of the reading at the KGB Bar in the East Village to an audience packed with talent scouts arranged by Rosenthal, and the subsequent summoning of eight publishing houses to wrestle for the rights to publish the book, speak of the fury to bring selected Latino voices to a market avid for marketable minority voices. The publication of his short stories in venues as prestigious as the *New Yorker* and the *Paris Review* soon attracted even more notice, placing Díaz in an almost untenable situation of having to meet the highest and most overblown expectations. His inclusion in two consecutive collections of *The Best American Short Stories* ("Ysrael" in 1996 and "Fiesta, 1980" in 1997) attests to the profound impact he has made on the American literary scene since the publication of *Drown*.

Like Toni Morrison, whose novels chronicle the black American experience, focusing on how characters struggle to find themselves and assert their cultural identity against an unjust society, Díaz is interested in narrating the great human loss of marginalization and closed options. Unlike Morrison, however, whose use of fantasy and highly poetic style lifts her characters toward the symbolic and mythic, Díaz is more concerned with depicting the petty humiliations and everyday deprivations of inner-city life. He is closer in outlook and style to two writers to whom he is frequently compared: Puerto Rican author Piri Thomas and Langston Hughes, both of whom are known for their eloquent portrayal of ghetto youth struggling against the conditions of life for urban black and Hispanic youth.

Thomas' *Down These Mean Streets* (1967), in particular, comes to mind when linking *Drown* to a literary tradition. In many ways *Drown* is a sort of throwback to the Nuyorican literature of the 1950s and 1960s. Thomas' classic of Latino anguish and despair was the first in a tradition of heart-wrenching memoirs depicting the destruction of the Puerto Rican soul in the American ghetto. The text dissected in harsh detail the drug-peddling culture, the devastation caused by heroin addiction, the brutality of prison life, the loss of the saving power of faith and family, and the constant struggle against the diminishing value of life that were part of the 1960s as lived by the young Puerto Rican community of Spanish Harlem. Díaz's *Drown*, though removed in time and space from Thomas' barrio, nonetheless revisits many of its themes and motifs, updating for a new audience, in a trimmed-down, more detached style, the vicissitudes of young immigrant life in the inner city. *Drown* chronicles the human cost of an immigrant people's displacement in an environment of cultural and racial discrimination and economic exploitation.

The trait that separates Díaz's work from this earlier tradition is the absence of a clear political intention, which is most obvious in the passionate, denunciatory style of Piri Thomas' work as compared to Diáz's cool, detached, minimalist prose. If *Down These Mean Streets* was a book of searing accusation against those forces in American society that condemned some ethnic minorities to alienation, discrimination, and disillusionment, it was also a book that assumed that these conditions could be altered through political action and consciousness-raising. There is no such faith in concerted community action in *Drown*; there is, as a matter of fact, little semblance of a community—in the sense of groups living lives of multileveled communication with each other. There are friends and neighbors who come across each other from time to time in these tales, but they merge and separate, like the proverbial ships that pass in the night, leaving little in their wake. James Woods, in his review for the *New Republic*, accurately points to the stories "skillfully" catching Díaz's characters "in their own glue of confusion, unable or unwilling to change anything."[7]

Drown opens with an epigraph from Cuban writer Gustavo Pérez Firmat—"The fact that I am writing to you in English already falsifies what I wanted to tell you"—a poignant statement affirming the centrality of language to a writer's understanding and articulation of experience. The epigraph, which bemoans Pérez Firmat's sense of loss of his "natural" [Spanish] language, announces Díaz's subject to be that of explaining that he does not "belong to English though I belong nowhere else." Its use in *Drown* sets up a curious paradox for Díaz's work, which does not dwell with particular pathos on his various immigrant characters' yearning for a lost home or language or on their removal from their place of origin.

In fact, Spanish has little impact on the stories in *Drown*; the texts may be peppered with unexplained and untranslated Spanish words, many of which are misspelled or are used in grammatically incorrect variations. They are not brought into the text to enrich the English language with new expressive possibilities, but as a re-creation of the easy slang of the minority community about which he writes.[8] This community's alienation and exile come from its marginalization from mainstream, middle-class American society, from a disempowerment that is endemic to national and immigrant minorities in the United States, and does not necessarily stem from a forced disconnection from the native language and environment. The characters in *Drown* belong quite comfortably in an English vernacular wrought out of the Latino community's experiences in the three decades that have elapsed since Thomas' work was initially published.

The element that sets *Drown* apart from other texts about immigrant life in the American inner city is a pointed and succinct, almost minimalist, style that is purged of any tendency to rhetorical flights of fancy, despite occasional lapses into questionable metaphors in describing the gritty landscape in which the various characters wait out their lives. On the whole, however, reviewers and readers agree that the collection's true originality lies in having created "a non-literary vernacular, compounded of African American slang, loosened Spanish and standard American storytelling" for his "cool and grimy" portrayals of contemporary urban America.[9]

In discussions of Díaz's spare language and style in *Drown*, much attention has been given to the impact of the lack of quotation marks or italics to identify dialogue or his use of four-letter words as part of his appeal "as an authentic voice of his community."[10] There is in this merging of voices, in this lack of distinction between narration and dialogue in Díaz's spare sentences, a brittleness that mirrors the bleakness and misery of the lives portrayed. Díaz claims to write "for the people he grew up with," in the language of immigrant adolescents with no desire to learn from or about the world. He claims for his book an authenticity of observation untainted by a desire to explain his world to outsiders: "I took extreme pains for my book to not be a native informant. Not: 'This is Dominican food. This is a Spanish word.' I trust my readers, even non-Spanish ones."[11] The reader unfamiliar with the milieu depicted in *Drown* must enter this world without a guide since neither narrator nor characters will explain or justify themselves.

There is in this first collection of stories, as there is in every first work, the stamp of a craft in the making, which, in the case of *Drown*, surfaces as the still-too-clear mark of professional writing programs like the one Díaz attended at Cornell. We can glimpse it in the only partly successful experiment with the imperative voice in "How to Date . . ." in a distrust of third-person narrative even when, as is "Edison, New Jersey," it could serve the narrative better; and in the too-faithful adherence to closely examined models. The best of these stories, nonetheless, surmount what James Wood has described as "the contemporary idea of the short story, as processed by writing programs, that it must present itself as a victim of its own confusion, as a bewilderment, a fragment,"[12] and point to Díaz's exceptional promise as a writer.

All of the stories in *Drown*, with the exception of "No Face," are narrated in the first person, which attests to their autobiographical nature. *Drown*, although not autobiography per se, is clearly an autobiographical book; the stories have their basis in Díaz's own experiences growing up in the Dominican Republic and, after age seven, in a tough Latino neighborhood in Perth Amboy. Five of the stories in *Drown* share the same narrator, the author's alter ego, Ramón de las Casas, known as Yunior, a young boy whose narratives of a somewhat blighted Dominican childhood become the tales of a rather traumatized inner-city New Jersey adolescent. In the New Jersey–based stories, the narrators, all of whom may or may not be Yunior, share Yunior's sensibility: the suspicious watchfulness and defensive stance, the blighted relationship with the father figure, and the uneasiness in relationships with women, which move from tenderness to violence.

Thematically, the stories in *Drown* center on the deprivation and tedium of life in the Dominican countryside and New Jersey: young children torture a deformed child in "Ysrael"; petty drug dealers languidly look for clients seeking to score in "Aurora"; days are spent searching for bargains in the mall in "Drown"; children vomit in cars while traveling to the Bronx to visit relatives in "Fiesta, 1980." Herein lies the strength—and occasionally the limitations—of these tales.

In "Ysrael," the story that opens the book, Yunior and his brother Rafa, exiled by their mother to the Dominican countryside during their summer vacation, look at the verdant landscape surrounding them, "at the mists that gathered like water, at the brucal trees that blazed like fires on the mountains," and declare it to be "shit"—"worse than shit."[13] This blank assertion sets the tone for the story of their dogged pursuit of a young deformed boy whose mask they want to remove to see the extent of his deformity. This, one of the most successful tales in the collection, works around two sets of failed connections—Yunior and Rafa/Yunior and Ysrael—and two failed quests—Rafa's search for sexual fulfillment and the search for the meaning behind Ysrael's horrible mutilation. Both quests are empty from the start—"worse than shit." Their pursuit of Ysrael—cruel and meaningless to begin with—is eroticized by its juxtaposition against Rafa's pursuit of girls on which to exercise his manhood; cruelty to the deformed Ysrael is another way to prove his incipient manhood.

Erotic themes dominate "Ysrael" and "No Face," the second story in the collection, which centers on the country boy disfigured by a hog, providing an interesting angle from which to read both stories in conjunction. Rafa's pursuit of the disfigured, tormented boy mirrors his pursuit of sexual pleasure from naïve young country girls. Yunior's reluctance to join in both pursuits leaves him open to charges of being a *pato*, a homosexual—just as Ysrael's mutilation is linked to images of castration. Ysrael's efforts to overcome the memory of the attack that led to his disfiguration—which focus on his efforts to act "like a man"—are coupled to a second attack by boys threatening to "make him a girl." The interweavings of multiple erotic strands in the two stories create a series of motifs which Díaz returns to in all the stories narrated by Yunior; they pair Yunior and Ysrael as mirror images of a sort, as Ysrael carries in the flesh the emotional mutilations Yunior has suffered during his fatherless childhood, which, although not visible to the eyes, remain just as profound. They prepare the ground for the themes Díaz will pursue in the stories centered on his womanizing, all-too-manly father: "Fiesta, 1980," "Aguantando," and "Negocios."

Similar themes are skillfully woven into "Fiesta, 1980," where Yunior returns to narrate another tale of sexual pursuit and betrayal. The tale, centered on Yunior's inability to travel in the family car without throwing up, links the vomiting to the bitter knowledge of his father's unfaithfulness with a Puerto Rican woman. Yunior, by now partly Americanized, sneers at his relatives' apartment in the Bronx as "furnished in Contemporary Dominica Tacky." But the tale, despite rueful details that hint at his assimilation, is not about the pains of immigration, but about the various ways in which Rafa is becoming like his father—toward the relentless pursuit of women and sex—while Yunior's identification with and sympathy for his mother leave him open to accusations of being a *pato*. Food deprivation—coupled here with Yunior's penchant for vomiting when not deprived—is mirrored in the text by the many secrets, the many silences Yunior must keep, and which threaten to burst out, destroying the false harmony of the family, just as his vomiting destroys their forced rapport as they travel together in the car.

Of the stories centered around Yunior's ambivalent yearning for a true father figure, "Aguantando" is the least successful. At most it is a well-written autobiographical piece that lacks the tension and nuanced insight evident in "Ysrael," "No Face," and "Negocios." "Negocios" offers a beautifully rendered portrait, deeply colored with poignant detail, of Yunior's father—a hard-working, flawed man, tyrannical and self-centered, weak and negligent of his family. The story also works well as a dual portrait in its finely etched rendition of Yunior's own anger, yearning, and ultimately love. This is the only story in the collection in which the immigrant experience takes center stage. Díaz depicts, with "calibrated restraint" (according to Gates), the father's dependence on his native language for strength and complexity of expression (and his concomitant loss when living in the English-speaking United States) and the cost to his son Yunior of his own half-assimilation. If Spanish and the possibility of a return to the Dominican Republic can offer refuge to his father, Yunior is fated to remain behind, with English and New Jersey looming as "the language and landscape of emotional deprivation." These themes are framed, quite successfully, by two scenes of abandonment: that of the father's leaving the family for the United States and that of his leaving his mistress many years later to return to the Dominican Republic. They are connected by the voice of Yunior, as he searches for a true picture of his father through which he can resolve the many ambivalences of their relationship, and by a return to the theme of betrayal—so skillfully used in "Fiesta, 1980"—where he must revisit his father's mistress' house to gather the last bits of information necessary to complete his portrait. Although the story follows, in its details of the father's life, a well-trodden path, it is saved from cliché and repetition by Díaz's tightly controlled, delicate touch.

The "New Jersey stories"—"Aurora," "Drown," "Boyfriend," "Edison, New Jersey," and "How to Date a Browngirl"—can be read as variations on the theme of masking and unmasking offered first in "Ysrael" and then developed in "No Face." Whether they have an older Yunior as a narrator, or not, they share a quality of stasis that stems from the character's paralysis of affect; damaged and under siege, they seek security in poses, in cordoning off their inner lives, in blankness. The narrative often emphasizes the masks these characters must assume and maintain, to the point that maintaining the mask assumes the centrality of life and experience—a protection against life and living.

In perhaps the best in this group, "Drown," the narrator, seduced by a male friend as they watch a porn video, seems intent on avoiding the friend when he returns from college on his summer holiday. The narrative never delves into the crisis or the loss of friendship it implies, but rather depends for its effect on the reader's willingness to read glimpses of real emotion behind the mask of coolness. These glimpses come, as they often do in Díaz's stories, through skillfully placed pairings. In the case of "Drown," the pain of loss is conveyed through both the recollections of the friendship between the two young men offered by the narrator and through the seemingly unrelated descriptions of the mother's yearning for the father who has left her despite knowing the relationship could bring her nothing but pain. Both tales, etched with betrayal, lure the narrator and his mother nonetheless with recollections of the true feeling that had existed between the two "couples" before betrayal wrenched them apart. Díaz uses video watching to good effect by pairing two scenes of video screenings—one leading to Beto's seduction of the narrator as they watch a porno film, the other an attempt at catharsis as the narrator and his mother seek solace for the anger of betrayal that consumes them while watching a dubbed version of the film *Bonny and Clyde*.

Díaz, in stories of emotional emptiness such as "Boyfriend," manages to convey a blankness of possibilities, a stunting of affect, that is not necessarily linked to the plight of immigration but to the loss of inner life—of characters who cannot bring themselves to shed the mask of detachment and risk further pain. The pain itself is often trivialized in these stories, as if the characters had mistaken frivolous emotion for the deepest-held passion, like the lovelorn dope smoker in "Boyfriend," who idles his time wallowing in his pain and eavesdropping on the beautiful and heartbroken neighbor downstairs but cannot reach out to her in companionship or sympathy. Like the narrators of "How to Date a Browngirl, Blackgirl, Whitegirl, or Halfie" and "Edison, New Jersey," the narrator of "Boyfriend" cannot "grow" in the story, cannot move beyond his stasis, because he is trapped in the slang of "coolness," devoid of the emotional and linguistic range through which to produce and convey emotion. Caught in their protective psychological masks, they remain imprisoned, "drowned." Even Díaz's most consistent attempt at portraying love and connection, "Aurora," the story of a small-town drug dealer whose passion for an elusive young addict deteriorates into violence, works only partially. It is marred by repetitive imagery and somewhat stultifying crudeness.

When the elements that inform Díaz's style—the bleak transparency of language, the delicate handling of detail, the stinging acuteness of a seemingly unimportant detail, the quiet pathos of lives reduced to bleak everydayness, the hint of anger, the intimation of complexity of emotion—come together almost seamlessly, as they do in "Edison, New Jersey," "Drown," "Negocios," and "Fiesta, 1980," the collection justifies the unprecedented hoopla that accompanied its publication. In Díaz, the Latino literary world has a burgeoning talent.

TEACHING THE WORK

1. In a number of interviews following his discovery as a writer, Díaz has claimed his public persona as that of a cool, down-home sort of guy whose themes and language span social classes and linguistic registers, a New York–New Jersey based Latino voice whose work is nurtured by a close connection to the working-class people to whom he belongs. In "Making It Work: More Orchard Beach Than Elaine's," an interview with Somini Sengupta of the *New York Times*, Díaz speaks of his "living on pennies, say, checking out a free jam session at Orchard Beach, being broke like his friends, as a "nourishing" existence which he has brought into his stories.[14] Direct students to identify specific examples of the use of language in the works that reflect this attitude. Discuss their significance.

2. Another important consideration in any discussion of *Drown* is that of genre. Although the texts collected in *Drown* belong to the genre of the short story, they do not fit traditional definitions of that genre. Close readings of these stories in the light of genre theory can yield interesting insights into the changing nature of literary genres. Analyze the texts in *Drown* as examples of current American conceptions of the short story and examine how Díaz's works link and differ from the writing traditions of the Dominican Republic and American ethnic literature. Good working definitions of the genre can be found in the many available dictionaries of literary terms and literary analysis guides.

3. Examine the many links between the stories narrated by the same character (Yunior) and their significance: the father-son/mother-son relationships and how they are used in the various texts to articulate the narrator's ambivalence about migration and cultural loss. Discuss the various dualities or pairings (Yunior/Rafa, Yunior/Israel, Yunior/Beto) through which Díaz seeks to give shape to various possibilities open to the narrator or to project emotional and psychological aspects of the narrator's dilemma: the intergenerational conflicts that Díaz uses to illustrate the difference between his narrator's response to migration and his parents.

4. Trace the impact of this intergenerational separation by exploring

the links between language and alienation in the stories. This exploration can follow two distinct paths: the loss of Spanish, thematically as well as technically, and Díaz's minimalist style. Both of these accentuate his character's deeply set alienation and hopelessness. Relate the text's numerous allusions to notions of manhood and sexuality to gender and sexual identities as defined by ethnicity.

NOTES

1. Barbara Stewart, "In Person: Outsider with a Voice." *New York Times* (8 December 1996): 13NJ.
2. Roberto Santiago, review of *Drown*, by Junot Díaz, *American Visions* 11, no. 5 (October–November 1996): 28.
3. Adam Mazmanian, "Best American Short Stories." Review. *Library Journal* 121 (1 October 1996): 129. See also "New Faces of 1996." *Newsweek* (15 January 1996): 63.
4. Somini Sengupta, "Making It Work: More Orchard Beach Than Elaine's." *New York Times*, 15 September 1996, 13:3.
5. Stewart, 13NJ.
6. Sengupta, "Making It Work," 13:3.
7. James Wood, review of *Drown*, by Junot Díaz, *New Republic*, 16 December 1996, 39.
8. Subsequent printings of *Drown* have corrected some of these spelling and grammar problems, but their appearance and, in some cases, reappearance in the corrected version points to a loss of connection to their original place and meaning.
9. Wood, review, 39.
10. David Stanton, "Junot Díaz: On Home Ground." *Poets & Writers* 26, no. 4 (1998): 26–37.
11. Sengupta, "Making It Work," 13:3.
12. Wood, review, 39.
13. Junot Díaz, *Drown* (New York: Riverhead Books, 1996). All subsequent references will be to this edition and will appear in parenthesis in the text.
14. Sengupta, "Making It Work," 13:3. Díaz has spoken repeatedly in interviews of the burden placed on him by his newly found fame. Speaking to David Stanton, in an interview for *Poets & Writers*, he bemoaned the trials of instant celebrity as having the negative effects of distancing him from the urban streets that inspired his stories.

SUGGESTIONS FOR FURTHER READING

Interviews and Criticism

Given the short time that has elapsed since the publication of *Drown*, little background information is available on the work and its author. Most of the available material comes from interviews given by Díaz in connection to the publication and publicizing of the book. Alexandria Lange's "Speaking Latin" can be found in *New York* magazine (29:36, 16 September 1996: 40). Somini Sengupta's "Making It Work: More Orchard Beach Than Elaine's" appeared in the *New York Times* (15 September 1996, 13:3). Barbara Stewart's "In Person: Outsider with a Voice" was published in the *New York Times* (8 December 1996: 13NJ).

In 1996 Díaz sat for a radio interview with fellow author Mark Winegardner, host of "Authors, a Radio Talk Show," in which the two young writers discussed their own work and that of the writers who served as their models (Grace Paley, Raymond Carver, Toni Morrison, and Pearl S. Buck). The interview is available as a recording under the title of "Junot Díaz with Mark Winegardner" (Macon, Georgia: Hyena Productions, 1996).

Two of Díaz's short stories have appeared in prestigious collections: "Ysrael" (*Best American Short Stories*, ed. John Edgar Wideman and Katrina Kenison, Boston: Houghton Mifflin, 1996) and "Fiesta, 1980" (*Best American Short Stories*, ed. Annie Proulx and Katrina Kenison, Boston: Houghton Mifflin, 1997). "How to Date a Brown Girl" is available in a compact disc recording, read by the author (see *The New Yorker Out Loud*. Vol. 2. New York: Mouth Almighty Records, 1998).

Since the publication of *Drown*, and as he continues to work on his forthcoming novel, Díaz has published pieces in several magazines, in particular "Otra Vida, Otra Vez" and "The Sun, the Moon, the Stars," both of which appeared in the *New Yorker* (28 June 1999 and 2 February 1998, respectively). In addition, *Drown* has been translated into several languages. The *New York Times* listed the book in the "Bear in Mind" section of their "Best Sellers List" for October 13, 1996, and in their "Notable Books of 1996."

Other Sources

Bandon, Alexandra. *Dominican Americans*. Parsippany, N.J.: New Discovery Books, 1995.

Bramen, Carrie Tirado. "Translating Exile: The Metamorphosis of the Ordinary in Dominican Short Fiction." *Latin American Literary Review* 26, no. 51 (1998): 63–78.

Dominican Studies: Resources and Research Questions. New York: CUNY Dominican Studies Institutes, 1997.

Luis, William. *Dance Between Two Cultures: Latino Caribbean Literature Written in the United States*. Nashville, Tenn.: Vanderbilt University Press, 1997.

Wilson, Rob. "Producing American Selves: The Form of American Autobiography." *Boundary 2* (Summer 1991): 104–29.

17

Using Latina Poetry in the Classroom

Bryce Milligan

ANALYSIS OF THEMES AND FORMS

History indicates that poetry is generally the first literary expression of politically driven movements, and this was certainly true of the Chicano movement of the 1960s and 1970s. "In any movement toward liberation," Seamus Heaney said in a 1990 Oxford lecture, "it will be necessary to deny the normative authority of the dominant language or literary tradition." The education provided by U.S. schools and universities has been dominated by English and Anglo-American fiction. Latina and Latino writers coming of age during the Chicano movement rebelled by creating their own genre: politically charged poetry featuring the bilingual idiom used in homes and in the streets from New York to Miami and Los Angeles. Code switching, as this sort of literary usage is called, is not uncommon in contemporary poetry; mainstream poets such as Ezra Pound and T. S. Eliot were famous for their multilingual poetry. On the other hand, young Latino/a poets were routinely criticized for using a bastardized language. It was several years before the creative genius of poets like Alurista, Angela de Hoyos, Ricardo Sánchez, Carmen Tafolla, Evangelina Vigil-Piñón and others was recognized as having aesthetically exceeded the common language of origin.

If the number of *abuelita* (grandmother) poems written throughout the movement period can be used as a gauge, then it was most often the *abuelitas* who instructed young Latinas in this country in history (both personal and public), cultural customs, and values. Vigil-Piñón's "apprenticeship" with her grandmother is perhaps the quintessential poem of this sort: "her words paint masterpieces."[1] Latina writers who came of age during the movement evolved out of a rich bicultural and bilingual soup wherein Spanish language literary expression was accepted and appreciated outside the mandatory English-only educational system.

The Chicano movement created a sense of cultural nationalism which found its first and most strident voice in poetry. Poets were rarely just poets; they were activists with an important role to play as *la voz de la raza* (the voice of the people). Works like Corky Gonzalez's "Yo soy Joaquín," Alurista's "El Plan Espiritual de Aztlán," and Angela de Hoyos' "Arise, Chicano" were used interchangeably as literary works and political documents. Both the political and literary aspects of the 1960s Chicano movement were male dominated. In the early 1970s, however, Chicano politicization encountered the American women's liberation movement. Liberated, politically experienced, college-educated Latinas began to explore new directions in bilingual poetry, drama, and fiction, but most especially in poetry. The stylistic and thematic homogeneity that had existed earlier in the Chicano movement was driven primarily by an almost unconscious need for collective self-definition as *la raza*, as a single people. While a collective sense of Latina sisterhood survives in the literature to this day, individual creative vision has replaced cultural/racial/political unity as the driving force. Likewise, most Latina writers have accepted English as their predominant mode of literary expression, although they have succeeded in reshaping the language to their own ends.

As poet Evangelina Vigil (now Vigil-Piñón) pointed out in her introduction to the 1983 "Woman of Her Word" issue of *Revista Chicano-Riqueña*, "Removed from the mainstream of American literature and barely emerging on the Hispanic literary scene, the creativity of Latina writers exists autonomously."[2] This early selection of the term "Latina" over "Chicana" was indicative of another change in the nature of the politicization: Chicanas no longer saw themselves as simply the feminist extension of the Chicano movement, but as an integral part of Third World feminism. At the same time, Latina writers of non-Mexican heritage began to publish in the United States—women with roots in Puerto Rico, Cuba, the Dominican Republic, and South and Central America— each bringing with her elements of her own national literary traditions.

Throughout the 1980s, Latina poets increased in both number and artistic sophistication. In this decade, such important poetic voices as Pat Mora, Ana Castillo, Sandra Cisneros, Evangelina Vigil-Piñón, Carmen Tafolla, Rosemary Catacalos, Marjorie Agosín, and many others burst upon the scene with their first books. Established poets, including Angela de Hoyos, Lucha Corpi, Alma Luz Villanueva, and Lorna Dee Cervantes, produced some of their finest works. Latina poetry in the 1990s has improved in quality, but the visibility of the poets has diminished as the fiction writers came to prominence. It is worth noting, however, that all of the major contemporary Latina fiction writers are, first and foremost, poets.

"An identity problem is obvious," states Beverly Sánchez-Padilla in her poem about the figurative mother of all mestizas, Malintzin, the translator, advisor, and lover of the conquistador Hernán Cortez.[3] Malintzin came to be known by the Spanish name Doña Marina, as well as by the derogative appellations La Malinche (the traitor) and La Chingada (the violated one or, even worse, the whore). Carmen Tafolla, in her poem on this topic, "La Malinche," asserts that Malintzin was highly aware of her role in history. Malintzin's predicament is a common theme in Latina writing, even among authors of non-Mexican origin. Condemned as a traitor by many writers over the years, Malintzin is for Tafolla a visionary realist who defeats the Spanish invasion in the only way possible, by giving birth to a new mestiza race which will survive the conquest and inherit its own ancestral lands. Indigenous peoples have always named themselves throughout the Americas, and in Tafolla's poem Malintzin names this new race "the people"—*la raza*.

One of the Latina writers who has taken a scholarly interest in the matter of identity is poet and novelist Ana Castillo. Defining herself as "mestiza/Mexic Amerindian," Castillo writes in *Massacre of the Dreamers: Essays on Xicanisma* that the group labeled as Latina or Hispanic in the United States can be neither "summarized nor neatly categorized."[4] The quest for identity persists as the single most important theme of Latina literature. Chicanas, in particular, have traced their roots from beyond such historical figures as Malintzin, Our Lady of Guadalupe, and Sor Juana Inés de la Cruz (the seventeenth-century poetess) into a purely American mythos, developing, in the process, the Aztec pantheon into a source of literary symbolism and allusion, in somewhat the same manner as earlier European mined Greco-Roman mythology. In her poem "Coatlícue," which is openly about identity, Sheila Sánchez-Hatch has successfully fused contemporary and mythological imagery.

It is clear that something other than geographical, historical, or even racial origins empower contemporary Latina identity. There is a recognizable culture held in common, even though individual manifestations of that culture in the literature may be ascribed to one or another ethnic or national origin. At the root of this common culture is the fact that Spanish, often the first language of U.S. Latinas or of their parents, constitutes a deeply cherished transnational/transhistorical linguistic umbilical cord. Except in the case of older writers and a few first-generation émigrés, Spanish is seldom the dominant language of either daily use or literary expression. Still there is indeed, throughout the literature created by U.S.-based Latina writers, an undercurrent of love for the Spanish language, whether or not the writer herself is fluent. This is evident in the code switching which occurs, especially in poetry, when a Spanish word or phrase is used within an English context when the Spanish is more accurate or more evocative than its English equivalent. This bilingualism, denigrated by terms like "Spanglish" and "Tex-Mex," is actually one of the most powerful linguistic tools at the disposal of these writers. Masters of this technique, such as Angela de Hoyos, Carmen Tafolla, and Evangelina Vigil-Piñón, have created distinct poetic idioms, at once reflective of the bilingual culture they inhabit and rising above it as a sort of linguistic critique, ennobling and empowering the language with nuance and beauty. Others writers, including Lucha Corpi, have chosen to write poetry in Spanish and fiction in English.

But this "linguistic umbilical cord" is evident in more than simply the usage of the Spanish language. Lillian Castillo-Speed, in her introduction to *Latina: Women's Voices from the Borderlands*, writes that Latina literature appears to English-language readers "to have been newly translated from Spanish, when in fact new Latina writers have taken the English language and have made it their own. It is more than just a combination of English and Spanish: it reflects the reality of women who live in two worlds."[5]

This is, in fact, the second most consistent theme of Latina literature: life for the U.S. Latina is nearly always bi-something—bilingual, bicultural, binational. Dividing these two worlds is *la frontera*, the border, which constitutes one of the most powerful and persistent images of Latina writing, functioning in both metaphorical and realistic contexts. A very real border divides the reality of Mexican-American women, or Chicanas, in half, often separating *la familia* into branches inhabiting two vastly different linguistic, economic, cultural, educational, and social worlds. Aside from geographical divisions, there is also a substantial gender-based division. Latin American machismo continues to forge a special bond among women family members, a bond that surfaces in the literature as both a consistent theme and a predominant subject. This is reinforced by powerful mother figures. As one writer put it, "No Latina can say to another, 'la cocina de mi mamá,' and be misunderstood. It is always the same kitchen, with the same rules and rituals."[6] Finally, there is the female bonding created by the historical influence of the male-dominated Catholic Church, which provides Latina writers with a rich source of imagery, a target for rebellion (and an almost inexhaustible well of guilt), and a set of established, personally relevant rituals such as *quinceañeras*, the traditional presentation of 15-year-old girls to society as marriageable young women.

One of the poets whose work has proven most useful in the classroom setting, from middle school through university, is Pat Mora. Her poetry, which consistently exhibits exceptional literary quality, is dense with cultural allusions and is intellectually substantial, yet it is also easy for the untutored reader to enjoy. Mora's first book, *Chants* (1984), opens with an invocation to the Chihuahuan desert, a prayer created in imitation of the "Indian women" whom she saw "long ago bribing/the desert with turquoise threads." The poet intones, "Guide my hands, Mother,/to weave singing birds," while secretly, she buries a "ballpoint pen/and lined yellowing paper," asking the land "to smile" on her as she composes these poems, to help her "catch her music with words." The desert thus forms a second persona early in the book, a mother-muse figure whose wild wisdom teaches the poet endurance.

Chants chronicles the development of a Tejana consciousness able to bridge the gap between mythic antiquity and the more immediate past— a past riddled with superstitions, with rules for both social and physical survival in hostile environments. Of course mental health, not to mention humanity, depends upon the poet not so much crossing the bridge as *being* the bridge. In the final poem in the book, "Legal Alien," Mora concludes that this is an uncomfortable position:

> an American to Mexicans
> a Mexican to Americans
> a handy token
> sliding back and forth
> between the fringes of both worlds
> by smiling
> by masking the discomfort
> of being pre-judged
> Bi-laterally.

Uncomfortable perhaps, but survivable, the will to survive being supplied by both the solitude of the desert and the bustling responsibilities of the poet's Anglo-dominated workplace. By intoning these chants, lyrics which describe situations and persons caught "between the fringes of both worlds," the poet ritualizes this duality. Mexican, Anglo, and Mestizo worlds, the past and the present, village superstitions and paneled office realities—all collide here in a tumult of images. Ultimately, Mora concludes, one can only live with the scar of this ambivalence. It is a conclusion valid wherever the American melting pot has failed to assimilate and homogenize independent cultures.

Mora, who was born and raised in El Paso, in sight of the Rio Grande, was constantly in contact with residents of La Ciudad de Juarez who crossed the river to work as day laborers. After receiving both undergraduate and graduate degrees from the University of Texas at El Paso (UTEP), Mora's jobs included being assistant to the president at UTEP and director of the university museum—which gives considerable weight to her repeated references to committees, paneled boardrooms, and other office imagery. Yet, she remains acutely aware of her position as a person living between two cultures.

Mora's dilemma is described from various perspectives in a number of her poems but perhaps nowhere so clearly as in "Aztec Princess." In this poem, a young woman upon the edge of independence is taken by her mother to the spot in the house where her own umbilical cord was buried—a sign, her mother tells her, that she would "nest inside." That night, the girl digs in the spot but finds nothing but "earth, rich earth." Placing it in a jar, she takes it out into the moonlight and whispers, "Breathe." This is a perfect reflection of the ambivalence of *Chants*— wishing to break free of the mystical implications of the buried umbilical cord, yet able to feel the necessity of a ritual act in order to achieve that freedom.

That such a ritual must be a logical necessity is supported in *Chants* by several poems describing both the ceremonial magic of *brujas* (witches) and the herbal cures of *curanderas* (healers). In "Bruja: Witch," Mora gives a first-person account of the shape-shifting of an old woman into the body of an owl, then back again. "Chuparrosa: Hummingbird," a more complex poem, begins, "I buy magic meat/of a chuparrosa from a toothless witch. . . ." The killing of the hummingbird is part of a love potion ritual to make her lover "see me, only me." It is painfully effective:

> You hover,
> Your eyes never wander.
> More and more
> on hot afternoons
> I sleep
> to escape your gaze.

The abrupt juxtaposition of these different worlds, different sensibilities, and different fates is crystal clear in El Paso, where one can shed a good deal of the twentieth century simply by crossing a river. Thus her second book, *Borders* (1986), refines the notion of the border as a metaphor for the no-man's zone that separates cultures, languages, sexes, and realities. As the poet puts it, "I live in a doorway."

Even as a child, Mora writes, precisely who held the power was clear, yet the road to such success remained a mystery. Like generations of aspiring young Chicanas, Mora grew up under the influence of female Anglo teachers. She recalls this in "Withdrawal Symptoms":

> We were hooked early,
> brown-eyed, round-faced girls
> licked our lips

tasting secret pleasures
even in first grade

rushed to school to push
tacks into bulletin boards
until our thumbs were sore
craving

. . .

all for gold stars, secret
winks from pale teachers

Mora is more than just a survivor of the Texas education system. She is a living witness to the Chicano-Anglo cultural collision. The addiction to "sticky sweet smiles" is endemic, so that when the little girl grows up and encounters an Anglo world of "bitter frowns/in committees and board rooms," she must ask herself, "Why am I the only Mexican American here?" Over and over again the poet describes crossing, as a successful Chicana in a superficial Anglo world, back into a world that is safer, more real somehow. From a boardroom inhabited by "careful women in crisp beige/suits, quick beige smiles" she crosses into "the other room" where "señoras/in faded dresses stir sweet/milk coffee, laughter whirls." In "Bilingual Christmas" Mora juxtaposes the images of an eggnog-and-rum-balls office party, with the poverty outside the windows where "Not carols we hear/whimpering/children too cold/to sing/on Christmas eve." "Echoes" is a vignette of the poet at a birthday party, where she witnesses the simplest sort of blind cruelty—"just drop the cups and plates/on the grass" her host says, "My maid/will pick them up." But for Mora, both the host's attitude and her own silence are disgusting. "Again and again I feel/my silence, the party whirring round me./I longed to hear this earth/roar, to taste thunder,/to see proper smiles twist." But it does not; instead, Mora writes, "[m]y desert land waits/to hear me roar, waits to hear/me flash: NO."

In *Chants*, Mora has developed a sense of cultural identity; in *Borders*, a longer work, she moves through a series of life experiences that define her as a woman and, ultimately, as a writer. In the fourth and final section of the book, she is away from the boardrooms, on her own where "motels are my convents," where "I wake early/mumbling phrases,/litanies/holding a pencil/rather than beads."

After earning a long string of literary awards, Mora left her beloved El Paso in 1989 to go with her husband (an archeologist) to Cincinnati, where she has been free to write without bearing the "bureaucratic weight" of her university jobs. As a Kellogg Foundation fellow, she has traveled the world studying minority cultures. She has also become the most prolific and best selling of all Latina children's authors.

Her latest collections of poetry, *Communion* (1991), *Agua Santa/Holy Water* (1995), and *Aunt Carmen's Book of Practical Saints* (1997), show an even more refined poetics. Gone are the thunder and flash of righteous indignation which punctuated the first two books; instead we are presented with reflective and diverse collections of powerful, imaginative, and well-crafted poems. Divided into three sections, *Communion* is full of place-specific poems, ranging from "Divisadero Street, San Francisco" to "The Taj Mahal" by way of Peru, Cuba, Pakistan, New York, and elsewhere. Some of her favorite themes reappear in portrait poems of various *brujas* and *curanderos*, or of "The Young Sor Juana." Several potent protest poems address domestic violence, as in "Emergency Room," where a young wife can stand naked and say,

> so I don't cover my breasts
> with my hands or a white sheet
> no
> you can look and touch
> i'm blue neck to knee
> he clothed me in bruises

Here Mora was clearly experimenting with punctuation and capitalization, something she rarely did in her early work. And there are explorations into traditional forms as well—a well-crafted villanelle, for example ("Strong Women").

Still, this substantial book was transitional, and it was clear that the poet was giving birth to a new voice. As she put it in the final poem of *Communion*, "I am gathering from within,/a light safe to follow." The power she gathered came to fruition in another format—the essay—in Mora's *Nepantla: Essays from the Land in the Middle* (1993) and in her most brilliant collection of poems to date, *Agua Santa/Holy Water*. In this book, Mora allows herself the luxuries of humor, of writing poems entirely in Spanish (a tribute to the *corrido* [ballad]), of intensely personal poems, of painting bitter portraits of those who would mistreat *los pobres*, the poor, of the world.

Clearly, Mora has achieved the status of an internationally respected poet, yet her work remains both accessible and illuminating to the general reader.

TEACHING THE WORK

Because of the clear relationship of its primary themes to the sociopolitical evolution of the last third of the twentieth century, Latina poetry can easily be used as a paradigm for the study of recent social movements, political history, and multicultural trends in American literature and in education. Themes of identity, family, and the sense of living between realities can be explored through the use of creative writing modeling exercises. Pat Mora's numerous portrait poems are also useful in this sense as modeling tools.

1. Using Pat Mora's poem, "Curandera," as a model, write a description of an unusual person who is both important to and isolated from your own community. Why is this person important to the community? Why is isolation necessary? Using the same poem as a model, describe in detail the things used by this person in his or her occupation (tools, materials, etc.) in such a way that we learn something about the way this person relates to the world. These descriptions can be used as raw materials to create poems.

2. Mora found symbolic significance in doorways, even writing that "I live in doorways." Discuss the borders that exist in the students' lives. What things divide the different aspects of their lives? For example, a student athlete may feel that it is his uniform that divides the student from the athlete. A musician may feel that it is the doorway to the recital hall. Most will cite something that divides their school existence from their "real" selves. Some will mention ethnic or religious differences. Once these borders have been identified, the questions become, "How are these things symbolic? Why does this thing mean more to me than it does to the person standing next to me?"

3. Latina poets often refer to personal, folk, and religious rituals, as Mora does in her poem, "Aztec Princess." Ask students to look for rituals in their own lives that they have adopted from observing others, or that they have invented for themselves. What are the roots of these rituals, and what is their importance? How do such rituals make our lives richer?

4. Discuss the use of more than one language in a single poem, story, or even in the students' own conversation. Why does one choose to use a word in one language rather than in another? English is full of words adopted from other languages. Have students record casual conversations and then identify the words that have come from other languages. Ask the students to compare the casual use of multilingual conversation to the careful code switching found in literary works.

5. Literary movements, whether stylistic or ethnic in nature, almost always begin with poetry rather than with fiction. Have students discuss why this may be so. Is poetry "closer to the soul" than fiction? Is it a more basic expression of the human condition? What can be expressed in poetry that cannot be expressed in a story? Why are most of the Latina fiction writers also poets?

NOTES

1. Evangelina Vigil, "apprenticeship," from *Nade y nade* (San Antonio: M&A Editions, 1978). Also in Bryce Milligan, with Mary Guerrero Milligan and Angela de Hoyos, eds., ¡*Floricanto Sí! A Collection of Latina Poetry* (New York: Penguin, 1998), 245.

2. Evangelina Vigil, ed., "Woman of Her Word: Hispanic Women Write," special issue of *Revista Chicano-Riqueña* 11, no. 3–4 (1983): 7.

3. Beverly Sánchez-Padilla, "Mali," in Milligan, ¡*Floricanto Sí!* 203–8.

4. Ana Castillo, *Massacre of the Dreamers: Essays on Xicanisma* (Albuquerque: University of New Mexico Press, 1994), 1–8.

5. Lillian Castillo-Speed, ed., *Latina: Women's Voices from the Borderlands* (New York: Simon & Schuster, 1995), 17–18.

6. Mary Guerrero Milligan, "Always the Same Kitchen" (unpublished essay).

SUGGESTIONS FOR FURTHER READING

Agosín, Marjorie. *Hogueras/Bonfires*, trans. Naomi Lindstrom. Tempe, Ariz.: Bilingual Review Press, 1990.

———. *Sargazo/Sargasso*, trans. Cola Franzen. Fredonia, N.Y.: White Pine Press, 1993.

———. *Starry Night*, trans. Mary G. Berg. Fredonia, N.Y.: White Pine Press, 1996.

———. *Toward the Splendid City*, trans. Richard Schaaf. Tempe, Ariz.: Bilingual Press, 1994.

Alvarez, Julia. *The Other Side/El Otro Lado*. New York: Dutton, 1995.

Castillo, Ana. *My Father Was a Toltec*. Albuquerque: West End Press, 1988.

———. *Women Are Not Roses*. Houston: Arte Público Press, 1984.

Cervantes, Lorna Dee. *Emplumada*. Pittsburgh: University of Pittsburgh Press, 1981.

———. *From the Cables of Genocide*. Houston: Arte Público Press, 1991.

Cisneros, Sandra. *Loose Woman*. New York: Random House, 1994.

———. *My Wicked Wicked Ways*. Bloomington: Third Woman Press, 1987.

Corpi, Lucha. *Variaciones sobre una tempestad/Variations on a Storm*, trans. Catherine Rodríguez-Nieto. Berkeley: Third Woman Books, 1990.

De Hoyos, Angela. *Arise Chicano! and Other Poems*, Spanish trans. Mireya Robles, Bloomington, Ind.: Backstage Books, 1975. 2d ed., San Antonio: M&A Editions, 1976.

———. *Chicano Poems: For the Barrio*. Bloomington, Ind.: Backstage Books, 1975. 2d ed., San Antonio: M&A Editions, 1976.

———. *Selected Poems/Selecciones*, Spanish trans. Mireya Robles. Xalapa, Veracruz: Universidad Veracruzana, 1975. 2d ed., San Antonio: Dezkalzo Press, 1989.

———. *Woman, Woman*. Houston: Arte Público Press, 1985.

Hatch, Sheila Sánchez. *Guadalupe and the Kaleidoscopic Screamer*. San Antonio: Wings Press, 1996.

Mora, Pat. *Agua Santa/Holy Water*. Boston: Beacon Press, 1995.

———. *Aunt Carmen's Book of Practical Saints*. Boston: Beacon Press, 1997.

———. *Borders*. Houston: Arte Público Press, 1986.

———. *Chants*. Houston: Arte Público Press, 1984.

———. *Communion*. Houston: Arte Público Press, 1991.

———. *Houses of Houses*. Boston: Beacon Press, 1997.

———. *Napantla: Essays from the Land in the Middle*. Albuquerque: University of New Mexico Press, 1993.

Ortiz Cofer, Judith, *The Latin Deli: Prose and Poetry*. Athens: University of Georgia Press, 1993.

———. *Reaching for the Mainland*. Tempe, Ariz.: Bilingual Press, 1995.

———. *Terms of Survival*. Houston: Arte Público Press, 1987.

Tafolla, Carmen. *Curandera*. San Antonio: M&A Editions, 1983. 2d ed., Santa Monica, Calif.: Lalo Press, 1993.

———. "La Isabela de Guadalupe y otras chucas." In *Five Poets of Aztlan*, ed. Santiago Daydi-Tolson. Binghamton, N.Y.: Bilingual Press, 1985.

———. *Sonnets to Human Beings and Other Selected Works*. Santa Monica, Calif.: Lalo Press, 1993.

Vigil-Piñón, Evangelina. *The Computer Is Down*. Houston: Arte Público Press, 1987.

———. *Nade y nade*. San Antonio: M&A Editions, 1978.

———. *Thirty an' Seen a Lot*. Houston: Arte Público Press, 1982.

Villanueva, Alma Luz. *Lifespan*. Austin: Place of Herons Press, 1985.

———. *Planet and Mother, May I?* Tempe, Ariz.: Bilingual Press, 1993. Reissues of early works.

Critical Anthologies

Anzaldúa, Gloria, ed. *Making Face, Making Soul/Haciendo Caras: Creative and Critical Perspectives of Feminists of Color*. San Francisco: Spinsters/Aunt Lute Books, 1990.

Castillo-Speed, Lillian, ed. *Latina: Women's Voices from the Borderlands*. New York: Simon & Schuster, 1995.

Fernandez, Roberta, ed. *In Other Words: Literature by Latinas of the United States*. Houston: Arte Público Press, 1994.

Herrera-Sobek, María, and Helena María Viramontes, eds. *Chicana Creativity and Criticism: New Frontiers in American Literature*. 2d ed., rev. Albuquerque: University of New Mexico Press, 1996.

Milligan, Bryce, with Mary Guerrero Milligan and Angela de Hoyos, eds. *Daughters of the Fifth Sun: A Collection of Latina Fiction and Poetry*. New York: Putnam/Riverhead Books, 1995; Berkley/Riverhead (paper) 1996.

———. *¡Floricanto Sí! A Collection of Latina Poetry*. New York: Penguin, 1998.

Rebolledo, Tey Diana, and Eliana S. Rivero, eds. *Infinite Divisions: An Anthology of Chicana Literature*. Tucson: University of Arizona Press, 1993.

Essays

Anzaldúa, Gloria. *Borderlands/La Frontera: The New Mestiza*. San Francisco: Aunt Lute Books, 1987.

Castillo, Ana. *Massacre of the Dreamers: Essays on Xicanisma*. Albuquerque: University of New Mexico Press, 1994.

Mora, Pat. *Nepantla: Essays from the Land in the Middle*. Albuquerque: University of New Mexico Press, 1993.

Trujillo, Carla, ed. *Living Chicana Theory*. Berkeley, Calif.: Third Woman Press, 1998.

18

Borders and Birthrights: Watching Cheech Marin's *Born in East L.A.*

Chon A. Noriega

ANALYSIS OF THEMES AND FORMS

When, on August 21, 1987, Universal Studios released Cheech Marin's directional debut, *Born in East L.A.*, it seemed as if the studio did not know what to do with the film.[1] After all, it was unlike the sex, drugs, and rock-'n-roll of the Cheech and Chong "occasions-on-film" that had earned almost $300 million since *Up in Smoke* (1978). Marin's past reputation conflicted with the "just say no" ethos of the Reagan era. To make matters worse, Universal changed studio heads mid-film, which all but guaranteed a lackluster promotion, since the film's success would accrue to the old, not the new, person in charge. *Born in East L.A.* was then dumped on the national market without the usual advance press screenings.

Caught off guard, the local press nonetheless responded favorably to the film, particularly in the Southwest, where the *Los Angeles Times* critic concluded, "It has more drive and energy than *La Bamba.*"[2] Coming one month after the box office success of Luis Valdez's *La Bamba* (1987), statements such as these fueled speculation about the emergence of a "Hispanic Hollywood." In the national press, however, *Born in East L.A.* hit a brick wall and received only two reviews. *People Weekly* dismissed the film as "a string of uneven skits," and *Cineaste* argued that the film was "well-intentioned" and "progressive," but little more than "loosely strung together shticks and vignettes" and, in the final analysis, was "politically naive."[3] These very different publications—one popular and conservative, the other elite and left of center—shared a common assumption: the film lacked a coherent narrative when judged against the correct aesthetics and politics.

Nevertheless, *Born in East L.A.* was the second highest grossing film in its first week, and it was the number one film in the Southwest for nearly four weeks. Aside from the surprise box office revenue, the film's social impact was discussed outside the Chicano and Spanish-language press, which praised it as an alternative and risky look at a "highly controversial issue" then dominating the news: the expiration on September 1, 1987, of the grace period for undocumented workers to apply for amnesty under the new immigration law.[4] Indeed, the film represents a calculated use of humor to respond to the Simpson-Rodino Immigration Reform Act and California's successful English-only initiative (both in 1986). But if the Hollywood film's political significance did not register outside of the Hispanic press in the United States, it did become a turning point for reconsidering oppositional cinema in Latin America.

In December 1987, *Born in East L.A.* won four major awards at the Ninth International Festival of New Latin American Cinema in Havana, Cuba, including, ironically enough, the Glauber Rocha award given by Prensa Latina, an international press organization based in Havana. The irony is twofold inasmuch as New Latin American Cinema represented a counter-cinema vis-à-vis Hollywood. Furthermore, New Latin American Cinema did not just speak about an underlying issue of underdevelopment; it transformed underdevelopment into an aesthetic logic aimed at *concientización* (political consciousness raising). In this manner, Glauber Rocha, an early filmmaker and theorist of *Cinema Novo* (New Cinema) in Brazil, spoke of an "aesthetics of hunger" and an "aesthetics of violence" as revolutionary responses to colonial oppression: "The moment of violence is the moment when the coloniser becomes aware of the existence of the colonised."[5] From the start, Chicanos were part of this vision, with Chicano cinema understood as a "national" category, allowing a paradoxical situation when Chicano filmmakers were able to work within *their* national industry, Hollywood. Thus, the awards received by *Born in East L.A.* were at once a sign of a strategic shift within New Latin American Cinema toward more popular and commercial forms, and of the continuing presence of "Chicano cinema" within Latin American film festivals since the 1970s. Paradoxically, the awards also suggested that the political ideals and goals of New Latin American Cinema could now be expressed through Hollywood.

Since its release and appearance at the festival, *Born in East L.A.* has generated considerable interest among Chicano scholars, while it has been all but forgotten in the U.S. mainstream. In fact, Cheech Marin and Luis Valdez have been unable to direct other theatrical release feature films in the intervening ten years.[6] Why has this neglect been the fate of most Chicano-directed feature films? At issue is the question of whether these films have a coherent structure worthy of a close reading. In other words, do these films make sense, or do Chicano critics make exceptions for them given the paucity of Chicano-themed or Chicano-produced feature films? After all, Marin's film is little more than a light comedy, right? A careful reconsideration of *Born in East L.A.* reveals that critics may not take enough into account, especially when it comes to allusions to Chicano history, culture, and aesthetics.

In *Born in East L.A.*, Rudy Robles (Marin) is deported to Mexico, although he is a third-generation Chicano who does not speak Spanish. The film's premise is based on a newspaper account Marin read in the *Los Angeles Times* while he was listening to Bruce Springsteen's "Born in the U.S.A." on the radio.[7] Thus the narrative is first and foremost about the ephemeral status of Chicano citizenship, and not, as many non-Latino critics assumed, "wetbacks" and "illegal aliens." As a critique of the English-only movement, *Born in East L.A.* reveals race, not language, to be the underlying factor, especially insofar as official language movements often walk hand in hand with immigration politics. As Dennis Baron notes in *The English-Only Question*, "[s]o central is language to political organization that in many societies defining language has become tantamount to defining nationality."[8] But this itself often obscures an implied equivalence among language, nation, and race or ethnicity. As Baron concludes, "Americanism evidenced by the adoption of English is not always enough" because official language legislation "inevitably [expresses] a nativism which rejects certain groups of Americans no matter what language they speak."[9]

In the final analysis, *Born in East L.A.* places these issues about the relationship between race and citizenship within a spatial logic more than a narrative one. In other words, the emphasis is on being somewhere (East L.A.) rather than becoming someone (a good citizen). As such, it focuses on constructing "borders" that frame events rather than on character and plot development. After Rudy is deported, the film depicts his various attempts to reason, purchase, and sneak his way back across the border. As a picaresque hero, Rudy experiences a number of unrelated adventures without an essential transformation of character. Instead, through his romance with Dolores, a would-be border crosser from El Salvador, Rudy makes a series of simple realizations that empower him to cross the border through sheer willpower. In between his deportation and his return, Rudy comes to realize three things: American society views him as more Mexican than American; Mexicans see him as American or *pocho*; and his attitudes toward women and immigrants have been callous. What organizes these picaresque scenes is an overarching satire on the paradox that Rudy must struggle to return to a position that remains a birthright. It is a birthright that is both entrenched (acculturation) and tenuous (citizenship), adding a racial dimension to Springsteen's working-class lament on citizenship in a postindustrial economy.[10] In effect, the picaresque or "loose" nature of the narrative mirrors the protagonist's own ambiguous status as citizen. The remainder of this chapter focuses on the opening and closing scenes of the film as well as a comedic framing device that separates these scenes from the narrative proper. These brief scenes use highly charged mise-en-scène, or direction, in order to provide an interpretive structure with which to read the "body" of the film. In the end, the "loosely strung together shticks and vignettes" are neither incoherent nor "politically naive," but rather determined, to a large degree, by the paradoxes and contradictions of Chicano birthright.

In its establishing shot, *Born in East L.A.* challenges Hollywood conventions of the barrio, initiating a shift from public to private space as the source for Chicano representation in Hollywood films. The film begins with a shot of the Los Angeles skyline, pans to the left to East L.A., tilts down and—through a series of dissolves—comes to rest on a house beside a church. Thus the home, with its fence, well-kept yard, and a tree, becomes the defining unit for the barrio, rather than a montage of graffiti, gangs, drug deals, and so on that signify "problem space." In essence, East L.A. is identified as an appropriate site for the American Dream. Similar shot sequences have been used to locate the barrio in social problem films since the 1950s, but these work against either metonymic or metaphoric associations between East Los Angeles and America. These films argue for ideological assimilation coupled with barrio segregation, both of which are depicted as choices made by the male protagonists.[11]

In its next shot, however, *Born in East L.A.* moves beyond a mere alternative to the usual external depictions of the barrio when it zooms in and cuts to the interior of the home. Inside, we see a household that cuts across several borders in terms of language usage, generation, popular culture, and cultural identity vis-à-vis Mexico and the United States. These borders are represented as a gentle conflict between Rudy and his mother, initially over her baroque interior decor, then over his duties to extended family members. The two argue while Rudy eats breakfast in the dining room. Rudy's mother wants him to pick up his cousin Javier, an undocumented worker who has recently arrived in the United States, since she and Rudy's sister are going to Fresno for the week. Rudy refuses, revealing that he does not speak Spanish, and makes several snide remarks about Mexican immigrants. Eventually he relents. Throughout the scene, the full shots of Rudy and his mother register details of the interior decor: devotional items, family photographs, kitsch lamps, a home altar. Once Rudy relents, the camera frames him at the table in a medium close-up in which the background consists of a home altar atop a bookcase filled with an encyclopedia set. Here in one concise image we see their argument both expressed and resolved within the mise-en-scène: the encyclopedias below represent the immigrant's rite of purchase into the objective knowledge of American society, and the altar above, with its lit candles, is an active and personal engagement of spiritual belief. This mise-en-scène establishes a hierarchical conflict between mother and son, with the mother's spiritual belief placed above the son's ideological assimilation. This symbolic resolution is literally acted out in their initial struggle over cultural expression within the home when Rudy gets into an argument with his mother over her placement of a dual-perspective picture of Jesus Christ in front of the telephone niche.

In the next scene, Rudy leaves for work in a low rider fashioned from a pink Volkswagen bug with the license plate "Pink Luv." Whereas his mother places belief over knowledge (encyclopedia) and technology (telephone), Rudy's pink bug engages in a public parody of Chicano masculinity. The conflict between mother and son, then, expresses itself as a split within the Chicano family between private and public, sincere and parodic, form and function, resistance and assimilation. Thus, the film poses much more than the question, "How will Rudy get home?"[12] Instead, home itself is at first called into question, until the film deports Rudy, re-figuring home as his object of desire. The film then asks, "How will Rudy be reconciled to domestic space?" This question places the issue of his relationship to women—initially, his mother and sister—within a familial context in which his absent father and nonexistent wife and children suggest a failure on Rudy's part to perform his expected gender role. His parodic low-rider bug, then, marks Rudy's simultaneous machismo and assimilation as a threat to the home that must be resolved in the public sphere.

In between the first and last scenes—the home and a Cinco de Mayo parade—and the narrative itself is a sequence in which a "sexy" French woman walks through the barrio. These two sequences overlap with the opening and closing credits, and coincide with the two times in the film in which Rudy occupies the public space of the United States. Thus, despite the brevity of her appearances, the French woman plays a complex allegorical function that frames the picaresque narrative, prefiguring Rudy's deportation and return on sexual, political, and cultural levels. Her appearance marks a shift in Rudy's behavior between his mother's home and the public sphere, and between the familial and the sexual. As he drives to work, Rudy pursues the French woman in his pink low-rider, issuing catcalls out of earshot. Whenever he loses sight of her, he stops to ask men on the corner if they have seen a red-headed woman in a green dress; in unison the men point the way.

The scene, modeled after the opening sequence in *The Girl Can't Help It* (1956) with Jayne Mansfield, reveals the woman's effect as an uncontrollable "object of desire" on both Rudy and the entire male barrio. The sequence ends with the French woman walking toward the camera and into Rudy's car shop. Behind her is a spray paint mural of the Mexican and U.S. flags with lowriders beneath them heading toward the Mexican side of the mural. As she approaches, her body increasingly occupies the space between the two flags, acting as the border. Both the border symbolism and the woman's allegorical status are reinforced in her iconographic coding as white skin, red hair, and a green dress—the colors of the Mexican flag. These colors, as well as her heavy French accent and her reappearance during the Cinco de Mayo parade at the end of the film, link her to the French occupation of Mexico in the 1860s. Cinco de Mayo, after all, celebrates the battle that initiated Mexico's overthrow of the French on May 5, 1862.

The allusion works on two levels. First, it posits a historical connection between the Chicano barrio and Mexico on the basis of colonialism, with the French woman serving as an allegorical figure for French colonialism in Mexico and, by extension, internal colonialism in East L.A. Second, Cinco de Mayo celebrations in the United States speak directly to the history of deportation as well as civil rights struggles since the 1930s. During Depression-era repatriation, the Mexican consulates sponsored Cinco de Mayo celebrations as fund-raising activities for their efforts to represent the Mexican and Mexican-American communities. Since the 1960s, these celebrations, along with Day of the Dead and Mexican Independence Day, have become symbolic expressions of Chicano cultural affirmation, resistance, and maintenance within the United States.

The French woman functions as a border symbol, embodying the dual or double-edged notion of "liberty" acted out by the French in the Americas in the mid-1800s. In addition to the occupation of Mexico, of course, the French presented the Statue of Liberty to the United States as a gift of freedom to the world (dedicated in 1886). On an iconographic level, the French woman shares the "exaggerated and slightly vulgar" stride of the statue while her position between the two flags and her red-white-and-green color scheme imply that, for Chicanos and Mexicans, the colonial experience still prevails over notions of universal liberty. Thus the French woman negotiates a complex relationship between Mexico and the United States, one that calls into question the symbolic purity of the Statue of Liberty in identifying the United States as a nation of immigrants. Within four years of the statue's dedication, the U.S. Census Bureau would declare the frontier closed, the borders set. Those borders, however, had been reached at the expense of Mexican and Native American lands, a fact which set in motion the contradiction between a Jeffersonian sense of liberty spreading around the globe, and an American expansion and exceptionalism that took liberties with other peoples' sovereignty. In referencing the period between 1862 and 1886, *Born in East*

L.A. shifts the discourse on Chicano citizenship from its usual origins in the Mexican-American War and the Treaty of Guadalupe Hidalgo (1848). This places the politics of immigration within an international and multiracial context rather than on the counter-nativist claims of Chicano nationalism.

After approaching Rudy's garage (and the camera) against the backdrop of the mural, the French woman turns and leans against her car. Situated on the right side of the screen, her car is on the U.S. side of the mural. With her legs spread, her left hand folded across her waist, and her right hand raised to the side of her head with a burning cigarette, the French woman strikes a pose similar to the Statue of Liberty with its tablets and torch. Here, positioned in front of the two flags, she suggests a welcome to Mexican immigrants in which the original invitation to assimilate is framed in sexual terms, seemingly addressed only to male Mexican nationals. But, contrary to this reading, the bottom portion of the mural itself depicts Chicano low riders driving from the United States to Mexico, with the mise-en-scène implying that they have passed between the woman's legs. It is at this point in the film's most vulgar sight gag that the mise-en-scène foreshadows Rudy's deportation and the terms of his eventual return. Rudy, who had been working beneath the car, slides out on his back in such a way that his head emerges between the French woman's feet. Taken as an allegory of citizenship, Rudy passes beneath the Statue of Liberty on his way to Mexico. The joke here is that the Statue of Liberty does not face Mexico, but Europe, hence the mutual surprise of Rudy and the French woman, captured in shot/reverse-shot to show his pleasure and her shock. Passing beneath the Statue of Liberty against the backdrop of the mural, then, presages Rudy's deportation and precludes his return within the usual terms of immigration and assimilation.

The last scene of the film, which depicts Rudy's return "home," provides the second half of this narrative frame. While in Mexico, Rudy had taught a group of "Indian" and "Chinese" workers called OTMs—Other Than Mexicans—how to pass as Chicano in order to avoid deportation. In addition to the obvious irony that Rudy himself could not "pass" as Chicano (and that many of the OTMs are played by Latino actors), these scenes, which are punctuated by stereotypical Chinese music, allude to the Chinese Exclusion Act of 1882, which lasted until 1943 (the same year as the Zoot Suit Riots), and represented the first denial of the right of free migration to the United States as well as one of the first victories of the emergent labor movement (as it sought to define its working-class agenda in racial terms as "white"). The Chinese Exclusion Act and subsequent laws prohibiting foreign contract labor resulted in a decisive shift within the unskilled labor force from Chinese to Mexican migrants. Mexican nationals—exempted as "foreigners *temporarily* residing in the

U.S."—provided a cheap labor pool for the rapid industrial development in the Southwest. Between 1880 and 1920, the Mexican population in the United States increased ninefold, while the national population doubled.[13] Given that Rudy identifies himself as the third generation born in the United States, he places his family history as U.S. citizens at the tail end of this period of Mexican migration. In this manner, *Born in East L.A.* foregrounds the confluence of race, labor, and citizenship, rather than an identity based on prior territorial claims. The film then establishes the limits of U.S. immigration policy and ideology with respect to racial others, revealing a hidden dynamic at the level of the working class that places various racial and ethnic groups in competition with each other.

In the end, Rudy leads a massive multiracial, multinational assault on the border. The scene visualizes Anglo-Americans' worst fear about illegal aliens swarming across the border to take away jobs, drain welfare funds, overburden social services, and increase urban crime. Marin, however, undercuts these associations, visually coding the scene as humorous, using music as an added counterpoint. Neil Diamond's "America," which played at the rededication ceremonies for the Statue of Liberty, describes these new immigrants' dream of America.

As with Marin's parody of "Born in the U.S.A.," the sincerely ironic use of Diamond's "America" expands the song's meaning to include non-European-descent citizens and immigrants. It is noteworthy, then, that the rededication of the Statue of Liberty occurs in the same year in which the Immigration Reform Bill and California's English-Only Initiative passed into law. Likewise, "America" replaces—literally, in the 1986 rededication—the Emma Lazarus lines inscribed on the statue's base in 1903:

> Give me your tired, your poor,
> Your huddled masses yearning to breathe free,
> The wretched refuse of your teeming shore.
> Send these, the homeless, tempest-tos't to me,
> I lift my lamp beside the golden door!

The status of these earlier immigrants suggests that they brought nothing with them. Their names were changed, and, like empty ciphers, they were expected to acculturate—to acquire the "American" language and culture. Diamond's song, especially in the context of *Born in East L.A.*, reveals a different set of expectations on the part of immigrants as well as inevitable cultural hybridity. For example, Dolores does not want to cross the border until she has saved enough money to be independent—not on welfare. In thus quoting two "American" popular songs, the film constructs its argument out of the contradictions and conflicts within the "mainstream" itself.

While "America" adds an ironic twist to the border crossing, the next scene further undermines the great fear of the mid-1980s, often expressed in the mainstream press as the fear of "latinization." Rudy and the OTMs are shown running down a hill into the United States, only to emerge in the next scene from a sewer hole into the barrio of East L.A. In other words, they move directly from the Mexican border to the Chicano barrio, invisible in the social space in between, which includes "white flight" suburbs and the military industrial complex. While immigration discourses often invoke and contend over a generic, "American" public space and its attendant rights, the actual struggle is more geographically specific and restricted, as the film suggests. After all, it is because the Mexicans and OTMs (Asians and Central Americans) will have to adapt and fit into the barrio and avoid other social spaces that Rudy is able to earn money in Tijuana teaching the OTMs how to act Chicano.

Having stormed the border, Rudy reemerges from the sewer amidst the Cinco de Mayo parade in East L.A. with Dolores and the OTMs. The Chinese OTMs quickly blend in as Chicanos at least as far as the police are concerned. It is at this point that the French woman reappears, causing the parade watchers—men, women, and children—to freeze, except for Rudy and Dolores, who embrace in front of a priest upon a church float. On an obvious level, the French woman is the whore to Dolores' Madonna. In fact, *dolores* means "pains" in English. The film conflates the sexual dichotomy with cultural nationalism, so that the whore also tempts Rudy with assimilation (pleasure), while the Madonna ensures cultural affirmation (pain). Although that conflation leads to Rudy's apparent reform, it also relieves him of responsibility. As a picaresque character, Rudy does not change as much as his circumstances change. It is Dolores, after all, who baptizes Rudy with a pail of water after a sexist remark, and who stands in silent witness to his subsequent acts of charity toward two Mexican women. What these brief scenes allow then is for Dolores to act as the witness for Rudy to resolve his Madonna/whore complex, first toward working-class Mexican women, then, by implication, toward the middle-class Mexican-American women in his own family and community. In the end, Dolores enables Rudy's spiritual return to the domain of the family, which he had taken for granted, if not actually ridiculed, in the opening scene. In addition to the mother's belief, Dolores facilitates a *latinidad* or panethnic "Latino" identity characterized by her insistence that Rudy learn Spanish.

In this manner, the first and last scenes in the film provide a narrative frame that moves from the private to the public symbol of the barrio: the home and the Cinco de Mayo parade. This shift in social space brings about a corresponding shift in the configuration of familial relations, from the mother-son-sister in the home to the priest-son-wife on the Church float. But this is not a shift from private to public as defined by

Richard Rodriguez in *Hunger of Memory*—that is, a shift from the language of a minority culture to that of the political and economic "mainstream."[14] Instead, the film depicts East L.A. as an alternative public sphere in its own right, one that stands between the ethnic family and the dominant culture.

If anything, then, *Born in East L.A.* manifests the ways in which Chicano expressions have understood cultural resistance and affirmation within oppositional terms that center on the role of women, family, and the home as sites of either redemption or betrayal. Ultimately, what the film argues is a familial, collective identity over and against a masculine, individual one and, presents this shift in nationalist terms as a choice between assimilation with deportation or cultural maintenance with segregation. While this choice is itself framed within the patriarchal terms of a madonna/whore dichotomy, the film also uses these terms to register a subtle shift from Chicano nationalism to a pan-Latino identity. Indeed, the fact that Dolores is from El Salvador alludes to the impact of recent Central American refugees, suggesting that to be born in East L.A. is no longer equated with Mexican descent (let alone descent from a single country of origin, if we imagine that Rudy and Dolores have children). The fact that the Spanish-language float is for an Evangelist church suggests other recent changes in the barrio. Nevertheless, the picaresque—with its emphasis on the material aspects of existence and its parody of social institutions—finds its resolution within the terms of melodrama wherein religious devotion and couple formation overcome the "outside" threat to the home. While conventional in terms of its gender politics, the film still offers something that most Chicano-themed films do not: a critique of institutional and societal racism in the United States that also pokes a little fun at the idea of a monolithic Chicano/Mexican-descent culture.

TEACHING THE WORK

1. *Born in East L.A.* lends itself to further close visual analysis, especially other portions of the scenes involving the French woman. For example, during the garage scene, the French woman leans against her car across from a poster of a Zoot suiter in front of his low rider. Compare the color coding for the two figures and cars. How might this juxtaposition between red and black be interpreted in terms of the statement in the poster, the exchange with Rudy, and the film as a whole? What other scenes lend themselves to similar readings?

2. Write about the opening sequence of other films that depict the barrio. These can include other Chicano-directed films and gang- or police-oriented films (for example, *Colors*). How do the opening se-

quences prepare us to interpret the rest of the film? How does the film depict the social space of the barrio? Who is identified as the protagonist, and what is his or her relationship to that space?

3. Nearly all Chicano-produced feature films are based on actual events or historical figures, including *Born in East L.A.*, which suggests a shared agenda with respect to crossing over into the mainstream. At the same time, these films conform to Hollywood genres: *Born in East L.A.* (comedy), *The Ballad of Gregorio Cortez* (Western), *Zoot Suit* (musical), *Stand and Deliver* (school film), *American Me* (gang), and *La Bamba, Selena*, and *Break of Dawn* (musical biographies). These films provide us with an opportunity to consider how we learn about history outside the classroom. In this sense, history becomes not some absolute truth but an argument that can be made within popular and public discourses. Select a film, identify the argument a filmmaker was attempting to make, and consider the role of genre. For example, does the fact that *Born in East L.A.* is a comedy undermine our sense that the film's issues are serious, or does humor allow viewers to consider ideas that they might reject or overlook?

NOTES

1. A much longer version of this chapter appears as " 'Waas Sappening?': Narrative Structure and Iconography in *Born in East L.A.*" in *Studies in Latin American Popular Culture* 14 (1995): 107–28.

2. Kevin Thomas, " 'East L.A.' Gets the Green Card," *Los Angeles Times*, 24 August 1987, sec. F, 1, 4.

3. Tom Cunneff, "Born in East L.A.," *People Weekly*, 14 September 1987, 14; and Dennis West and Gary Crowdus, "Cheech Cleans Up His Act," Interview, *Cineaste* 16, no. 3 (1988): 34–37.

4. Juan Rodriguez Flores, "En el estreno de la pelicula 'Born in East L.A.,' " *La Opinión*," 22 August 1987, sec. 3, 1; Maggie Cardenas, "Born in East L.A.," *Unidad/Unity*, 12 October 1987, 12; and Ruben Guevara, "Interview with Cheech Marin," *Americas 2001* (June 1987): 18–21. On the end of the "grace period," see Marita Hernandez, "Amnesty—The First Wave Battles Red Tape," *Los Angeles Times*, 1 September 1987, A9, A16; and Jess Bravin, "No Mass Firings of Aliens Seen as Exemption Ends," *Los Angeles Times*, 1 September 1987, B3, B16.

5. Glauber Rocha, "The Aesthetics of Hunger," trans. Julianne Burton, in *Twenty-Five Years of the New Latin American Cinema*, ed. Michael Chanan (London: British Film institute/Channel Four Television, 1983), 13.

6. See Rosa Linda Fregoso, "*Born in East L.A.* and the Politics of Representation," *Cultural Studies* 4, no. 3 (October 1990): 264–80; Eddie Tafoya, "*Born in East L.A.*": Cheech as the Chicano Moses," *Journal of Popular Culture* 26, no. 4 (Spring 1993): 123–29; and Christine List, "Self-Directed Stereotyping in the Films of Cheech Marin," and Victor Fuentes, "Chicano Cinema: A Dialectic of Voices and Images of the Autonomous Discourse Versus Those of the Dominant," in

Chicanos and Film, ed. Chon A. Noriega (Minneapolis: University of Minnesota Press, 1992), 183–94, 207–17.

7. Interview by author with Richard "Cheech" Marin, October 16, 1990, Malibu, California.

8. Dennis Baron, *The English-Only Question. An Official Language for Americans?* (New Haven, Conn.: Yale University Press, 1990), 6.

9. Ibid., 62.

10. On the political ambiguity of the song's lyrics and reception, see John Lombardi, "St. Boss: The Sanctification of Bruce Springsteen and the Rise of Mass Hip," *Esquire* (December 1988): 139–54, esp. 146.

11. Chon A. Noriega, "Internal 'Others': Hollywood Narratives About Mexican-Americans," in *Mediating Two Worlds: Cinematic Encounters in the Americas,* ed. John King, Ana M. López, and Manuel Alvarado (London: British Film Institute, 1993), 52–66.

12. Rosa Linda Fregoso, *The Bronze Screen: Chicana and Chicano Film Culture* (Minneapolis: University of Minnesota Press, 1993), 55–56. Fregoso continues, "The film poses an even more scathing question: what type of society deports its citizens merely on the basis of the color of their skin?" While Fregoso focuses attention solely on the role of "institutional racism," I want to show how the film interrelates questions about the Chicano home and U.S. citizenship.

13. James D. Cockcroft, *Outlaws in the Promised Land: Mexican Immigrant Workers and America's Future* (New York: Grove Press, 1986), 47–48.

14. Richard Rodriguez, *Hunger of Memory: The Education of Richard Rodriguez* (New York: Bantam Books, 1982).

SUGGESTIONS FOR FURTHER RESEARCH

Criticism

Fregoso, Rosa Linda. *The Bronze Screen: Chicana and Chicano Film Culture.* Minneapolis: University of Minnesota Press, 1993. Explores cultural studies and feminist approaches to Chicano cinema.

List, Christine. *Chicano Images: Refiguring Ethnicity in Mainstream Film.* New York: Garland Publishing, 1996. Genre and thematic analysis of Chicano feature films.

Noriega, Chon A., ed. *Chicanos and Film: Representation and Resistance.* Minneapolis: University of Minnesota Press, 1992. Essays on Chicano representation and self-representation in Hollywood and Mexican cinemas.

Noriega, Chon A., and Ana M. López, eds. *The Ethnic Eye: Latino Media Arts.* Minneapolis: University of Minnesota Press, 1996. Essays on Chicano, Puerto Rican, and Cuban-American media, including experimental video, documentary, and feature-length narrative.

Literary Sources

Paredes, Américo. *"With His Pistol in His Hand": A Border Ballad and Its Hero.* Austin: University of Texas Press, 1958. The source for the film adaptation, *The Ballad of Gregorio Cortez.*

Valdez, Luis. *Zoot Suit and Other Plays*. Houston: Arte Público Press, 1992. Includes the stage version of *Zoot Suit*.

Other Feature Films Available on Home Video

American Me (Edward James Olmos, 1992)
The Ballad of Gregorio Cortez (Robert M. Young, 1982)
La Bamba (Luis Valdez, 1987)
Break of Dawn (Isaac Artenstein, 1988)
Mi Familia/My Family (Gregory Nava, 1995)
Selena (Gregory Nava, 1997)
Stand and Deliver (Ramon Menendez, 1987)
Zoot Suit (Luis Valdez, 1981)

Appendices: Other Areas of Study for U.S. Latino Authors

APPENDIX A: SAMPLE COURSE OUTLINE OF U.S. LATINO LITERATURE

The following is a sample course syllabus for the study of Latino writings in English produced in the United States. Writings include autobiography, drama, poetry, fiction, and essay. The course is based on a 1997 anthology, *The Latino Reader*, as well as five additional extended readings.

TEXTS

Alvarez, Julia. *How the Garcia Girls Lost Their Accents* (Chapel Hill, N.C.: Algonquin Books, 1991).

Anaya, Rudolfo. *Bless Me, Ultima* (New York: Warner Books, 1994).

Augenbraum, Harold, and Margarite Fernández Olmos. *The Latino Reader: An American Literary Tradition from 1542 to the Present* (Boston: Houghton Mifflin, 1997).

Cisneros, Sandra. *The House on Mango Street* (New York: Vintage Books, 1991).

García, Cristina. *Dreaming in Cuban* (New York: Alfred A. Knopf, 1992).

Thomas, Piri. *Down These Mean Streets* (New York: Vintage Books, 1991).

OUTLINE

Class 1: Background. History of the Latino presence in the United States; a background of the Latin American and Caribbean peoples' experience; U.S. expansion, immigration, and the foundation of ethnic minorities; analysis of the terms "Hispanic" and "Latino." Readings: *The Latino Reader*, "An American Literary Tradition."

Class 2: The seeds of a tradition. *Conquistadores*, explorers, and missionaries. Readings: *The Latino Reader*, "Encounters"; Alvar Núñez Cabeza de Vaca, "The Account" (1542–1555); Fray Mathias Sáenz de San Antonio, "Lord, If the Shepherd Does Not Hear" (1724); "The Comanches" (ca.1780).

Class 3: Nineteenth-century cultural nationalism. Part I. Readings: *The Latino Reader*, "Prelude"; José María Heredia, "Niagara" (1824); Eulalia Pérez, "An Old Woman Remembers" (1877); María Amparo Ruiz de Burton, "The Squatter and the Don" (1885).

Class 4: Nineteenth-century cultural nationalism. Part II. Readings: *The Latino Reader*, José Martí, "A Vindication of Cuba" (1889) and "Simple Verses" (1891); Pachín Marín, "New York from Within" (1892); "The Ballad of Gregorio Cortez" (ca. 1901).

Class 5: Early twentieth-century writing. Part I. Readings: *The Latino Reader*, "Latino United States"; Leonor Villegas de Magnón, *The Rebel* (ca.1920); selected poetry of William Carlos Williams (1923–1927); Arthur A. Schomburg, "José Campeche" (1934).

Class 5: Early twentieth-century writing. Part II. Readings: *The Latino Reader*, "Memoirs" by Bernardo Vega (ca.1944); Cleofas Jaramillo, *Romance of a Little Village Girl* (1955).

Class 6: Early ethnic consciousness. The foundations of U.S. Latino literature. Chicano authors. Readings: *The Latino Reader*, Rodolfo "Corky" Gonzales, "I Am Joaquín" (1967); Tomás Rivera, . . . *y no se lo tragó la tierra* (1971).

Class 7: Chicano narrative. Rudolfo Anaya, *Bless Me, Ultima* (1972), novel.

Class 8: Puerto Rican authors. Readings: Piri Thomas, *Down These Mean Streets* (1967), memoir.

Class 9: Puerto Rican authors, continued. *The Latino Reader*, Pedro Juan Soto, "God in Harlem" (1956); Pedro Pietri, "Puerto Rican Obituary" (1973).

Class 10: Cuban-American authors. Readings: *The Latino Reader*, Lourdes Casal, "For Ana Veldford" (1981); Dolores Prida, *Beautiful Señoritas* (1991).

Class 11: Cuban-American authors, continued. Cristina García, *Dreaming in Cuban* (1992), novel.

Class 12: Latina authors. Forging a female voice within Latino literature. Readings: *The Latino Reader*, Sandra María Esteves, "From the Commonwealth" (1979) and "A la Mujer Borrinqueña" (1980); Cherríe Moraga, "A Long Line of Vendidas" and "Loving in the War Years" (1983).

Class 13: Latina authors, continued. Sandra Cisneros, *The House on Mango Street* (1983), novel.

Class 14: Language and assimilation. Bilingualism, "Spanglish," and ethnic identity. Readings: *The Latino Reader*, Richard Rodriguez, *Hunger of Memory* (1982); Edward Rivera, *Family Installments* (1982); Tato Laviera, "My Graduation Speech" (1979) and "AmeRícan" (1985); Rosario Morales and Aurora Levins Morales, "Ending Poem" (1986).

Class 15: "Border" culture: the multicultural vision that is being created outside of the mainstream in the changing space of the "Borderlands." Readings: *The Latino Reader*, Gloria Anzaldúa, *Borderlands/La Frontera: The New Mestiza* (1987).

Class 16: Recent Latino voices. New visions created by changes in immigration from Latin America and the Caribbean; the expansion of Latino writing. Readings: *The Latino Reader*, Judith Ortiz Cofer, "American History" (1993); and Julia Alvarez, *How the Garcia Girls Lost Their Accents* (1991), novel.

SELECTED BIBLIOGRAPHY

Flores, Juan. *Divided Borders: Essays on Puerto Rican Identity* (1993).

Gutiérrez, Ramón, and Genaro M. Padilla. *Recovering the U.S. Hispanic Literary Heritage* (1993).

Horno Delgado, Asunción, et al. *Breaking Boundaries: Latina Writings and Critical Readings* (1989).

Limón, José E. *Mexican Ballads, Chicano Poems* (1992).

Mohr, Eugene. *The Nuyorican Experience: Literature of the Puerto Rican Minority* (1982).

Paredes, Américo. *With His Pistol in His Hand: A Border Ballad and Its Hero* (1958).

Rebolledo, Tey Diana. *Women Singing in the Snow* (1995).

Shorris, Earl. *Latinos: A Biography of the People* (1992).

Stavans, Ilan. *The Hispanic Condition: Reflections on Culture and Identity in America* (1995).

Tatum, Charles. *Chicano Literature* (1982).

APPENDIX B: LATINO GAY AND LESBIAN AUTHORS AND THEIR WORKS

Though no novels by gay and lesbian Latinos were included in the main body of this book, in the past two decades that subheading has made up a significant area of exploration. Following is a selected list of works that will provide avenues of research and shed light on important spheres of sexuality within the U.S. Latino community.

Anzaldúa, Gloria. *Borderlands/La Frontera: The New Mestiza*. San Francisco: Spinsters/Aunt Lute Foundation Books, 1987.

———. *This Bridge Called My Back: Writings by Radical Women of Color*. New York: Persephone Press, 1981.

Anzaldúa, Gloria, and Cherríe Moraga, ed. *Making Face, Making Soul/Haciendo Caras: Creative and Critical Perspectives by Feminists of Color*. San Francisco: Spinsters/Aunt Lute Foundation Books, 1990.

de la Peña, Terri. *Latin Satins*. Seattle: Seal Press, 1994.

———. *Margins*. Seattle: Seal Press, 1992.

Islas, Arturo. *LA Mollie and the King of Tears*. Albuquerque, N.M.: University of New Mexico Press, 1996.

———. *Migrant Souls*. New York: William Morrow, 1990.

———. *The Rain God*. Stanford, Calif.: Alexandrian Press, 1984.

Manrique, Jaime. *Bésame Mucho* (edited, with Jesse Dorris). New York: Painted Leaf Press, 1999.

———. *Colombian Gold*. New York: Clarkson N. Potter, 1983.

————. *Eminent Maricones: Arenas, Lorca, Puig and Me.* Madison: University of Wisconsin Press, 1999.

————. *Latin Moon in Manhattan.* New York: St. Martin's Press, 1992.

————. *My Night with Federico García Lorca.* Hudson, N.Y.: Groundwater Press, 1995.

————. *Twilight at the Equator.* Boston: Faber & Faber, 1997.

Moraga, Cherríe. *Loving in the War Years: lo que nunca pasó por sus labios.* Boston: South End Press, 1983.

Muñoz, Elías Miguel. *Brand New Memory.* Houston: Arte Público Press, 1998.

————. *Crazy Love.* Houston: Arte Público Press, 1988.

————. *En estas tierras/In This Land.* Tempe, Ariz.: Bilingual Review/Press, 1989.

————. *The Greatest Performance.* Houston: Arte Público Press, 1991.

————. *Los viajes de Orlando Cachumbambé.* Miami: Ediciones Universal, 1984.

Nava, Michael. *The Burning Plain.* New York: G. P. Putnam's Sons, 1997.

————. *The Death of Friends.* New York: G. P. Putnam's Sons, 1996.

————. *Golden Boy.* Los Angeles: Alyson, 1988.

————. *The Hidden Law.* New York: HarperCollins, 1992.

————. *How Town.* New York: Harper & Row, 1989.

————. *The Little Death.* Los Angeles: Alyson, 1986.

Obejas, Achy. *Memory Mambo.* Pittsburgh: Cleis Press, 1996.

————. *We Came All the Way from Cuba So You Could Dress Like This.* Pittsburgh: Cleis Press, 1994.

Ortiz Taylor, Sheila. *Coachella.* Albuquerque: University of New Mexico, 1998.

————. *Faultline.* Tallahassee, Fla. Naiad Press, 1982.

————. *Imaginary Parents.* Albuquerque: University of New Mexico Press, 1996.

————. *Slow Dancing at Miss Polly's.* Tallahassee, Fla.: Naiad Press.

————. *Southbound.* Tallahassee, Fla. Naiad Press, 1990.

————. *Spring Forward/Fall Back.* Tallahassee, Fla.: Naiad Press, 1985.

Rechy, John. *Bodies and Soul.* New York: Carroll & Graf, 1983.

————. *City of Night.* New York: Grove Press, 1963.

————. *The Fourth Angel.* New York: Viking, 1973.

————. *Marilyn's Daughter.* New York: Carroll & Graf, 1989.

————. *The Miraculous Day of Amalia Gomez.* New York: Arcade, 1991.

————. *Numbers.* New York: Grove Press, 1967.

————. *Our Lady of Babylon.* New York: Arcade, 1996.

————. *Rushes.* New York: Grove Press, 1979.

————. *The Sexual Outlaw.* New York: Grove Press, 1977.

————. *The Vampires.* New York: Grove Press, 1971.

APPENDIX C: LATINO LITERARY RESOURCES ON THE WORLD WIDE WEB

The following is a partial list of recommended Internet web sites that focus on U.S. Latino realities. Among the many meta-sites (sites functioning as clearinghouses or bibliographies), e-journals, directories, and electronic newspapers are available. These were evaluated for accuracy and usefulness for teachers and students. Only web sites in English or bilingual English/Spanish available at the time of publication of this book were selected. Several include their own search engines and point to other useful sites on the Internet.

META-SITES AND DIRECTORIES

The Azteca Web Page
http://www.azteca.net/aztec/
Useful for research in Chicano and Mexican-American culture and history as well as general information.

Boricua.com
http://www.boricua.com/
Information on the different Puerto Rican communities throughout the United States; directory of Puerto Ricans on the Internet, calendar, and general cultural facts.

CLNet (Chicano/Latino Net)
http://latino.sscnet.ucla.edu/
An important site for research, community outreach, and the arts; main focus is Chicano and general Latino material. Makes available a wide variety of information.

Chicano/Latino Web Sites
http://hypatia.ss.uci.edu/clstudies/websites/html
Helpful and useful links to sites in culture, community, politics, as well as Chicano/Latino studies programs.

Chicano!: Related World Wide Web Sites, Resources for Teachers and Parents
http://www.pbs.org/chicano/weblink2.html
Links to resources based on the PBS program on Chicanos; wide ranging and diverse.

Cuba Web
http://www.cubaweb.com/eng/index/html
Cuban-American and Cuban resources: viewpoints, bookstore, calendar of events, and chat forums.

IPRNet (Institute for Puerto Rican Policy Network)
http://www.iprnet.org/IPR/
Major research and policy site for U.S.–specific Puerto Rican issues. Articles, news, events, and an online newsletter.

Latin American/Hispanic/Chicano Resources on the Internet
http://multimedia.tamu-commerce.edu/library/latin.htm
Listing of databases, archives, documents, resource sites, Chicano/Hispanic history/culture links/sites, literature, art and education, organizations, and business.

Latino and Chicano Links, Multicultural Paths
http://curry.edschool.virginia.edu/go/multicultural/sites/ latino.html
Links to news magazines, research material, and collaborative projects.

Latino Net Pages
http://www.latinonetpages.com/
A listing of Latino links on the arts, education, film, music, dance, politics, and sports, among others.

Latino Web
http://latinoweb.com/
A massive site with a wide range of material from the arts to education, history, magazines, and personal pages. Includes a listing of Latino radio and television sites and information on many U.S. Latino groups.

Electric Mercado
http://www.mercado.com
Latino cultural information and marketplace. Books, food, culture, articles, and other web resources on U.S. Latinos.

E-JOURNALS, E-NEWS

El Andar
http://www.mercado.com/andar/
Cultural and literary journal; focuses on Chicano and Mexican issues, but recently expanded to include U.S.–Latino and Latin American issues.

LatinoLink
http:/www.latino.com/index/html
E-zine with articles that focus on news, culture, and entertainment regarding many U.S. Latino groups.

Pocho Productions' Virtual Varrio
http://www.pocho.com/index.2.html
Satiric Chicano humor and comic art; information and chat rooms.

APPENDIX D: OTHER AREAS OF INDEPENDENT STUDY

The literary works included in this book represent a small sample of the thousands of literary pieces produced by Latinos during the 450 years they have lived in North America. They also represent one possible avenue of study particularly relevant for high school and college students.

There are, however, more concentrated areas of study that may be appropriate for students and teachers interested in pursuing them. Following are a few ideas that may spark interest, with a few suggestions under each that will provide an opening for these studies. It should be noted that most of the listed publications are surveys that will lead the student, through citations and bibliographies, to additional and more specific texts.

The Spanish colonial period along what is often called the far northern frontier of the Spanish empire in the Americas lasted for about 250 years, from the 1520s to just after 1800 in the West and until 1898 in the East. Literary works from the period range from Alvar Núñez Cabeza de Vaca's *The Account* to plays adapted from original Spanish drama to chronicles of exploration and missionary activity to folk tales passed down through the generations. Despite their shortcomings, two good books with which to begin a study of these literary works are Herbert Eugene Bolton's *The Spanish Borderlands: A Chronicle of Old Florida and the Southwest* (New Haven, Conn.: Yale University Press, 1919) and Henry Raup Wagner's annotated bibliography *The Spanish Southwest 1542–1794* (reprint, New York: Arno Press, 1967). A good collection of essays on the New Mexican literary tradition of this period can be found in Erlinda Gonzalez-Berry's *Pasó por Aqui: Critical Essays on the New Mexican Literary Tradition, 1542–1988* (Albuquerque: University of New Mexico Press, 1989).

The tradition of publishing literary work in daily and weekly Spanish-language newspapers and popular magazines was particularly strong between 1850 and 1940. Microfilms of many of the newspapers themselves can be found in various research libraries across the country through the state's Newspaper Project, begun in 1994. Two very good surveys of literary works in Southwestern newspapers can be found in A. Gabriel Meléndez's *So All Is Not Lost: The Poetics of Print in Nuevomexicano Communities 1834–1958* (Albuquerque: University of New Mexico Press, 1997) and Doris Meyer's *Speaking for Themselves: Neomexicano Cultural Indentity and the Spanish-Language Press, 1880–1920* (Albuquerque: University of New Mexico Press, 1996). A useful survey book on a single literary publication in the East is Vernon A. Chamberlin and Ivan A. Schulman's *La Revista Ilustrada de New York* (Columbia, Mo.: University of Missouri Press, 1976).

Stories about Mexican-American bandits can be particularly fun for students. Among the research on *bandidos latinos* are the many stories of Joaquin Murrieta, a legendary Mexican-American bandit in 1850s California, who was first lionized in John Rollins Ridge's *The Life and Adventures of Joaquin Murrieta* (reprint, Norman: University of Oklahoma Press, 1955); Tiburcio Vasquez, active in California in the 1870s; Vicente Silva, a cutthroat bar owner and wife-killer active in New Mexico in the 1880s whose exploits were chronicled in Manuel Cabeza de Baca's; *Vicente Silva y sus cuarenta bandidos*; and Gregorio Cortez, who led the Texas Rangers on a merry chase in 1899, though he was most likely innocent of all charges, profiled in Américo Paredes' *With His Pistol in His Hand: A Border Ballad and Its Hero* (Austin: University of Texas Press, 1958).

The literature of exile has been particularly poignant in the East among Cubans and Puerto Ricans who, throughout the nineteenth century, felt the sting of political exile while their islands lay under the yoke of the fast-deteriorating Spanish empire. Though these exiles tended to cluster in New York in the nineteenth century, their influence has also been felt in many other places along the Eastern seaboard, including Boston, New Haven, Philadelphia, and, of course, Miami, particularly in the contemporary period. Among these were the Spanish-language anthology of poetry *El laúd del desterrado* (The Exile's Lute) (not translated, reprint, Houston: Arte Público Press, 1996), the works of José Martí, the works of Francisco Gonzalo "Pachín" Marín (see Harold Augenbraum and Margarite Fernández Olmos, *The Latino Reader* [Boston: Houghton Mifflin, 1997, 108–13]), and, more recently, Reinaldo Arenas' *Before Night Falls* (New York: Viking, 1993).

The plight of migrant workers in the southwest has received a good deal of political attention through the efforts of the late César Chávez. Among literary texts are Raymond Barrio's *The Plum, Plum Pickers* (Sunnyvale, Calif.: Ventura Press, 1969; reprint, Binghamton, N.Y.: Bilingual Review Press, 1984), an excellent evocation despite the fact that Barrio is of Spanish heritage, not Chicano; Miguel Mendez's; *Pilgrims in Aztlán* (Tempe, Ariz.: Bilingual Review/Press, 1992); and Ramon "Tianguis" Pérez's *Diary of an Undocumented Immigrant* (Houston: Arte Público Press, 1991). Economic migration, however, is not limited to farmworkers, and in the East, one should note that the fathers in such works as Oscar Hijuelos' *Our House in the Last World* and Edward Rivera's *Family Installments* are, in essence, migrant workers as well, who seek economic benefits from their migration to an urban area of the United States.

The uniqueness of the lands that lie along the border of Mexico and the United States, where cultures both meld and clash—where the standards of living of two adjacent countries are so vastly different—are of particular interest to Texas-Mexican writers, though they approach their work in vastly different ways. Rolando Hinojosa, the dean of U.S. Latino letters, has created the Klail City Death Trip, a series of brief novels that, taken together, paint a vivid portrait of the Texas border region and the mixing of working- and middle-class Anglo and Mexican cultures in the fictional Belken County. These include *Klail City* (Houston: Arte Público Press, 1987) and *Becky and Her Friends* (Houston: Arte Público Press, 1989). A particularly interesting work about the border is Aristeo Brito's *El Diablo en Tejas/The Devil in Texas* (Tempe, Ariz.: Bilingual Press, 1990).

Finally, the varying religious and mythological traditions within Latino cultures also play a prominent role in the works of many Latino writers, who invoke images of gods, goddesses, and tricksters that are often alien to and misunderstood by the majority of the American public. The literature derived from these ceremonies is sometimes confused with South American magic realism, and in North America this literature tends to be highly syncretic. In novels by writers whose ancestry is Caribbean, spiritual and religious influences often come from Africa. In Judith Ortiz Cofer's *The Line of the Sun* (Athens: University of Georgia Press, 1989) a barrio ceremony, lifted directly from the religion of Puerto Rico, ends in disaster. In the Southwest, where the influences are decidedly Native American, and Chicanos often see themselves as native to the region, Native American symbols abound. Rudolfo Anaya's *Bless Me, Ultima* (see Chapter 5), Ana Castillo's *So Far from God* (New York: W. W. Norton, 1993), and even John Rechy's *The Miraculous Day of Amalia Gomez* (New York: Arcade, 1991) evidence these influences. The spiritual element that often resides in Latino literature, a search for meaning connected to religion and inherent in such practices as Cuban Santería and *shamanismo*, has produced such disparate works as Cristina Garcia's novel *Dreaming in Cuban* (see chapter 15) and Carlos Castaneda's series of "memoirs" about the *espiritista* he called "Don Juan." The exploration of spirituality in literature is a growing avenue of study in American literature, and students can find new critical studies that they may relate to U.S. Latino literature.

Index

About the Editors and Contributors

HAROLD AUGENBRAUM is Director of the Mercantile Library of New York and its Center for World Literature. Among his publications are *Latinos in English* (1992), *Growing Up Latino: Memoirs and Stories* (1993), *Bendíceme, América* (1993), and *The Latino Reader: An American Literary Tradition from 1542 to the Present* (1997). He is also an editor of the forthcoming *Norton Anthology of Latino Literature of the United States*.

MARGARITE FERNÁNDEZ OLMOS is Professor of Spanish at Brooklyn College of the City University of New York. A recipient of a Ford Foundation Fellowship and a Postdoctoral Fellow of the National Research Council, she has lectured and written extensively on contemporary Caribbean and Latin American literatures. Fernández Olmos is coeditor with Doris Meyer of *Contemporary Women Authors of Latin America: New Translations* and *Introductory Essays* (1983). Her other works include *Remaking a Lost Harmony: Stories from the Hispanic Caribbean* (1995), *Sacred Possessions: Vodou, Santeria, Obeah and the Caribbean* (1997), both coedited and translated with Lizabeth Paravisini-Gebert), *The Latino Reader: An American Literary Tradition from 1542 to the Present* (1997), coedited with Harold Augenbraum, *Rudolfo A. Anaya: A Critical Companion* (Greenwood 1999), and a forthcoming collection of essays, *Healing Cultures: Art and Religion as Curative Practices in the Caribbean and Its Diaspora*.

MYRNA-YAMIL GONZÁLEZ is a Ph.D. candidate at the Graduate and University Center of the City University of New York and Adjunct Professor at Brooklyn College. She has published several articles in *Culturadoor*.

IRAIDA H. LÓPEZ is Assistant Professor at Medgar Evers College of the City University of New York. She is completing a manuscript on contemporary Hispanic autobiography in the United States. Her interview with Cristina García appeared in *Bridges to Cuba/Puentes a Cuba* (1995).

BRYCE MILLIGAN is the director of the literature program for the Guadalupe Cultural Arts Center, in San Antonio, Texas. He is publisher/editor of Wings Press, which awards the annual Premio Poesía Tejana, a novelist, and a poet.

CHON A. NORIEGA is Associate Professor and Vice Chair in the UCLA Department of Film and Television. He is author of *Shot in America: Telecommunications, Chicano Cinema, and the State* (1999) and editor of six books, including *Urban Exile: Collected Writings of Harry Gamboa, Jr.* (1988). Since 1996, he has been editor of *Aztlán: A Journal of Chicano Studies*.

RAFAEL OCASIO is Associate Professor of Spanish at Agnes Scott College. Among his publications are articles in the *Journal of Caribbean Studies*, a chapter on revolutionary Cuban children's literature in *Imagination, Emblems and Expressions: Essays on Latin American, Caribbean, and Continental Culture and Identity* (1993), a comparative study of the work of Nicholasa Mohr and Judith Ortiz Cofer in *Literature and Ethnic Discrimination* (1997), and four interviews with Judith Ortiz Cofer.

GENARO M. PADILLA is Vice Chancellor for Undergraduate Affairs at the University of California at Berkeley. He wrote *My History, Not Yours: The Formation of Mexican American Autobiography* (1993), edited *The Short Stories of Fray Angélico Chávez* (1987), and coedited *Recovering the Hispanic Literary Heritage of the United States* (1993).

LIZABETH PARAVISINI-GEBERT is Professor of Hispanic Studies at Vassar College. Her books include *Phyllis Sharod Allfrey: A Caribbean Life* (1996), *Jamaica Kincaid: A Critical Companion* (1999), and the forthcoming *Women at Sea: Travel Writing and the Margins of Caribbean Discourse*.

GUSTAVO PÉREZ FIRMAT is the David Feinson Professor of Humanities at Columbia University. He is the author of several books, including *Life on the Hyphen, Next Year in Cuba*, and *Cincuenta lecciones de exilio y desexilio*.

BEATRICE PITA teaches in the Spanish Section of the Department of Literature at the University of California at San Diego. With Rosaura Sánchez, she has edited and written the introduction to María Amparo

Ruiz de Burton's two novels, *The Squatter and the Don* (1992) and *Who Would Have Thought It?* (1995).

ASELA RODRÍGUEZ DE LAGUNA is Associate Professor of Spanish at Rutgers-Newark, where from 1992 to 1999 she was Director of the Hispanic Civilization and Language Studies Program. She is author of *George Bernard Shaw en la literatura hispánica* (1981) and *Notes on Puerto Rican Literature: Images and Identities—An Introduction* (1987) and editor of *Images and Identities: The Puerto Rican in Two World Contexts* (1987), among other works.

HEATHER ROSARIO-SIEVERT is Professor of English at Hostos Community College of the City University of New York. She is author of *Honor My Father* (1995) and "Anxiety, Repression, and Return: The Language of Julia Alvarez," which appeared in *Readerly/Writerly Texts* (1987).

AILEEN SCHMIDT is Professor of Literature at the University of Puerto Rico. Her studies of women's autobiography in Cuba and Puerto Rico (the topic of her forthcoming book) have appeared in a Casa de las Américas (Havana) collection of essays on women's writing and in the *Revista de Ciencias Sociales*. Schmidt's research also includes the subject of feminist police fiction.

HECTOR A. TORRES is Associate Professor of English at the University of New Mexico at Albuquerque. He is the author of the entry on Gloria Anzaldúa in the *Dictionary of Literary Biography* and is currently at work on a book on Chicana narrative.

EVANGELINA VIGIL-PIÑÓN's translation of Tomás Rivera's . . . *y no se tragó la tierra/And the Earth Did Not Devour Him* was published by Arte Público Press in 1987. Among her books of poetry are *Nade y nade* (1978), *Thirty an' Seen a Lot* (1982), and *The Computer Is Down* (1987). She edited the anthology *Woman of Her Word: Hispanic Women Write* (1983) and from 1984 to 1996 she served as poetry editor of *The Americas Review*. Vigil-Piñón is Public Affairs Director with ABC-KTRK in Houston.

ALFREDO VILLANUEVA-COLLADO is Professor of English at Eugenio Maria de Hostos Community College in New York. His literary criticism has appeared in *Discurso Literario, Revista de Estudios Hispánicos, Revista Chicano-Riqueña,* and *Revista Iberoamericana,* among other publications.